Jesus: The Great Debate

Dr. Grant R. Jeffrey

Frontier Research Publications, Inc.
P.O. Box 129, Station "U", Toronto, Ontario M8Z 5M4

Jesus: The Great Debate

Library of Congress Cataloging in Publication Data:
Jeffrey, Dr. Grant R.
Jesus: The Great Debate
1. Apologetics   2. Eschatology   3. Witnessing
1. Title

August 1999 Frontier Research Publications, Inc.

ISBN 0-921714-56-4

Unless otherwise indicated, Scripture quotations are from the
Authorized King James Version.

Cover design: The Riordon Design Group
Printed in Canada: Harmony Printing Limited

Table of Contents

Acknowledgments   7

Introduction   9

 1 The Criteria of Historical Evidence about Jesus 29
 2 The Fundamental Issue of When The Gospels
   Were Written 49
 3 Remarkable Evidence in the Dead Sea Scrolls 59
 4 The Date of Christ's Nativity, Ministry, and Crucifixion . . 71
 5 Evidence from the Ancient Christian Tombs 79
 6 The Search for the Real Tomb of Jesus 93
 7 The Mysterious Shroud of Turin 113
 8 The Historical Evidence About Jesus 159
 9 Evidence from Jewish Sources 179
10 Ancient Jewish Messianic Expectations 191
11 The Genealogy of Jesus: His Legal Right to the
   Throne of David 221
12 Fulfilled Prophecies about Jesus as the Messiah 229
13 Jesus – The Son of God 245
14 The Evidence of Transformed Lives 255
15 The Impact of Jesus' Life on World History 259
16 The Verdict Is Yours 271

Selected Bibliography 275

Acknowledgments

Jesus: The Great Debate is the most comprehensive examination of the historical, archeological, and scientific evidence about Jesus of Nazareth. This book reflects thrirty-five years of research involving thousands of books, articles, and Bible commentaries. However, the inspired Word of God is the major source and continual guide to my studies.

The Gospels and their claims about Jesus Christ are subject to a relentless attack in our generation in the universities, the seminaries, and the media. Yet everything we believe as Christians, our hope for salvation and heaven itself depends upon the total truthfulness and trustworthiness of the sacred Scriptural account about Jesus of Nazareth. I believe it is time for Christians to stand up and launch a vigorous defence of the inspiration of the Bible and boldly proclaim that our faith in Jesus Christ and His resurrection is grounded upon a strong foundation of historical fact. *Jesus: The Great Debate* is a small contribution to that defence of Christianity that all believers are called upon to perform. This book continues the theme established in my books *The Signature of God* and *The Handwriting of God* that the evidence in the Gospels together with a wealth of historical, archealogical, and scientific evidence should convince any inquiring mind that Jesus Christ is the promised Messiah, the true Son of God.

My parents, Lyle and Florence Jeffrey, have inspired in me a profound love for Jesus Christ and the Holy Word. Over the years they have been a continual encouragement in my research and writing.

A special thanks to my editorial assistant, Adrienne Jeffrey Tigchelaar, who has provided valuable research and editorial services throughout this project.

I dedicate *Jesus: The Great Debate* to my lovely wife, Kaye, who is my constant inspiration, my faithful partner in ministry and the Vice President of Frontier Research Publications, Inc. As we travel the world to conduct research and minister in various nations, she continually encourages me in my efforts to share this research.

I trust that the information revealed in the following pages will encourage you to personally study the Gospels and come to know Jesus of Nazareth in a deeper way.

Dr. Grant R. Jeffrey
Toronto, Ontario
August 1999

Introduction

The last decade of this millennium has featured a veritable explosion of books that explore the quest for the historical Jesus. The widespread interest in Jesus has produced a powerful debate between agnostic historians and liberal theologians, and conservative Christian scholars. One of the greatest subjects of dispute is the question of what historical evidence qualifies as acceptable proof of the life of Jesus of Nazareth. Many liberal and agnostic scholars reject most of the evidence found in the four Gospels and the rest of the New Testament. They also declare that, apart from the New Testament, there is almost nothing that qualifies as acceptable historical evidence about Jesus. However, conservative Christian historians accept the four Gospels, the epistles of Paul, and the contributions of Jewish and pagan historical sources as reliable evidence about His life. In addition, the contributions from the field of archeology and science reveal much about Jesus and those who interacted with Him during His short life.

Without question, Jesus is the most controversial person in human history. The life of Jesus of Nazareth began in the controversy of His virgin birth and ended thirty-three years later with the remarkable claim that He actually rose from the dead on the third day following His death on the cross. Jesus began His ministry with the miracle of turning water into wine at a wedding feast in Cana. Later, Jesus created more controversy with His divine healings, including the miracle of opening the eyes of a blind boy. The ancient prophet Isaiah had foretold that one of the unique signs of the coming Messiah would be that he would "open the eyes of the blind" (Isaiah 42:7). Until that point in history no one had ever healed someone born blind. To the religious leaders of Israel this miracle was tantamount to Jesus claiming He was the true Messiah. His miraculous healings of so many people afflicted with disease confounded the religious leaders of the day. His fulfillment of the dozens of messianic prophecies, His death on the cross, and His astonishing resurrection from the dead polarized Jewish society. While thousands acknowledged Him as the Son of God, many others violently rejected His claims to be the true Messiah and equal with God.

Jesus' claim to be the Son of God ultimately launched the greatest religious movement in human history. Two thousand years have passed, yet today over a billion people throughout the world worship this poor Galilean teacher as the King of Kings, the Lord of Lords, and the Son of God. Followers of Christ can be found in every nation on earth and in every culture, language, and profession. Over 20 percent of the world's population — from simple peasant farmers in the Sudan to brilliant, well-educated professors at Oxford — are committed Christians who believe that Jesus is the Son of God and that the Gospel record is correct. At the same time, there are millions of people, from all walks of life, who reject the Bible's claims about Jesus. Many people simply cannot believe the Gospels' claims about His virgin birth, His miracles, and most of all, His resurrection from the dead.

The purpose of this book, *Jesus: The Great Debate,* is to present the tremendous amount of historical, archeological, and scientific evidence that points to the reality of the life, death, and resurrection of Jesus Christ. After reviewing this material, I believe most readers will agree that we possess more authentic historical material about the life of Jesus than almost any other person from ancient history. In fact, we know more about the last eight days of the life of Jesus of Nazareth than we do about any other person in the ancient world of Rome, Egypt, or Greece.

The questions remain: Did Jesus really live? Are the accounts about His miraculous healings and raising people from the dead true? Did He actually die on the cross? What is the evidence that

He truly rose from the dead? What historical evidence is there to support the Bible's extraordinary claim that Jesus is the Son of God and the true Messiah?

The Claims of Agnostic Historians

1. *The agnostic historians claim that there is little surviving historical evidence about Jesus.*

However, there is a significant amount of surviving historical evidence about Jesus. Four Gospel accounts from four separate individuals who claim that they personally knew Jesus and were eyewitnesses to many key events provide historical evidence. There are reliable references to Jesus from His enemies, including Roman historians and governors, as well as pagan historians who describe the remarkable darkness that occurred during His crucifixion. Significant Jewish references about the life and death of Jesus have been found in the Talmud, the Dead Sea Scrolls, and the works of contemporary Jewish historian Flavius Josephus. Archeological evidence confirms many of the details of the Gospels' account about Jesus. Finally, scientific evidence about the mysterious Shroud of Turin may actually prove details of Jesus' crucifixion.

2. *Agnostic historians suggest that we cannot place confidence in the authority of Gospel accounts of Jesus because none of the four original Gospels have survived.*

They maintain that the oldest surviving copies of the Gospels date from approximately A.D. 200, therefore we can't know what happened to them between the time of their composition and the creation of surviving copies in A.D. 200. The truth is that we have over five thousand existing copies of the Greek New Testament that date back to the first few centuries of the early Church. No other ancient manuscript has survived with more than ten genuine copies. The wealth of surviving manuscripts of the New Testament, as well as over one hundred thousand letters from Christians that contain more than 99 percent of the eight thousand verses of the New Testament, provides overwhelming proof that the text of the New Testament is historically reliable.

3. *These liberal historians argue that the authors of the four Gospels are unknown.*

According to them, the current names were given to the

Gospels during the later part of the second century to give them authority. Therefore we don't know who wrote the Gospels. However, the historical writings of the early Church provide strong evidence that the four Gospels were indeed written by the individuals whose names are ascribed to them.

4. *The agnostic historians claim that the four Gospels are not really independent eyewitness accounts, but are in fact copied from one initial source, namely the Gospel of Mark. Others suggest a hypothetical source document named Q, of which there is no historical evidence other than conjecture.*

The critics dispute the historical accuracy of the four Gospels on the basis that they often differ from each other in their description of small details. However, as any judge or lawyer will tell you, any four eyewitness accounts of an event that agree in *every* detail would be thrown out of court as a collaboration. Any eyewitnesses of an event, such as a car accident, naturally will describe the same event with different details and occasional discrepancies, although they each honestly describe what they saw of the actual event. The agnostic critics also reject statements in the Gospels that are similar to each other on the basis that they believe they must have been copied from one original source; at the same time, they inconsistently reject statements from the Gospel of John on the basis that none of the other Synoptic Gospels describe the same event or message.

We know that the Jews in the first century were accustomed to memorizing the teachings of their rabbis. They practiced powerful memory systems that enabled them to recount the sayings of their teachers with great accuracy. This would account for the similarity of the Gospels. The minor verbal differences are easily explained as well. For example, historians and theologians often point to differences in the Gospels, such as the reference to the "fig tree." Matthew 24:32 says, "Now learn a parable of the fig tree," whereas Luke 21:29 says, "Behold the fig tree, and all the trees. . . ." However, for someone like myself who often gives a message on a particular topic to different audiences in cities across America, the minor differences in the Gospels' recounting of Christ's messages are perfectly understandable. If I speak to an audience in New York about Matthew 24 and the next week address an audience in Los Angeles about the same topic, the body of the message will be the same, but a number of my specific statements and illustrations will differ. We must remember that Jesus of Nazareth, as an itinerant preacher, would have likely given the same message, such as the Sermon on the Mount, to several different audiences on different days. Slight variations in His expression of the message would be normal.

5. *The agnostics believe that the fundamental problem with the Gospels' account of Jesus is the presence of numerous supernatural events and prophecy.*

Underlying most of the criticism of modern agnostic historians and theologians is a fundamental attitude that totally dismisses the possibility of supernatural miracles, prophecy, or the claim of Jesus to be the Son of God. It is not simply a question of their examining the historical and textual evidence and rejecting it on the basis of its failure to prove the early churches' claims about Jesus Christ. These agnostic scholars reject the Gospels' supernatural claims before they even begin their investigation. They usually do not even seriously consider the eyewitness evidence of the miracles about Jesus on the basis of their previously declared position that supernatural events cannot possibly occur.

The Problem of Miracles

The event we commonly call a "miracle" is usually called "a sign," "a wonder," "a work," or "a power," in the original Greek language of the Gospels, reflecting the fact that the writers intended to refer to the supernatural event as a purposeful act of God to reveal His power and message to humanity. The Gospel writers often emphasized the astonishment experienced by witnesses of a supernatural "sign" (see Mark 2:12). It is important to note that the word "wonders" is never applied to miracles by itself. The word "wonders" always appears in the Gospels in connection with the word "signs" but never on its own. The consistent evidence presented by the Evangelists is that a miracle is never produced by God solely as a "wonder" but rather as a demonstration of God's supernatural power to authenticate His revealed message or His Messenger, Jesus Christ.

The language we use may actually deceive us regarding the truth about miracles. Theologians and historians often speak of "laws of God" of "laws of nature." They then declare that it is logically impossible that such "laws of God" could ever be overthrown through miracles produced by a higher law, a specific supernatural intervention of God into the affairs of man. They claim these observed "laws of God" cannot be violated, even by God Himself. While this sounds reasonable, it is not. So-called "laws of God" or "laws of nature" are only observations about how nature normally behaves, and cannot restrict the purposeful and supernatural actions of the Supreme Intelligence of the Universe. Such "laws of God or nature" exist only for humans, but not for a supernatural God who created this universe. As other Christian theologians have noted with truth, the creation of a human baby is no less a miracle than the regeneration of life within the dead corpse of Lazarus by the supernatural power of Jesus of Nazareth.

The continuing creative activity of God, which is usually veiled behind the constant actions of what we call "the laws of nature," reveals itself in the presentation of a miracle which demonstrates the supernatural act, as well as the Hand of God Himself. The daily manifestation of the preserving miraculous power of God creating the precisely required amount of oxygen in our atmosphere, the proper amount of heat from the sun, and the exact amount of magnetism required to facilitate the electro-chemical interactions of the cells within our body are only a few of the millions of examples of the continuous demonstration of the supernatural power of God to allow human life to exist and prosper on the earth.

The philosopher John Mill explained that "a miracle is no contradiction to the law of cause and effect. It is a new effect, supposed to be introduced by the introduction of a new cause."[1] While the occurrence of absolute miracles is totally impossible in the normal course of events without the direct supernatural intervention of God, there are other miracles recounted in the Bible that are providential miracles. These providential miracles are normal events which are supernaturally caused by God to occur at a specific time to affect a Divine purpose such as the discovery of a coin in the mouth of a fish that Jesus instructed His disciple to find (Matthew 17:27). The fact that a coin was found in a specific fish precisely when Jesus commanded His disciple to catch such a fish is an example of a providential miracle in which an unusual event is caused by God to occur at the exact time the Lord commands to demonstrate His power and underline the significance of Christ's message.

A miracle is not a violation of the laws of nature, because such "laws" are simply our observation of how things normally behave. If we believe that a supernatural God exists with the power to create everything in the universe, then His ability to intervene in that universe at rare intervals to effect specific supernatural acts is not illogical nor impossible. The fact that the normal experience of humanity does not reveal miracles only confirms their extremely rare nature. It is significant that the miracles that occur according to the Scriptures always happen with a purpose of healing, divine deliverance, or as a sign or wonder that affirms the supernatural credentials of Jesus as the Son of God. A biblical sign or wonder is a very unusual event which God brings about to authenticate His revealed message to a skeptical humanity.

The normal evidence of nature demonstrates and illustrates the existence and attributes of God. The rare but purposeful miracles, as described in the Scriptures, demonstrate the supernatural intervention of God into the normal order of events in which He usually acts. Miracles such as restoring the sight of the young man born blind or reviving Lazarus after death are certainly not greater manifestations of the supernatural power of God than the creation of the earth, the birth of a baby, or the creation of a new sun; but these examples are certainly a different type of manifestation of God's supernatural power. It could be stated that other manifestations, such as the birth of a baby, are examples of a continuous demonstration of His eternal supernatural power in His universe. As the apostle Paul declared, "For the invisible things of him from the creation of the world are clearly seen, being understood by the things that are made, even his eternal power and Godhead; so that they are without excuse" (Romans 1:20).

Modern Historical Critics' Rejection of the Supernatural

This trend of rejecting the supernatural has existed for the last century and a half. The critics' complete denial of the supernatural elements from the Gospels is not due to a detailed examination of the eyewitness records and the detection of contradictions and weaknesses in the disciples' statements. The critics reveal by their statements that their primary objection is their a priori rejection of the possibility of supernatural events occurring at all.

We need to consider the illogical nature of the argument presented by many of these scholars. If a supernatural God truly exists, then logically, all of the miraculous events of the Bible are possible. The philosopher Baruch Spinoza (1632–1677) established the philosophical foundation for the modern anti-supernatural interpretations of the Bible. Spinoza believed that miracles, as God's purposeful violations of His Divine natural laws, were impossible by definition in that God would not contradict His own unchanging laws. Spinoza was the first philosopher to declare that it was unnecessary to even examine the evidence in the Bible for specific miracles. He believed that one should reject the possibility of the supernatural because of its inherent impossibility. Another influential philosopher, Scottish historian David Hume, also rejected the possibility of supernatural events on the basis that miracles were impossible by definition. Hume argued that a miraculous event, no matter how well attested by historical eyewitness evidence, could not be proven to be a miracle because you could not prove that a natural law had actually been overthrown.

In other words, Hume declared that miracles are impossible by definition, but, if the evidence of the miracle is overwhelming, then you simply redefine the definition of natural law to include the miraculous event. Then you declare that the miracle isn't really a miracle after all. That such an argument should prove enormously popular among modern philosophers and religious historians proves to what absurd lengths people will go to escape the evidence of the supernatural. Many of the agnostic historians will not even consider or comment on the fulfillment of dozens of Old Testament prophets' specific predictions about the life and death of Jesus of Nazareth on the basis that such prophecies are theoretically impossible in a universe in which the supernatural cannot occur. The influence of Hume's anti-supernatural philosophy has powerfully affected the majority of the modern historical studies of Jesus Christ. This naturalistic and anti-supernatural philosophy became widespread during the Enlightenment, a period that followed the French Revolution in 1800. It is still a powerful influence among scholars today.

This anti-supernatural attitude in connection with studies

about the life of Jesus first appeared in Germany. Professor Herman Samuel Reimarus' naturalistic history of Jesus, *Fragments: The Intention of Jesus and His Disciples*,[2] attempted to present the life of Christ by eliminating all miraculous elements from the accounts in the Gospels. Reimarus claimed that the writers of the four Gospels falsely created the supernatural elements to create Jesus Christ as the Son of God. The most important and influential nineteenth century anti-supernatural study of Christ's life was produced in 1835 by David Friedrich Strauss; it was called *The Life of Jesus Critically Examined*.[3] This book strongly argued that it was absurd to believe the scriptural accounts of supernatural events in the life of Jesus Christ. Strauss also denied that Mark's Gospel could have been an accurate rendition of eyewitness accounts and the genuine recollections the apostle Peter related to Mark. David Strauss declared that a fundamental principle in examining the Gospel record should be the rejection of any evidence that refers to supernatural events or miracles concerning the life of Jesus.

In his *Criticism of the Gospels and History of Their Origin*, published in 1851, author Bruno Bauer totally rejected the reliability of the Gospel of Mark.[4] He suggested that it was a fictional creation of the early Church and that Jesus of Nazareth likely never existed. Another European writer, E. Renan of France, wrote a popular book, *The History of the Origins of Christianity* in 1863. In it, he denied the historical truth of the miracles as well as the resurrection of Christ.[5] Another popular study of Christ in the last century was Rev. F. W. Farrar's *Life of Christ*,[6] published in 1874, which took a somewhat traditional view of the supernatural elements of the Gospels' accounts without directly dealing with the evidence or refuting the liberal arguments against the miracles. The popular writer and philosopher Albert Schweitzer wrote his influential book, *The Quest of the Historical Jesus*, in 1906. He presented Jesus' apocalyptic message as one that must be understood in terms of His prophetic expectation of the immediate intervention of God into human history to establish the kingdom of God on earth with Jesus ruling from the Throne of David.[7] Schweitzer believed that Jesus, as a human messenger of God, was simply mistaken about God's timing. While acknowledging the final realization of the kingdom of God in the future, Schweitzer believed that Jesus, because He was not truly the Son of God, did not understand the eschatological plan of God for humanity.

During the early decades of this century, two influential theologians strongly rejected the Gospel accounts about Jesus. One, Rev. Karl Barth, claimed that the only important theological element in the life of Jesus was His death on the cross. Barth suggested that the attempt to determine the truth about the historical evidence of Jesus is a useless quest and should be abandoned. The other, Professor Rudolf Bultmann, perhaps the most influential Protestant theologian of this century, concluded that "we can know almost nothing concerning the life and personality of Jesus except that he existed and died on a cross." He denied the Gospels and rejected any other historical evidence from pagan or Jewish sources. Bultmann suggested that historical evidence about the life, death, and resurrection of Jesus from the New Testament is historically and theologically irrelevant to Christianity. Bultmann wrote in *Jesus and the Word*, "we can know almost nothing concerning the life and personality of Jesus, since the early Christians sources show no interest in either, are moreover fragmentary and often legendary and other sources do not exist."[8]

Professor Bultmann, after rejecting all biblical and nonbiblical evidence that supports the historical reality of Christ's life and resurrection, claimed that the only important message of Christianity is the call to live "authentically." Bultmann declared that the "kerygma," the essential spiritual proclamation of the early Church, is simply a call to humans to live honestly or authentically before God and our neighbors. While acknowledging that scholars should not automatically reject anything before examining the data, he declared that there was only one exception, the supernatural: "history is a unity in the sense of a closed continuum of effects." In a later comment about the issue of supernatural events, Bultmann wrote, "this closedness means that the continuum of historical happenings cannot be rent by the interference of supernatural, transcendent powers and that therefore there is not a 'miracle' in this sense of the word."[9]

The modern debate about the historicity of Jesus is exemplified by the continuing public discussion between the liberal scholar Professor Marcus Borg, a leading member of the Jesus Seminar and the conservative historian N. T. Wright, a great critic of the liberal

Jesus Seminar.[10] An example of Professor Borg's conclusions is revealed in his statement, "If someone asks me, Do you believe Jesus was God? the answer is no. I view Jesus differently. Rather than being the exclusive revelation of God, He is one of many mediators of the sacred." Although Borg publicly identifies himself as a Christian he admits that he does not believe in God and denies that Jesus of Nazareth was uniquely the Son of God as the Gospels declare.

The Jesus Seminar

The rejection of the supernatural and, consequently, the rejection of biblical authority and the historical accuracy of the Bible continues to this day among liberal Christians. For example, The Jesus Seminar, a group of seventy-five New Testament liberal scholars, meets semi-annually in America to determine whether or not any of the Gospel quotations of Jesus' words are authentic or credible. These scholars meet to examine individual "sayings" of Jesus as recorded by the four canonical New Testament Gospels as well as the non-canonical apocryphal (nonbiblical) gospel of Thomas from the second century. Each academic votes to accept or reject the plausibility of these individual statements. The Jesus Seminar is sponsored by the Westor Institute, a private California study center. It was founded by Robert Funk, a very liberal and agnostic New Testament scholar who has authored numerous books that question the authority and accuracy of New Testament Gospel accounts about the life and teachings of Jesus. For example, in the introduction to Robert Funk's book *The Five Gospels: The Search for the Authentic Words of Jesus,* he wrote:

> The Christ of creed and dogma, who had been firmly in place in the Middle Ages, can no longer command the assent of those who have seen the heavens through Galileo's telescope. The old deities and demons were swept from the skies by that remarkable glass. Copernicus, Kepler and Galileo have dismantled the mythological abodes of the gods and Satan and bequeathed us secular heavens.[11]

Robert Funk also derided the orthodox beliefs of all traditional Christians over the last two thousand years in his ridicule of those who accept the Gospel's statements about Jesus' birth, miracles, and resurrection. Funk wrote:

> The redemptive function of Jesus' death is usually expressed in mythological language. It is termed mythological because it refers to an act that was performed by God, or by God's son, on behalf of humankind. Such an act can be neither verified (nor falsified) on the basis of empirical data by facts established by historical investigation. His death as redemptive event was not an act visible to the disinterested observer. All such mythological acts lie outside sciences and hence of the historian. When, on the other hand, literalists claim that certain biblical stories are descriptively true, they are making claims that are an affront to common sense. Such stories include accounts of Mary's conception while still a virgin, Jesus' exorcisms of demons, references to seven heavens in the vault above the earth and to Sheol or hell below the earth, and Jesus' resurrection as the resuscitation of a corpse. If this form of understanding were not so deeply entrenched in the literalistic mind, it would make us snicker.[12]

Another indication of the underlying attitudes of these seminarians regarding the authenticity of Jesus' words is revealed by the comments of Professor Arthur Dewey of Xavier University, a member of the Jesus Seminar. As reported in an article in *Time* magazine in April 1994, Dewey stated that, while rejecting the accuracy of most of Christ's words as recorded in the Gospels, the scholars believe Jesus was occasionally "humorous."[13] One commented, "There is more of David Letterman in the historical Jesus than Pat Robertson." These particular liberal scholars are openly contemptuous in their rejection of the authenticity of the Bible based on their own theological anti-supernatural opinions. However, the Jesus Seminar participants merely represent the tip of the iceberg of modern academic scholars who generally reject, in whole or in part, the Scriptures. These agnostic attitudes have permeated, not only the academic world, but also our modern media and religious seminaries.

In 1985, Jesus Seminar participants began to use a system of colored beads to indicate their personal opinion and vote on the validity of particular statements of Jesus. If a scholar thought that Jesus would "certainly" have made such a statement, he dropped a red bead into the box, indicating his opinion that the statement was "authentic." A pink bead signified the scholar's opinion that Jesus "might" have made a statement close to what the Gospel writer recorded. If a particular scholar believed that the statement in question may have been close to what Jesus thought, but not what He actually stated, he dropped a grey bead in the box. Finally, when they completely reject a given statement in the Gospels as something they believed that Jesus would not have said, the scholars dropped a black bead into the box, indicating that it was not "authentic."

Time magazine's April 6, 1996 issue reported that during the Jesus Seminar's 1995 meeting in Santa Rosa, California, the scholars had decided that the Gospels of Matthew, Mark, Luke, and John were "notoriously unreliable: the judges . . . had to throw out the Evangelists' testimony on the Nativity, the Resurrection, the Sermon on the Mount."[14] The article repeats "the assertion, published by the 75-person, self-appointed Seminar three years ago, that close historical analysis of the Gospels exposes most of them as inauthentic." The exclusion criteria used by these liberal scholars to exclude statements as inauthentic are as follows: they automatically reject any prophetic statements, statements by Jesus on the cross, descriptions of His trial, the Resurrection, and any claim by Jesus to be the Messiah or the Son of God. Their most basic rule for exclusion is: "When in sufficient doubt, leave it out." Since these scholars automatically reject any statement regarding supernatural events, they are forced to reject great portions of the Gospel record about the life of Jesus. However, if the view of the Jesus Seminar is correct — that almost nothing definite can be known about the life of Jesus of Nazareth — the basis for all Christian belief is destroyed. Fortunately, the evidence presented in this book will show that they are wrong.

Incredibly, this group has chosen to publish a new version of the Gospels that displays the "authentic words of Jesus" in various colors of ink reflecting their "validity." Not surprisingly, very little of their final text is in red letters, indicating authentic statements. For example, when these liberal academics examined the text containing the Lord's Prayer, they rejected every single word as spurious except for the opening phrase, "Our Father." In effect, these scholars declare by their votes whether or not they themselves would have made these Gospel statements if *they* were Jesus! American cable channel Cinemax 2 ran a program in April 1996, called "The Gospel According to Jesus," that records people reading from a new version of the Bible created by author Stephen Mitchell, based on Jesus Seminar research. In this version, Mitchell eliminated almost all of the Gospel statements and most of the miracles by Jesus as recorded in the New Testament. Not surprisingly, it was a very short book.

Evangelical scholar Professor Michael Green, of Regent College, Vancouver, B.C., rejects the analysis of the proponents of the Jesus Seminar. Green stated that the Gospels are the best authenticated of all ancient documents that survived from that period. Green wrote, "We have copies of them going back to well within the century of their composition, which is fantastic compared with the classic authors of the period. And in striking contrast to the two or three manuscripts we have attesting the text of these secular writers, we have hundreds of the New Testament. They give us the text of the New Testament with astonishing uniformity." Additionally, Professor Green noted the remarkable historical harmony of the facts found in the Gospel records: "The artless, unplanned harmony in their accounts is impressive and convincing."

Eighteen centuries ago, the Bishop of Lyons, Iraneus, wrote about the widespread acceptance of the reliability of the Gospel's records about the life and death of Jesus as follows: ". . . so firm is the ground upon which these Gospels rest, that the very heretics themselves bear witness to them."[15] Professor Frederic G. Kenyon referred to more than five thousand surviving Greek manuscripts of the New Testament that are available to scholars today and declared: "The number of manuscripts of the New Testament . . . and of quotations from it in the oldest writers of the church, is so large that it is practically certain that the true reading of every doubtful passage is preserved in some one or another of these ancient authorities."[16]

Bishop John Spong's Attack on Fundamental Biblical Beliefs

Episcopalian Bishop John Spong is well known for his prominent attacks on evangelical Christians who believe the fundamental doctrines of the Word of God. Bishop Spong claims that there are three main paths for Christians to take in addressing the Bible. These alternatives are described in his own words as "ignorant fundamentalism" and "vapid liberalism." The third alternative is his own "unique" but still strongly liberal path. However, Spong's third path is merely another example of a modernist liberalism that expresses a wholesale rejection of the miraculous and contempt for the orthodox doctrines of Christianity. The bishop claims his desire is to free Christians from "2000 years of misunderstanding." Spong declares that the Gospel writers and the apostle Paul never intended their "stories" to be taken literally. As a result of his denial of the truthfulness of the New Testament accounts, Bishop Spong openly admits that he rejects the foundational doctrines of the orthodox Christian faith. He denies the virgin birth, the miracles and prophecies, as well as the supernatural details of Jesus' crucifixion and resurrection. He also rejects the Genesis account of the beginning of man's sin, and states that "the fall of man . . . no longer makes sense." He then dismisses as "no longer believable" the Bible's revelation in which "Christ has been portrayed as the divine rescuer — sent to save the fallen human creature from sin and to restore that creature to the goodness of his or her pre-fall creation."[17] As a result of his rejection of the literal meaning of Scripture, Spong feels no need to submit to the Bible's condemnation of homosexuality. Therefore, the bishop proudly proclaims his endorsement of homosexuality and admits that he oversees twenty-three openly homosexual priests in his Newark, New Jersey Episcopalian diocese.

While Spong despises fundamentalist, orthodox Christians as "uninformed, unquestioning, and ignorant," he is forced to admit that the fundamentalist churches that teach traditional biblical doctrines are growing rapidly at the very time when most liberal mainstream churches are shrinking annually. Bishop Spong reluctantly acknowledges that biblical literalism appeals to people's need for certainty regarding spiritual matters.

Many liberal theologians and modern religious writers agree with Bishop Spong, condemning as "ignorant" any believers who uphold the orthodox, biblically based beliefs in salvation through faith in Christ's atoning death on the cross that have sustained billions of Christians for the last two thousand years.

However, anyone who observes the religious scene exhibited today in North America and Europe will recognize the utter failure of this anti-literal, anti-Bible, and anti-Christian religious viewpoint to motivate people to join the shrinking congregations of liberal mainline denominations. Spong himself reluctantly admits that the fundamentalist, Bible-believing churches are growing at an unprecedented rate, while the liberal mainline churches that reject the Bible's teaching "shrink every day in membership." He complains, "The only churches that grow today are those that do not, in fact, understand the issues and can therefore traffic in certainty. They represent both the fundamentalistic Protestant groups and the rigidly controlled conservative Catholic traditions." In other words, Spong believes the successful and growing Bible-believing churches "do not, in fact, understand the issues," primarily on the basis that they still espouse traditional, orthodox Christian beliefs which he personally rejects.

The truth is that once someone divorces their "Christianity" from the recorded statements about Jesus as found in the Bible, they have, in reality, created a new religion based on an imaginary Christ who exists solely in their own minds. In other words, Spong's new liberal "Christianity," divorced from the authority of biblical statements and stripped of the supernatural, would be virtually unrecognizable to the disciples of Jesus Christ or to the vast majority of His followers over the last two thousand years.

Some Critics Discredit the Gospels

Many writers question whether it is truly necessary to know if the Gospels' revelations about Jesus are historically accurate. The Hindu religious philosopher Sri Aurobindo expressed aspects of this modern viewpoint in his writings:

> Such controversies as the one that has raged in Europe over the historicity of Christ would seem to a spiritually-minded Indian largely a waste of time; he would concede to it a considerable historical, but hardly any religious, importance; for what does it matter in the end whether a son of the carpenter Joseph was actually born in Nazareth or Bethlehem, lived and taught and was done to death on a real or trumped-up charge of sedition, so long as we can know by spiritual experience the inner Christ, live uplifted

in the light of His teaching and escape from the yoke of the natural Law by that atonement of man with God of which the crucifixion is the symbol? If the Christ, God made man, lives within our spiritual being, it would seem to matter little whether or not a son of Mary physically lived and suffered and died in Judea.[18]

But it does matter whether or not Jesus of Nazareth truly lived, died, and rose from the dead. If the Gospel's record about Jesus is nothing more than a curious myth, then Christianity is a fraudulent religion that has deceived countless billions of faithful souls over the last two thousand years. If Jesus did not rise triumphantly from the empty tomb, then our hope of salvation is nothing more than a dream based on the greatest lie in history. The position espoused by many modern religious philosophers such as Aurobindo is that the "idea" or myth of Jesus is the truly important thing. They suggest that Christianity would not be significantly weakened by abandoning the position that the Gospels record the truth about Jesus' teachings and His call to salvation through faith in His atoning death on the cross. However, once we abandon the solid ground of the teachings of the Scriptures about Christ's words and deeds, we are left adrift on a sea of unlimited speculation.

Ultimately, if Christianity is divorced from historical events as described in the written text of the Gospels, then every man is free to create his own "Christ" in his own image. Tragically, while such an imaginary "Christ" may be satisfactory and even comfortable to a religious philosopher, a mythological Jesus cannot reconcile humanity to God because it would only be a private myth with no more reality or substance than last night's dream. Fortunately, the discoveries of science and archeology during the last few decades as presented in this book provide powerful evidence that the Bible's historical record is reliable and that the Jesus Christ of the Gospels truly lived and taught in Judea two thousand years ago and lives today. The mystery of Jesus is that He is both part of history and He also transcends it.

As we face the beginning of a new millennium, perhaps the most important question is this: Can an intelligent person believe the Bible's claims about Jesus Christ, based on solid historical and archeological evidence? The tremendous developments in our century of sophisticated archeological research and powerful scientific instruments, such as electron microscopes, computer-enhanced photography, and carbon-dating techniques have allowed us to lift the veil on many of the mysteries surrounding the life, death, and resurrection of Jesus. For the first time in history we can scientifically examine the archeological and historical evidence, including the tombs of the first Christians and the possible burial shroud of Jesus. Questions regarding Jesus' true identity have fascinated humanity for the past two thousand years. This book, *Jesus: The Great Debate*, attempts to answer these critical questions by examining all of the archeological, historical, and scientific evidence that has been discovered in order to determine the truth about Jesus.

Some people suggest that there is no need to scrutinize the Gospels to prove their historical accuracy. They suggest that we should simply and blindly accept the Christian faith without regard to the evidence. However, I have never believed in accepting anything on unquestioned blind faith. The Scriptures do not suggest that God expects us to "leap into the darkness" in blind faith. Rather, the Scriptures ask us to examine the historical and textual evidence of the Bible and come to a personal conclusion about Jesus of Nazareth, based on the light of His revealed truth. Then, the Scriptures invite us to place our faith and trust in Jesus Christ as God. It is significant that the writers of the New Testament continually appeal to the evidence that Jesus has fulfilled many of the Old Testament prophecies about the coming of the Messiah as evidence for His credentials. The apostle Peter reminds us "to be ready always to give an answer to every man that asketh you a reason of the hope that is in you with meekness and fear" (1 Peter 3:15).

The Claims of the New Testament Writers

In the book of Acts we read, "Yea, and all the prophets from Samuel and those that follow after, as many as have spoken, have likewise foretold of these days" (Acts 3:24). Luke, the writer of the Gospel of Luke and the book of Acts, declares that Jesus "shewed himself alive after his passion by many infallible proofs, being seen of them forty days, and speaking of the things pertaining to the kingdom of God" (Acts 1:3). Luke and Peter both refer to the fact that they were eyewitnesses to the events they recorded about Jesus. Luke wrote: "Even as they delivered them unto us, which from the beginning were eyewitnesses, and ministers of the word"

(Luke 1:2). The apostle Peter appealed to the reliability of the eyewitness evidence he presented to his readers: "For we have not followed cunningly devised fables, when we made known unto you the power and coming of our Lord Jesus Christ, but were eyewitnesses of his majesty" (2 Peter 1:16). After years of studying of the New Testament, I have come to the same conclusion as the great English writer Charles Dickens, who wrote, "The New Testament is the best book the world has ever known or will know."

For thirty-five years I have examined the evidence about the life of Jesus of Nazareth. As I study His life, His teachings, and His resurrection, I am convinced by the wealth of evidence that Jesus, as presented to us in the Gospels is, in fact, the true Messiah. In this book I will present the results of my exhaustive research, which has taken me to the libraries and museums of Canada, the United States, England, Europe, and Israel. I have spent countless hours exploring archeological sites in Israel, including Bethlehem, Nazareth, and Cana, the area where He began His unique ministry; Capernaum, where He taught in a synagogue; and Jerusalem, where He died and rose from the dead. I have had the privilege of exploring the Dead Sea Caves, where thousands of ancient biblical manuscript fragments, found in 1947, that confirm the astonishing accuracy of the text of the Scriptures. During my last two trips to Israel, I examined the tombs of first-century Jewish Christians and the tomb of Caiaphas the High Priest who presided at the Sanhedrin trial of Jesus. I have interviewed a key individual who participated in the scientific examination of the fascinating and controversial Shroud of Turin. It is my hope that this presentation of archeological, historical, and scientific evidence will enable you to come to a reasoned and knowledgeable decision about your personal response to the claims of Christ.

Notes

1. John Mill, *Logic*, 2 vols. 2:187.

2. Herman Samuel Reimarus, *Fragments: The Intention of Jesus and His Disciples*, ed. C. H. Talbert (Philadelphia: Fortress Press, 1971).

3. David Friedrich Strauss, *The Life of Jesus Critically Examined* (London: Chapman, 1846).

4. Bruno Bauer, *Criticism of the Gospels and History of Their Origin* (Berlin: Hempel, 1851).

5. E. Renan, *The History of the Origins of Christianity* (New York: Random House, 1863).

6. F. W. Farrar, *Life of Christ* (New York: Dutton Publishers, 1874).

7. Albert Schweitzer, *The Quest of the Historical Jesus* (London: A. & C. Black, 1910).

8. Rudolf Bultmann, *Jesus and the Word* (New York: Scribner's, 1958).

9. Rudolf Bultmann, *Existence and Faith: Shorther Writings of Rudolf Bultmann*, ed. S. M. M. Ogden (New York: World, 1966) 289–291.

10. Marcus Borg and N. T. Wright, *The Meaning of Jesus* (San Francisco: HarperSanFrancisco, 1998).

11. Robert W. Funk, *The Five Gospels: The Search for the Authentic Words of Jesus* (San Francisco: HarperSanFrancisco, 1991).

12. Robert W. Funk, *Honest To Jesus* (San Francisco: HarperCollins, 1966).

13. Arthur Dewey, *Time* Apr. 1994.

14. *Time* 6 Apr. 1996.

15. Iraneus, *Ante-Nicine Fathers* (Grand Rapids: Wm. B. Eerdmans Publishing Co., 1986).

16. Frederic G. Kenyon, *The Story of the Bible* (Grand Rapids: Eerdmans Co., 1967).

17. John Shelby Spong, *Rescuing the Bible from Fundamentalism* (San Francisco: HarperCollins, 1991) 35.

18. Sri Aurobindo, *The Human Cycle*. (New York: Dutton Press).

1

The Criteria of Historical Evidence about Jesus

Several decades ago one of the most brilliant professors in England, a well-known atheist, converted to Christianity. After studying the evidence, Professor C. S. Lewis could no longer deny the existence of Jesus Christ. Ultimately, he became one of the most compelling and effective witnesses to the historical truth of Christianity. However, he was constantly confronted by people who rejected Jesus Christ's claims that He is God, but nevertheless professed a great reverence for Jesus as an inspired, ethical, and moral teacher. Lewis recognized the inherent logical contradiction in this widely espoused opinion. In response, he wrote the following comment about this untenable position in his book *Mere Christianity*:

> You must make your choice. Either this man was and is the Son of God: or else a madman or something worse. You can shut Him up for a fool, you can spit at Him and kill Him as a demon; or you can fall at His feet and call Him Lord and God. But let us not come with any patronizing nonsense about His being a great human teacher. He has not left that open to us. He did not intend to.[1]

If Jesus was only a normal human being, yet claimed repeatedly that He was God and that He could forgive man's sins, then He must have been mad or a very evil man. However, the evidence from the Gospels about his inspired moral teachings demonstrates conclusively that He was neither mad nor evil. In fact, the considered opinion of the wisest philosophers and religious leaders throughout history is that Jesus of Nazareth was the most holy and moral human being who ever walked on earth. The logical conclusion is that His statements about Himself must be true.

Most individuals who take the time to examine carefully the life and teachings of Jesus as reported in the Gospels eventually come to a conclusion that He was more than just a man. The impact of His life and teachings upon untold generations of humanity in every nation and culture of the world demonstrate His supernatural influence on humanity. Even the greatest of the generals, kings, intellectuals, and statesmen have ultimately acknowledged that Jesus was more than just a man. For example, during his imprisonment on the island of St. Helena, the great general and emperor of France, Napoleon Bonaparte, told his companions that Jesus of Nazareth far surpassed all other great men of antiquity:

> I think I understand somewhat of human nature and I tell you all these were men, and I am a man, but not one is like Him; Jesus Christ was more than man. Alexander, Cæsar, Charlemagne, and myself founded great empires; but upon what did the creations of our genius depend? Upon force. Jesus alone founded His empire upon love, and to this very day millions would die for Him.[2]

In the same vein he wrote, "I search in vain in history to find the similar to Jesus Christ or anything which can approach the Gospel." Napoleon also spoke about the vitality and power of the Gospels:

> The Gospel is no mere book but a living creature, with a vigor, a power, which conquers all that opposes it. Here lies the Book of Books upon the table, I do not tire of reading it, and do so daily with equal pleasure. The soul, charmed with the beauty of the Gospel, is no longer its own: God possesses it entirely: He directs its thoughts and faculties; it is His. What a proof of the divinity of Jesus

Christ! Yet in this absolute sovereignty He has but one aim — the spiritual perfection of the individual, the purification of his conscience, his union with what is true, the salvation of his soul. Men wonder at the conquests of Alexander, but here is a conqueror who draws men to Himself for their highest good; who unites to Himself, incorporates into Himself, not a nation, but the whole human race.[3]

On another occasion the emperor wrote, "The nature of Christ's existence is mysterious, I admit; but this mystery meets the wants of man. Reject it and the world is an inexplicable riddle; believe it, and the history of our race is satisfactorily explained."

Agnosticism and Atheism

Many people today respond to the claims of Christianity by saying, "I just don't know whether or not I can believe the Bible." An atheist declares confidently that he totally rejects the claims of the Bible and Christ regarding truth and salvation. However, the agnostic claims that based on the evidence he has seen thus far he cannot decide whether to believe or not. To paraphrase Paul Little in his insightful book *Know Why You Believe*, the question that confronts anyone who claims "they just don't know the truth about Jesus and the Bible" is to ask whether you are an "ordinary" agnostic or an "ornery" one. The ordinary agnostic honestly declares that he has not seen enough evidence to convince him that God exists and that the Gospels are true. However, he is willing to acknowledge that others may have seen enough evidence to convince them of this fact. In other words, the ordinary agnostic says, "I don't know, but you may know." However, the ornery agnostic says, "I don't know, and you can't know either."[4] The writer G. Lowes Dickinson declared, "The mistake of agnosticism, it seems to me, has been that it has said not merely, 'I do not know,' but 'I will not consider.'"[5]

Writer Richard Downey revealed the fundamental problem with agnosticism as an approach to revealed truth: "Agnosticism denies to the human mind a power of attaining knowledge which it does possess. . . . Agnosticism, as such, is a theory about knowledge and not about religion."[6] Possibly Francis Thompson best described the fundamental problem with the philosophical approach of agnosticism in that it can never arrive at a satisfactory conclusion that provides confidence that it has found the truth. Francis Thompson acknowledged that, "Agnostism is the everlasting perhaps."[7]

The Importance of the Gospel's Historical Claims

Simon Greenleaf was one of the greatest lawyers in western history. Although he wrote his classic book on the proper evaluation of legal evidence in our judicial system over a century ago, *A Treatise on the Law of Evidence* is still an unsurpassed masterpiece. The *London Law Magazine* wrote of this book, "Upon the existing Law of Evidence (by Greenleaf) more light has shone from the New World than from all the lawyers who adorn the courts of Europe." Although Greenleaf set out initially to overthrow the Gospel record about Jesus Christ, his in-depth evaluation of the evidence forced him to acknowledge the historical accuracy of the Gospels and convert to Christianity. As a result, Greenleaf wrote a thought-provoking book on the historical reliability of the Gospels as legal evidence if presented in a court of law. *The Testimony of the Evangelists* addresses the importance of the historical quest to discover the truth about Jesus of Nazareth. He correctly points out that the claims of the Gospels regarding life, death, salvation, heaven, and hell are so momentous that it is vital that we as individuals examine the evidence to determine whether the Gospel record is true or not. Nothing less than our soul's eternal destiny is at stake. As Greenleaf wrote,

> The things related by the Evangelists are certainly of the most momentous character, affecting the principles of our conduct here, and our happiness forever. The religion of Jesus Christ aims at nothing less than the utter overthrow of all other systems of religion in the world; denouncing them as inadequate to the wants of man, false in their foundations, and dangerous in their tendency. It not only solicits the grave attention of all, to whom its doctrines are presented, but it demands their cordial belief, as a matter of vital concernment. These are no ordinary claims; and it seems hardly possible for a rational being to regard them with even a subdued interest; much less to treat them with mere indifference and contempt. If not true, they are little

else than the pretensions of a bold imposture, which, not satisfied with having already enslaved millions of the human race, seeks to continue its encroachments upon human liberty, until all nations shall be subjugated under its iron rule. But if they are well-founded and just, they can be no less than the high requirements of heaven, addressed by the voice of God to the reason and understanding of man, concerning things deeply affecting his relations to his sovereign, and essential to the formation of his character and of course to his destiny, both for this life and for the life to come.[8]

The Proper Criteria to Judge Evidence in the Gospels

In light of the supreme importance of our inquiry, we need to free our minds from previous prejudice as far as that is possible and begin a search for the truth about the claims about Jesus. The most fundamental questions we should address are the following: Are the Gospels a true and reliable record of the events and teachings of Jesus? Were the Gospels written by the followers of Christ in the first few decades following His death? Or, were the Gospels composed more than a hundred years after the events by editors of the early Church who had a religious agenda and who had never seen Jesus in the flesh? Are descriptions of the miracles, healings, and resurrections from the dead accurate portrayals of eyewitness evidence or are they simply myths created more than a century later to bolster the reputation of their religious leader? The question of when the Gospels were written is so important to our quest for truth that an entire chapter will be devoted to explore the evidence related to this vital question.

Consider the words of the Gospel writer Luke who challenged his readers to evaluate the "miracles" of Jesus of Nazareth as evidence that He was the promised Messiah because these events occurred "in the midst of you." Luke wrote: "Ye men of Israel, hear these words; Jesus of Nazareth, a man approved of God among you by miracles and wonders and signs, which God did by him in the midst of you, as ye yourselves also know" (Acts 2:22). It would have been fatal to Luke's purpose of evangelism to point to these "miracles and wonders and signs" as well-known historical events that had occurred "among you" unless he was confident that his readers had personally witnessed these supernatural events and that they would confirm these remarkable events to others.

However, before delving further into this matter, it is important that we establish the proper criteria for an historical examination of this kind. Many critics of Christianity, and even some Christians, have fallen into the habit of applying inappropriate standards to the question of evidence regarding the Gospels. For example, some people ask the question: Can you establish scientifically to an absolute standard of demonstrated proof that Jesus rose from the dead, et cetera? This question reveals a misunderstanding of the proper evaluation of historical evidence. Demonstrative scientific evidence cannot be offered to prove that President Abraham Lincoln was assassinated in the Ford Theatre in Washington in 1865. The problem we face is that demonstrative scientific evidence requires a hypothesis capable of being tested repeatedly in a laboratory by other scientists to verify the results. The nature of historical events is that they can never be repeated and, therefore, cannot be tested by scientific methods. The great error of skeptics is that they demand scientific proof about historical accounts about Jesus in the Gospels when such absolute proof about any historical event is impossible to obtain. However, the question about the historicity of the Gospels' claims about Jesus is a question of fact — precisely the type of question that has been considered and judged by courts of justice every day for thousands of years.

Courts judge the truthfulness of witnesses and questions of fact according to a fundamental rule summarized by legal expert Simon Greenleaf: "In trials of fact, by oral testimony, the proper inquiry is not whether it is possible that the testimony may be false, but whether there is sufficient probability that it is true."[9] Unfortunately, many arguments against the genuineness of the Gospel account are based on a cavalier approach that quickly rejects the accuracy of the historical record about Christ whenever the *slightest* doubt is raised by *anyone* about *any* detail in the Gospel account. Unwilling to acknowledge that the evangelists' accounts are probably true, they contemptuously reject the Gospels' statements because they believe that it is *possible* that they might be false. If this unreasonable basis for judging truth were applied to the records of other historical events, such as the assassination of Abraham Lincoln, we would have to throw out as unreliable virtually all the statements of actual witnesses that allow us to understand what happened during that tragic event.

A vital principle that should govern any serious inquiry into historical events is the principle of what actually constitutes historical proof. Simon Greenleaf defines this legal principle in his book *The Testimony of the Evangelists*: "A proposition of fact is proved, when its truth is established by competent and satisfactory evidence."[10] Competent and satisfactory evidence is the type and amount of evidence that would satisfy a normal, unprejudiced juror beyond any reasonable doubt. If the Gospel accounts about Christ can provide "competent and satisfactory" evidence that would satisfy an average jury beyond a reasonable doubt, then we can assume that historical proof has been established.

Another important principle concerning the credibility of witnesses is outlined by Greenleaf: "In the absence of circumstances which generate suspicion, every witness is to be presumed credible, until the contrary is shown; the burden of impeaching his credibility lying on the objector."[11] This point is vital. Many skeptical writers who reject Gospel accounts about Jesus do so automatically because they presume that the statements of the four Gospel writers are unreliable and lacking in credibility. On the other hand, if these critics find a single nonbiblical source that apparently contradicts the statements of the evangelists, that evidence tends to settle the issue automatically against the historical accuracy of the Gospels. However, according to Greenleaf's criteria, critics of the Gospels bear the burden of evidence to prove that Gospel statements are false. When the liberal critics are judged by this appropriate legal standard, many of their arguments lose their validity.

A final fundamental principle articulated by Greenleaf applies to all ancient documents: "Every document, apparently ancient, coming from the proper repository or custody, and bearing on its face no evident marks of forgery, the law presumes to be genuine, and devolves on the opposing party the burden of proving it to be otherwise."[12]

In other words, the assumption should be that the ancient document is authoritative, reliable, and accurate in its contents unless sufficient evidence is produced to contradict that assumption. When we consider the case for the Bible's reliability, the evidence is overwhelming. The Scriptures have been in use publicly for two thousand years in thousands of independent churches. Moreover, many different sects quickly sprang up and their members constantly appealed to Scripture to argue and defend their differing doctrinal interpretations of the text's meaning. This provides ample proof that the genuine text of the Scriptures has been reliably preserved down through the centuries until today. The existence of these sects guaranteed that no one could change the biblical text without it being instantly detected by their opponents. The principles of law also provide clear guidance on the questions raised by the fact that, at this time, we do not possess the original manuscripts of the Gospels. The courts of Western nations grant that copies of ancient documents that are universally received as legitimate (such as the Bible) are to be given the same value as evidence as the original manuscripts.

The Accuracy of the Bible Manuscripts

Over the last four thousand years, Jewish scribes, and later Christian scribes, took great care to correctly copy and transmit the original manuscripts of sacred Scriptures without any significant error. The Jewish scribes who hand-copied the manuscripts of the Old Testament were called "Masoretic" (from the Hebrew word for "wall" or "fence") because their extreme care in meticulously counting the letters of the Bible created a "fence around the law" to defend its accuracy. When a scribe completed his copy, a master examiner would painstakingly count every individual letter to confirm that there were no errors. If an error was found, the incorrect copy was destroyed to prevent its being used as a master copy.

The Roman emperors did everything in their power to destroy the new faith of Christianity by burning both Christians and the manuscripts of the Bible. In A.D. 303, the Roman Emperor Diocletian issued an official command to kill Christians and burn their sacred books. Professor Stanley L. Greenslade, editor of the *Cambridge History of the Bible*, records the history of this persecution: "An imperial letter was everywhere promulgated, ordering the razing of the churches to the ground and the destruction by fire of the Scriptures, and proclaiming that those who held high positions would lose all civil rights, while those in households, if they persisted in their profession of Christianity, would be deprived of their liberty"[13]

Nevertheless, the Christians' enthusiasm and dedication to the Scriptures in those first centuries following Christ motivated them to produce numerous manuscripts that were widely copied, distributed, and translated throughout the empire. From the moment of its writing by the apostles, the New Testament became the most widely quoted book in history; its popularity continues today. In A.D. 70, only four decades after Jesus died on the cross, Bishop Ignatius of Antioch, the minister responsible for several churches in Syria, quoted extensively from the New Testament in his writings. Clement, the Bishop of Rome (mentioned by Paul in Philippians 4:3), also quoted extensively from the New Testament within forty years of Christ's resurrection.

Historians have recovered almost one hundred thousand manuscripts and letters from the first few centuries of this era that were composed by Christian writers. These numerous letters and books written by the early Christian Fathers contain an astonishing 99 percent of the almost eight thousand verses in the New Testament, demonstrating the profound love of the Scriptures in the life of the young Church. Scholars Norman Geisler and William Nix, drawing from the research of biblical scholar Sir David Dabrymple, documented the number of New Testament verses that were quoted by the early Church Fathers in the second and third centuries: "A brief inventory at this point will reveal that there were some thirty-two thousand citations of the New Testament prior to the time of the Council of Nicea."[14] One Christian writer, Origen, quoted individual New Testament verses more than seventeen thousand times according to Geisler and Nix.

Dabrymple declared, "You remember the question about the New Testament and the Fathers? That question roused my curiosity, and as I possessed all the existing works of the Fathers of the second and third centuries, I commenced to search, and up to this time I have found the entire New Testament, except eleven verses."[15] In other words, even if the Romans had succeeded in destroying the New Testament, we could still reliably reconstruct over 99 percent of its text from these surviving quotations. This fact shows the absolute reliability and integrity of the surviving text of the New Testament as it exists today.

The Inspiration of Scripture

Generations of Christian believers have shared an unshakable conviction that the Scriptures contain the infallible, inspired, and authoritative words of God. The Bible itself claims that "all scripture is given by inspiration of God, and is profitable for doctrine, for reproof, for correction, for instruction in righteousness" (2 Timothy 3:16). The Greek word translated "inspired" literally means "God breathed," indicating the Lord's direct supernatural supervision of the writing by the biblical author. The Bible claims that its words were not written by men in an ordinary manner, but that God inspired men to record His written revelation to mankind for all time. Just as God created only one sun to provide light to our planet, He gave us only one book, the Bible, to enlighten our world spiritually. The great philosopher Immanuel Kant acknowledged the enormous gift that God has given humanity: "The Bible is the greatest benefit which the human race has ever experienced."[16] The brilliant scientist Sir Isaac Newton was a true Christian who had a profound faith in the Word of God and in his personal relationship with Jesus Christ. Isaac Newton wrote, "We account the Scriptures of God to be the most sublime philosophy. I find more sure marks of authority in the Bible than in any profane history whatsoever."

Tragically, during this century many pastors, professors, and laymen have lost their faith and confidence that the Bible is truly inspired. Dr. Kennedy, a Regius Professor of Classics at Cambridge University, in the early decades of this century warned of the relentless battle that was about to begin over the authority of the Bible: "The inspiration of Scriptures will be the last battle ground between the Church and the world." Unfortunately, today, many in our churches and seminaries have admitted defeat in this battle, surrendering at the hands of skeptics who express contempt for the concept of the authority and inspiration of the Word of God and Jesus' claim to be the Son of God.

This widespread rejection of the truthfulness of the Scriptures in modern times reveals the folly of men who "have forsaken me the fountain of living waters, and hewed them out cisterns, broken cisterns" of vain philosophy (Jeremiah 2:13). Today the broken cisterns of existential philosophy present us with a hopeless world view in which humanity has been set adrift as an evolutionary accident in a dying universe without meaning or purpose.

In the New Testament the apostle Peter declared that "Knowing this first, that no prophecy of Scripture is of any private interpretation, for prophecy never came by the will of man, but holy men of God spoke as they were moved by the Holy Spirit" (2 Peter 1:20–21). The prophet Jeremiah declared, "Then the Lord put forth His hand and touched my mouth, and the Lord said to me: 'Behold, I have put My words in your mouth'" (Jeremiah 1:9). God confirmed that He directly inspired His servants, the prophets, to record His words and instructions "word for word." One of the strongest statements about the Bible's authority is found in the words of Jesus Himself who declared, "The Scripture cannot be broken" (John 10:35). The brilliant philosopher, John Locke, described his opinion of the nature of the Scriptures. "They have God for their author, salvation for their end, and truth, without any mixture of error, for their matter." Scottish geologist Hugh Miller also wrote, "The gospel is the fulfillment of all hopes, the perfection of all philosophy, the interpreter of all revelations, and a key to all the seeming contradictions of truth in the physical and moral world."[17]

Evidence of the Accuracy of the Scriptures

A wealth of evidence proves the accuracy and authenticity of the Gospel records about Jesus. Evidence we will examine includes the following:

1. Many ancient inscriptions and manuscripts that support the historical accuracy of the Scriptures.

2. Little-known archeological discoveries of the actual tombs of people mentioned in the Gospel account of Christ's trial and crucifixion.

3. The ancient pagan and Jewish writings that provide remarkable confirmation of the biblical accounts about the death of Jesus.

3. The fulfillment of many detailed messianic prophecies about Jesus that authenticate the Scriptures.

4. The transformed lives of the writers of the Bible.

5. The unprecedented influence of Jesus Christ on the lives of individuals, Western culture, and the history of the world.

6. Ancient manuscripts from the Dead Sea Scrolls that refer to the crucifixion of Jesus Christ and contain quotations from the Gospels.

7. New scientific discoveries about the ancient burial cloth known as the Shroud of Turin that suggest it may have covered the body of Christ.

The evidence provided in this book will confirm that we know more about the life, death, and resurrection of Jesus of Nazareth through multiple historical eyewitness statements and documentary evidence than any other person of the ancient world. As a result of the details in the four Gospels and the multitude of documents from Roman, pagan, and Jewish sources, we know an astonishing number of historical details about the life of Christ. However, at Jesus' birth the prophet Simeon warned, "Behold, this child is set for the fall and rising again of many in Israel; and for a sign which shall be spoken against" (Luke 2:34). Jesus Himself warned during His life that He would become the center of the greatest debate that would divide families and the world. The balance of this book demonstrates the powerful historical, archeological, and scientific evidence that reveals that Jesus was the true Messiah and the Son of God as He claimed.

Archeological Evidence That the Bible Is Reliable

The field of biblical archeology has exploded in the past century and a half. The discoveries have provided tremendous new insights into the life, culture, and history of the ancient biblical world. Most importantly, while archeology can never "prove" the inspiration of the Bible, these discoveries have confirmed the historical accuracy of thousands of individual biblical statements.

Archeologists digging at sites in the Middle East have made remarkable discoveries, including the tombs of Caiaphas the High Priest and others mentioned in the Gospels. Many new discoveries in Israel and the surrounding nations have provided confirmation of the accuracy of the Word of God, according to Dr. Nelson Glueck, the most outstanding Jewish archeologist of this century:

> It may be stated categorically that no archæological discovery has ever controverted a Biblical reference. Scores of archæological findings have been made which confirm in clear outline or in exact detail historical statements in the Bible. And by the same token, proper evaluation of Biblical descriptions has often led to amazing discoveries. They

form tesseræ in the vast mosaic of the Bible's almost incredibly correct historical memory.[18]

Confirming Glueck's statement, another respected scholar, Dr. J. O. Kinnaman, said, "Of the hundreds of thousands of artifacts found by the archeologists, not one has ever been discovered that contradicts or denies one word, phrase, clause, or sentence of the Bible, but always confirms and verifies the facts of the biblical record."

Only fifty years ago many liberal scholars rejected the historical accuracy of the Bible because they claimed that the Scriptures spoke about kings, places, and individuals that could not be confirmed from any other historical or archeological records. Recent discoveries, however, have confirmed many biblical details, events, and personalities. For example, many modern scholars have contemptuously rejected the Bible's statements about King David. As an example, Professor Philip R. Davies wrote, "I am not the only scholar who suspects that the figure of King David is about as historical as King Arthur."[19] Textbooks used in many universities and seminaries have openly rejected historical statements in the Scriptures about King David or Solomon. Examples of this approach include the books *In Search of Ancient Israel*, by Philip R. Davis, and *The Early History of the Israelite People*, by Thomas L. Thompson. He wrote, "The existence of the Bible's 'United Monarchy' during the tenth-century [B.C.] is . . . impossible." For example, in 1997 Israeli Professor Nadav Na'a,an ignored the most recent discoveries and declared that there were no surviving inscriptions that referred to the first kings of Israel:

> It is true that no extra-Biblical source mentions either David or Solomon. This is not surprising. Detailed accounts of first-millennium international affairs appear for the first time in the ninth century B.C.E. All Syro-Palestinian inscriptions of the tenth century refer to local affairs and shed no light on political events. In other words, even if David and Solomon accomplished the deeds attributed to them in the Bible, no source would have mentioned their names.[20]

However, Israeli archeologists were astonished to discover an ancient stone inscription at Tell Dan, near the ancient city of Dan, at the foot of Mount Hermon in northern Israel. This inscription fragment from a stone column victory monument was written in the Aramaic language and mentions "the house of David." It was created by an enemy of Israel in approximately 900 B.C., to describe their defeat of a Jewish army. An article in *Biblical Archeological Review* (March–April 1994) reported, "Avraham Biran and his team of archæologists found a remarkable inscription from the 9th century [B.C.] that refers both to the 'House of David' and to the 'King of Israel.' This is the first time that the name David has been found in any ancient inscription outside the Bible. That the inscription refers not simply to a 'David' but to the House of David, the dynasty of the great Israelite king, is even more remarkable."[21] A review of recent archeological books and articles reveals that evidence has also been found in this century that confirms the historical existence of the following biblical kings: Ahab, Ahaz, Omri, Hezekiah, Hoshea, Jehu, Jeroboam II, Manasseh, and Pekah.

Professor Millar Burrows wrote about the underlying reason most scholars reject the authority of the Bible: "The excessive skepticism of many liberal theologians stems not from a careful evaluation of the available data, but from an enormous predisposition against the supernatural. . . . On the whole, however, archæological work has unquestionably strengthened confidence in the reliability of the scriptural record."[22]

The remarkable truth is that the life of Jesus of Nazareth occurred in historical time as opposed to some mythological period in the distant past. There is no other period in the ancient past that is so well documented as the first century of the Christian era during the rule of the Roman emperors. Some of the greatest historians of the ancient world were contempories of Jesus and His disciples, including the Roman writers Livy and Seneca, as well as the Jewish historian Flavius Josephus, whose works have survived through the centuries.

The evidence reveals that the Gospel writer Luke was an accurate historian who mentions well-attested historical figures, including Pontius Pilate, King Herod, Tiberius Cæsar, the High Priests Annas and Caiaphas, as well as James, the brother of Christ, John the Baptist, and Jesus of Nazareth, all of whom are also mentioned by Jewish historian Flavius Josephus in A.D. 73. Even the existence of a relatively obscure person such as Lysanias, tetrarch of Abilene, who is mentioned in the third chapter of Luke's Gospel, has been historically confirmed by the discovery of two archeological inscriptions bearing his name and office. The greatest critics of Christianity in the early centuries, including Celsus, who debated Christian writers in the second century of the Christian era, never once ventured to suggest that Jesus of Nazareth did not live or die in Jerusalem. Surely if the pagans had possessed any evidence that contradicted the basic account of Christ's life, they would have openly challenged the Christian writers with those facts. However, the pagans never claimed that Jesus was a mythical figure because they, too, were familiar with the historical facts of Christ's life and the claims of the thousands in Israel who had witnessed His miraculous feeding of the five thousand and the hundreds who had seen Jesus alive for forty days after His resurrection from the grave.

In fact, when you carefully consider the Gospel claims about the feeding of the five thousand, it becomes obvious that these supernatural claims would have been instantly rejected as absurd if it were not for the fact that thousands of people in Israel were eyewitnesses to these events. Claiming such miracles, had they never occurred, would have been the surest way to destroy the new religion of Christianity. The fact that Christianity constantly affirmed the greatest miracles in history, including the resurrection of Jesus Christ, while thousands of eyewitnesses to these events were still alive, provides the strongest evidence that these remarkable events must have actually occurred as recorded in the Gospels. As this book will demonstrate, the Gospels were written, distributed, and translated into other languages within thirty to forty years of the crucifixion of Jesus — at a time when thousands of Jews who witnessed these events in Christ's life and ministry were still alive. Christianity could never have survived, let alone flourish, if it had been based on a lie.

The Effect of the Attempt to Discredit the Gospels

Professor E. B. Pusey, in his brilliant defense of the authenticity of the Scriptures against the higher critics of his day, wrote about the continual attacks on the inspiration of Scripture from those who still claimed to be ministers of the Gospel:

The faith can receive no real injury except from its defenders. Against its assailants, those who wish to be safe, God protects. If the faith shall be (God forbid!) destroyed in England, it will not be by open assailants, but by those who think that they defend it, while they have themselves lost it. So it was in Germany. Rationalism was the product, not of the attacks on the Gospel but of its weak defenders. Each generation, in its controversies with unbelief, conceded more of the faith, until at last it was difficult to see what difference there was between assailants and defenders. Theology was one great graveyard; and men were disputing over a corpse, as if it had life. The salt had 'lost its savour.' The life was fled.[23]

The widespread agnosticism and atheism that is found almost everywhere within our modern government, media, universities, and seminaries has contributed to the increasing moral collapse of our society. The philosopher Thomas Hobbes wisely described the inevitable and disastrous spiritual effects on society caused by growing agnosticism and a gradual abandonment of the authority of Scriptures in the life of our nations: "No arts, no letters, no society, and which is worst of all, continual fear and danger of violent death, and the life of man solitary, poor, nasty, brutish and short."[24] The inevitable consequences of our current national apostasy were accurately predicted in his writings.

In 1830 the government of France faced a crime wave and overflowing prisons as a consequence of the virtual elimination of public religion following the French Revolution. The French authorities sent a well-respected judge, Alexis de Tocqueville, to study the society, beliefs, and the prisons of the United States of America to find out why there was so little crime and so few jails in the vibrant young nation, which had experienced its own revolution only a few decades before France. America seemed a veritable paradise in comparison to the corruption and criminality that swept France following the French Revolution, a period in history in which the church and religion in general were repudiated by the French. After several years of careful study, he wrote his celebrated book entitled *The Democracy of the United States* in 1840. Alexis de Tocqueville wrote about the reason for America's greatness as a nation and its remarkably low crime rate:

I sought for the greatness of the United States in her commodious harbors, her ample rivers, her fertile fields, and boundless forests — and it was not there. I sought for it in her rich mines, her vast world commerce, her public schools system and in her institutions of higher learning — and it was not there. I looked for it in her democratic Congress and her matchless Constitution — and it was not there. Not until I went into the churches of America and heard her pulpits flame with righteousness did I understand the secret of her genius and power. America is great because America is good, and if America ever ceases to be good, America will cease to be great![25]

A century and a half after de Tocqueville recorded his observations, America has publicly abandoned the Bible as the moral anchor of her society, government, courts, and education. It should surprise no one that, after decades of eliminating the Bible from our schools and teaching our children that there are no absolute rights and wrongs, we now face a widespread breakdown in public and private morality, along with rising levels of violent youth crime, as witnessed in the appalling shooting tragedy at schools such as Columbine, Colorado.

President Andrew Jackson shared the same opinion as de Tocqueville about the vital position of the Scriptures in the life of his nation. As he lay on his deathbed, President Jackson pointed to the Bible on the table by his bed and said to his companion, "That Book, Sir, is the rock on which our Republic rests." Another scholar, Sir William Jones, described the Gospels as follows: They contain more sublimity, more exquisite beauty, purer morality, more important history, and finer strains both of poetry and eloquence, than could be collected within the same compass from all other books that were ever composed in any age, or in any idiom."

Notes

1. C. S. Lewis, *Mere Christianity* (Grand Rapids: Baker Book House, 1977).

2. Napoleon Bonaparte, *Bertrand's Memoirs* (Paris, 1844).

3. Napoleon Bonaparte, *Bertrand's Memoirs* (Paris, 1844).

4. Paul Little, *Know Why You Believe* (Downer's Grove: Intervarsity Press, 1967).

5. G. Lowes Dickinson, *Religion* (1905).

6. Richard Downey, *Critical and Constructive Essays* (1934).

7. Francis Thompson, *Paganism Old and New* (1910).

8. Simon Greenleaf, *The Testimony of the Evangelists* (New York: J. C. & Co., 1874).

9. Simon Greenleaf, *The Testimony of the Evangelists* (New York: J. C. & Co., 1874).

10. Simon Greenleaf, *The Testimony of the Evangelists* (New York: J. C. & Co., 1874).

11. Simon Greenleaf, *The Testimony of the Evangelists* (New York: J. C. & Co., 1874).

12. Simon Greenleaf, *The Testimony of the Evangelists* (New York: J. C. & Co., 1874).

13. Stanley L. Greenslade, *Cambridge History of the Bible* (Cambridge: Cambridge University Press, 1963).

14. Norman L. Geisler and William E. Nix, *A General Introduction to the Bible* (Chicago: Moody Press, 1968).

15. Norman L. Geisler and William E. Nix, *A General Introduction to the Bible* (Chicago: Moody Press, 1968).

16. Immanuel Kant, *Critique of Pure Reason* (1770).

17. Hugh Miller, *The Headship of Christ* (Edinburgh: William P. Nimmo, 1857).

18. Nelson Glueck, *Rivers in the Desert* (New York: Grove, 1960) 31.

19. Philip R. Davis, *Biblical Archæology Review* July–Aug. 1994: 55.

20. Nadav Na'a,an, "Cow Town or Royal Capital," *Biblical Archeological Review* July–Aug. 1997.

21. *Biblical Archeological Review* Mar–Apr. 1994: 26.

22. Millar Burrows, *What Mean These Stones?* (New York: Meridian Books, 1956) 258–259.

23. E. B. Pusey, *The Prophet Daniel* (Plymouth: Devonport Society, 1864) 25.

24. Thomas Hobbes, *Leviathan* (1651).

25. Alexis de Tocqueville, *The Democracy of the United States* (1840).

2

The Fundamental Issue of When the Gospels Were Written

During the earlier years of this century many liberal scholars concluded that the Gospels were unreliable as historical evidence largely because they believed that the Gospels were written at least one hundred years after the events they describe. The scholars concluded that these "second" century Gospel documents must be based, therefore, on hearsay and oral traditions, rather than on eyewitness accounts. This unwarranted prejudice led a whole generation of liberal scholars to reject the historical authority of the Gospels.

Sir Frederic G. Kenyon, former director of the British Museum, was possibly the most respected New Testament textual scholar of our century. He concluded that the Gospels were composed within a few decades after the events of Christ's life and that the early church widely distributed them to its congregations within a relatively short period of time. Kenyon wrote:

The interval, then, between the dates of original composition and the earliest extant evidence becomes so small as to be in fact negligible, and the last foundation for any doubt that the Scriptures have come down to us substantially as they were written has now been removed. Both the authenticity and the general integrity of the books of the New Testament may be regarded as finally established.[1]

It is reassuring at the end to find that the general result of all these discoveries and all this study is to strengthen the proof of the authenticity of the Scriptures, and our conviction that we have in our hands, in substantial integrity, the veritable Word of God.[2]

Professor Merrill F. Unger declares that the recent discoveries of archeology have proven the complete accuracy and historical authority of the Gospels as reliable eyewitness accounts. Unger wrote, "The Acts of the apostles is now generally agreed in scholarly circles to be the work of Luke, to belong to the first century and to involve the labors of a careful historian who was substantially accurate in his use of sources."[3]

The well-respected language scholar, Dr. Robert Dick Wilson, formerly professor of Semitic philology at Princeton Theological Seminary, made the following comment:

After forty-five years of scholarly research in biblical textual studies and in language study, I have come now to the conviction that no man knows enough to assail the truthfulness of the Old Testament. When there is sufficient documentary evidence to make an investigation, the statement of the Bible, in the original text, has stood the test.[4]

A. N. Sherwin-White was a great classical historical scholar at Oxford University. After he studied the evidence for and against the historical accuracy of the book of Acts, he said, "For Acts the confirmation of historicity is overwhelming . . . any attempt to reject its basic historicity even in matters of detail must now appear absurd."[5]

Dr. John A. T. Robinson, a distinguished scholar and lecturer at Trinity College in Cambridge, originally concluded that the Gospels were written at least one hundred years after the death of Christ. However, an article in *Time* magazine, March 21, 1977, reported that Professor Robinson decided to re-examine the matter. Robinson was shocked to discover that much of the past scholarship on the New Testament was academically untenable because it was based on a "tyranny of unexamined assumptions" and what he felt must have been an "almost willful blindness." Robinson concluded that the apostles were the genuine writers of the New Testament books and that they wrote their accounts in the years between A.D. 32 and A.D. 64, at a time when thousands of eyewitnesses of Jesus' miracles and resurrection were still alive to give their accounts. As a result of his new analysis, Robinson believed that a re-examination of the evidence would necessitate "the rewriting of many introductions to — and, ultimately, theologies of — the New Testament."[6]

Modern scholars now possess more than five thousand ancient manuscript copies of various portions of the New Testament that have survived in the Greek language. There are an additional fifteen thousand manuscripts in other languages such as Latin and Syriac that have survived from the first few centuries of the Christian era. No other important ancient text, whether historical or religious, has more than a few dozen copies that have survived almost two thousand years until our generation. The twenty thousand surviving manuscripts of the New Testament reveal minute differences of spelling, and other minor variations. However, this huge number of biblical manuscripts provides the strongest textual evidence possible, allowing scholars to check and trace the origin of the various readings to ascertain the original text. Most importantly, these minor discrepancies, mostly caused by careless copying over the centuries, are usually trivial. It is significant that not one of these small textual differences affects or brings into question a single important fact or doctrine of the Bible.

The importance of these New Testament scholars' conclusions supporting an early date for the Gospels (before A.D. 70) cannot be overstated. It would have been almost impossible to successfully distribute a blatantly false story about Christ's miracles, His death, and His resurrection throughout the Roman Empire while thousands of His faithful followers and thousands of non-Christian observers of these events were still alive to dispute it. Furthermore, the evidence is overwhelming that the Greek originals of the Gospels and the New Testament Epistles were widely copied, distributed, and translated immediately into Hebrew, Syriac, Latin,

Coptic, and other languages. These New Testament documents were treasured by the churches and read in their Sunday services within the first century. If anyone had wanted to introduce a false miracle, an imaginary event, or a theologically deviant doctrine into the Gospels, they would have faced an almost impossible task. In order to successfully introduce a false statement, the forger would have to simultaneously forge and insert this counterfeit passage into every single manuscript copy of the Gospels in every country and language without being detected or challenged by any Christian.

To put this in proper perspective, imagine that some modern writer wanted to create a false story in the 1990s about President Kennedy performing miracles and being raised from the dead for a period of forty days following his tragic assassination in November 1963. To succeed with his plan the writer would have to accomplish two virtually impossible tasks: (1) He would have to simultaneously acquire every one of the thousands of books and newspaper reports about the president and secretly insert his counterfeit passage in this material without being detected by a single reader; and (2) He would have to simultaneously convince millions of people around the world to accept this forgery as true, despite the fact that people who were alive when Kennedy lived and died would have independent recollections that contradict this invented story.

It is obvious to anyone who considers the problem carefully that it would be almost impossible to successfully produce such a forgery about President Kennedy's life that would convince anyone who witnessed the events, let alone the whole population of the world. However, the liberal scholars who suggest that the Gospel records were altered to introduce new doctrines and statements about Christ's virgin birth and resurrection are proposing something that is just as impossible. In light of the tremendous opposition and the continuing persecution of their new faith, the early Christians had every reason to inquire into the truthfulness of the Gospel record about Jesus Christ.

Johannes von Muller once wrote, "Christ is the key to the history of the world. Not only does all harmonize with the mission of Christ, but all is subordinate to it." In his comment on the sustained and unrelenting attacks on the authority of the Bible from the modern academic community, Professor Bernard Ramm made the following comment about the failure of these attacks to make a serious dent in the popularity and influence of the Scriptures: "A thousand times over, the death knell of the Bible has been sounded, the funeral procession formed, the inscription cut on the tombstone, and committal read. But somehow the corpse never stays put."[7] Samuel Taylor Coleridge once wrote, "Christianity is not a theory or speculation, but a life; not a philosophy of life, but a living presence."

The Bible repeatedly declares that Scripture is inspired directly by God Himself and that it is free from error. Several examples will prove this point. The Torah reveals that God supernaturally wrote a portion of the Scriptures — the Ten Commandments — on tablets of stone with His finger. Moses recorded this event: "And he gave unto Moses, when he had made an end of communing with him upon mount Sinai, two tables of testimony, tables of stone, written with the Finger of God" (Exodus 31:18). King David also confirmed the absolute accuracy and authority of the testimony of God as recorded in the Bible in the following passage: "The law of the Lord is perfect, converting the soul: the testimony of the Lord is sure, making wise the simple" (Psalms 19:7). David also declared, "For ever, O Lord, thy word is settled in heaven" (Psalms 119:89). Centuries later, the Gospel writer Matthew, who ministered for almost three and one-half years with Jesus of Nazareth, recorded Christ's words: "For verily I say unto you, Till heaven and earth pass, one jot or one tittle shall in no wise pass from the law, till all be fulfilled" (Matthew 5:18). Christ's statement declares that the very words and the spelling of the words in the original Hebrew and Greek languages were inspired by Almighty God.

The Gospel writer John, the beloved disciple of our Lord, recorded Jesus' statement, "For had ye believed Moses, ye would have believed me: for he wrote of me. But if ye believe not his writings, how shall ye believe my words?" (John 5:46–47). It is fascinating to note that Jesus Christ compared the ancient words of Moses with His own words and declares that both statements are equally inspired and authoritative. Finally, the apostle Peter declared the authority and inspiration of the written Scriptures: "Knowing this first, that no prophecy of the scripture is of any private interpretation. For the prophecy came not in old time by the will of man: but holy men of God spake as they were moved by the Holy Ghost" (2 Peter 1:20–21). In this passage, the apostle Peter confirmed that the authors of the Bible were supernaturally directed by the power of God's Holy Spirit. This epistle of Peter describes the inspiration of Scripture in his statement that the holy men of God spoke as they were moved by the Holy Spirit.

One important clue that supports an early date in the first century for the writing of the four Gospels is found, in the Gospels' failure to mention the Roman destruction of Jerusalem and the Jewish state in A.D. 70. If the Gospels were written after A.D. 66, when the Roman legions invaded Galilee, or after A.D. 70, when the Romans burned the city and Temple, the Gospel writers naturally would have referred to the fact that these events fulfilled Jesus' earlier prophecies made in A.D. 32 regarding the impending destruction of the Jewish Temple. However, the three Synoptic Gospels are totally silent about the catastrophic events of Jerusalem's destruction, a disaster that affected every Jewish citizen throughout the land of Judea. The silence of the Gospels about this tragic fulfillment of Christ's prophecy provides convincing evidence to any unbiased observer that the Gospel writers must have written their manuscripts at some point prior to the Jewish-Roman War in A.D. 66–70.

The well-known Jewish historian Flavius Josephus, who lived at the time of the apostle Paul described the sacred books of the Old Testament, and declared that these writers wrote "according to the *pneustia* (inspiration) that comes from God." In another passage Josephus wrote, "After the lapse of so many centuries, no one among the Jews has dared to add or to take away, or to transpose any thing in the sacred Scriptures."[8] The writer of the famous novel *Ben Hur*, Lew Wallace, was another skeptical inquirer who attempted to disprove the Gospel account about Jesus. Wallace wrote of his quest for the historical truth that led him inexorably to the conclusion that Jesus was truly the Son of God and mankind's only spiritual hope.

> After six years given to the impartial investigation of Christianity, as to its truth or falsity, I have come to the deliberate conclusion that Jesus Christ was the Messiah of the Jews, the Saviour of the World, and my personal Saviour.[9]

Sir William Ramsay, a brilliant English scholar, travelled as a young man to Asia Minor over a century ago with the sole purpose of disproving the Bible's history as described by Luke in his Gospel and in his book of Acts. Young Ramsay and his skeptical professors were convinced that the New Testament record must be terribly inaccurate. He believed that Luke could not possibly be correct in his Gospel history about Christ or in his account in the book of Acts about the growth of the Church during the first decades following the death of Christ. Ramsay began to dig in the ancient ruins of Greece and Asia Minor, searching for ancient names, boundary markers, and other archeological finds that would prove conclusively that Luke had "invented" his Gospel history of Christ and His Church. To his amazement, Ramsay discovered that the statements of the New Testament Scriptures were accurate in the smallest detail. Although Ramsay began his research as a confirmed skeptic, his extensive archeological discoveries throughout the Middle East finally forced him to declare that the archeological and historical evidence was overwhelming. Luke's account in the Gospel and the book of Acts was accurate and reliable:

> Luke is a historian of the first rank; not merely are his statements of fact trustworthy; he is possessed of the true historical sense . . . In short this author should be placed along with the very greatest of historians."[10]

As a result, Sir William Ramsay became both a Christian and a great Bible scholar. His books have become classics in the study of the history of the New Testament.

Another scholar, Dr. William F. Albright, was unquestionably one of the world's most brilliant biblical archeologists. In 1955 he wrote, "We can already say emphatically that there is no longer any solid basis for dating any book of the New Testament after circa A.D. 80." Additional discoveries over the next decade convinced him that all the books in the New Testament were written "probably sometime between circa A.D. 50 and 75." Significantly, Albright concluded that the writing of the New Testament within a few years of the events it described made it almost impossible for errors or exaggerations to have entered the text. He wrote that the duration between the events of Christ's life and the writing about them was "too slight to permit any appreciable corruption of the essential center and even of the specific wording of the sayings of Jesus."[11]

> The deathless Book has survived three great dangers: the negligence of its friends; the false systems built upon it; the warfare of those who have hated it.
>
> — Isaac Taylor

Notes

1. Frederic G. Kenyon, *The Bible and Archealogy* (New York: Harper & Row, 1940).

2. Frederic G. Kenyon, *The Story of the Bible*, Special U.S. Edition (Grand Rapids: Eerdmans Co., 1967) 133.

3. Merrill F. Unger, *Archeology and the New Testament* (Grand Rapids: Zondervan Publishing House, 1962).

4. Robert Dick Wilson, *A Scientific Investigation of the Old Testament* (Chicago: Moody Press, 1959).

5. Rubel Shelley, *Prepare To Answer* (Grand Rapids: Baker Book House, 1990).

6. John A. T. Robinson, *Time* 21 Mar. 1977.

7. Bernard Ramm, *Protestant Christian Evidences* (Chicago: Moody Press, 1957) 239.

8. Flavius Josephus, *Antiquities of the Jews* (A.D. 93).

9. Lew Wallace, *Ben Hur* (1908).

10. Sir William Ramsay, *The Bearing of Recent Discovery on the Trustworthiness of the New Testament* (Grand Rapids: Baker Book House, 1953) 80.

11. William F. Albright, *Recent Discoveries in Bible Lands* (New York: Funk and Wagnalls, 1955).

3

Remarkable Evidence in the Dead Sea Scrolls

If someone had asked a minister in 1947 to prove that the original Hebrew Scriptures of the Old Testament were copied without error throughout thousands of years, he might have had some difficulty in providing an answer. At that time, the oldest Old Testament manuscript used by the King James translators was dated approximately A.D. 1100. Obviously, that manuscript from A.D. 1100 was a copy of a copy of a copy, et cetera. How could we be sure that the text in the copy of the Scriptures from A.D. 1100 was identical to the original text, as given to the writers by God and inspired by Him?

An extraordinary discovery that changed this religious dilemma occurred in the turbulent year before Israel became a nation. In 1947, a Bedouin Arab shepherd boy found a hidden cave in Qumran near the Dead Sea that ultimately yielded over one thousand priceless manuscript fragments dating back before A.D. 68, when the Roman legions destroyed the Qumran village during the Jewish war against Rome. *(See picture 1 in photo section.)*

This shepherd boy discovered the greatest archeological find in history. When the scholars examined these ancient Hebrew scrolls, they found that this Qumran site contained a library with hundreds of precious texts of both biblical and secular manuscripts that dated back before the destruction of the Second Temple and the death of Jesus Christ. Once the Bedouins recognized the value of the scrolls, they began to search for additional documents in every valley and cave near the Dead Sea. The most incredible find was discovered in Cave Four at Qumran — an immense library of biblical manuscripts that contained almost all of the books of the Old Testament (with the exception of the book of Esther). In fact, multiple copies of several biblical texts from the books of Genesis, Deuteronomy, and Isaiah were found. The Dead Sea Scrolls provided evidence of original biblical texts that had lain undisturbed in the desert caves for almost two thousand years. Furthermore, the scholars discovered that the manuscript copies of the most authoritative Masoretic Hebrew text, Textus Recepticus (Received Text), used by the King James translators in 1611, was virtually identical to these ancient Dead Sea Scrolls. After carefully comparing the biblical manuscripts, they discovered that, aside from a tiny number of spelling variations, there were no significant differences between the original scrolls in the caves and the Hebrew texts used to produce the Authorized King James Version of 1611.

It is known that the Dead Sea community of Qumran was inhabited by the Essenes, a Jewish community of ascetics, who lived primarily in three communities: Qumran at the Dead Sea, the Essene Quarter of Jerusalem (Mount Zion), and an area near Damascus. They are thought to have existed from approximately 200 B.C. until the destruction of their communities in Jerusalem and Qumran by the Roman armies in A.D. 68. During the first century there were three significant Jewish religious groups: the Pharisees, the Sadducees, and the Essenes. The Essenes established the center of their religious community near the shores of the Dead Sea. In their love for the Word of God they faithfully copied each Old Testament scroll in their Scriptorium in the village of Qumran. New evidence indicates that these men were aware of Jesus of Nazareth and several of the writings about Him that became known as the New Testament. The Christian historian Eusebius, who wrote around A.D. 325, believed that the Essenes were influenced by Christianity.[1]

When the scrolls were first discovered, many Christian scholars naturally wondered if they might contain evidence relating to

Christianity. Despite intense scholarly interest, the hopes of Christian scholars were frustrated for almost fifty years by the decision of the small group of original scroll scholars to withhold release and publication of a significant number of these precious scrolls. Some scholars speculated that the unpublished scrolls might contain evidence about Christ, but the original scroll scholars vehemently denied these claims. While some scroll scholars had published part of their assigned texts, after forty-five years the team responsible for the huge number of scrolls discovered in Cave Four had published only twenty percent of the five hundred Dead Sea Scrolls in their possession.

A public relations campaign led by the *Biblical Archeology Review* magazine demanded the immediate release of the unpublished scrolls to other scholars. Finally, the last of the unpublished scrolls were released to the academic world. To the great joy of many scholars, the scrolls contained references to the New Testament and to Jesus of Nazareth. *(See picture 2 in photo section.)*

The Crucified Messiah Scroll

One of the most extraordinary of these scrolls (released in 1991) refers directly to the crucifixion of Jesus Christ.

This five-line scroll contains information about the death of the Messiah. It refers to "the Prophet Isaiah" and his famous prophecy (chapter 53) that identifies the Messiah as one who would suffer for the sins of His people. Many scholars believed that the Jews (during the first century) expected that, when He finally came, the Messiah would rule forever without dying. This scroll reveals that the Jewish Essene writer understood the dual role of the Messiah. It identifies the Messiah as the "Shoot of Jesse" (King David's father) and the "Branch of David." More importantly the scroll declares that he was "pierced" and "wounded," an obvious reference to crucifixion. Undoubtedly, this is a reference to Jesus because no other messianic figure was ever crucified.

The scroll also describes the Messiah as a "leader of the community" who was "put to death." It identifies the Messiah as "the sceptre," a probable reference to the Genesis 49:10 prophecy: "The sceptre shall not depart from Judah, nor a lawgiver from between his feet, until Shiloh come; and unto him shall the gathering of the people be."

This scroll was translated by Dr. Robert Eisenman, Professor of Middle East Religions at California State University. He wrote, "The text is of the most far-reaching significance because it shows that whatever group was responsible for these writings was operating in the same general scriptural and Messianic framework of early Christianity."[2] As another professor, Dr. Norman Golb of the University of Chicago, said, "It shows that contrary to what some of the editors said, there are lots of surprises in the scrolls, and this is one of them."

The "Son of God" Scroll

Another fascinating scroll discovered in Cave Four and known as "4Q246" refers to the Jewish hope for a future Messiah. This is another of the scrolls that remained unpublished until recently. Its text refers to the Messiah as "the son of God" and the "son of the Most High." These remarkable words are identical with those recorded in the Gospel of Luke.

Scroll 4Q246: The Son of God Scroll

He shall be called the son of God,
and they shall designate [call] him son of the Most High.
Like the appearance of comets, so shall be their kingdom.
For brief years they shall reign over the earth and shall trample on all;
one people shall trample on another and
one province on another until the people of God shall rise
and all shall rest from the sword."[3]

Luke 1:32, 35

He shall be great, and shall be called the Son of the Highest: and the Lord God shall give unto him the throne of his father David. . . . And the angel answered and said unto her, The Holy Ghost shall come upon thee, and the power of the Highest shall overshadow thee: therefore also that holy thing which shall be born of thee shall be called the Son of God.

One of the great differences between Christian and Jewish conceptions of the promised Messiah is His relationship to God. While Jews believe the Messiah will be a great man with a divine mission, like Moses, Christians believe that the Bible teaches that the Messiah would be uniquely "the Son of God." Generally, Jews believe that the Christian concept of a "son of God" violates the primary truth of monotheism, found in Deuteronomy 6:4: "Hear, O Israel: The Lord our God is one Lord." Christians believe that Jesus' claim to be the Son of God is not a violation of Deuteronomy 6:4. Rather, Christians believe in the Trinity, the doctrine that the Father, the Son, and the Holy Spirit are revealed in the Bible as One God, revealed in three personalities. It is fascinating in this regard to consider the presence of these statements in this first century Jewish text: "He shall be called the son of God, and they shall designate [call] him son of the Most High." The important question of how Jesus of Nazareth thought of Himself is addressed in detail in Chapter 13.

The presence of these statements in the Dead Sea Scrolls suggests that some of the Essenes had either accepted the messianic claims of Jesus that He was the Son of God or had anticipated this concept. Either possibility opens up new areas for future scholarly exploration. Another possibility that must be considered is this: Is it possible that the author of "scroll 4Q246" is quoting the words of the Gospel of Luke, which were widely circulated by A.D. 68? Luke the physician claimed that he wrote the Gospel of Luke as an eyewitness to the events he described. In Luke 1:1–3, he says,

> Forasmuch as many have taken in hand to set forth in order a declaration of those things which are most surely believed among us, Even as they delivered them unto us, which from the beginning were eyewitnesses, and ministers of the word; It seemed good to me also, having had perfect understanding of all things from the very first, to write unto thee in order, most excellent Theophilus.

The virtually identical wording of Luke and this Essene scroll regarding the divinity of the Messiah stands as a tremendous witness to the early existence and transmission of the Gospel records within thirty-five years of the death of Christ. If the three Synoptic Gospels were written and distributed within thirty-five years of the events of the life of Jesus (as the Gospels claim), then they provide the best eyewitness historical records we could ever hope to possess.

Dead Sea Scrolls Fragment 4Q521

Another remarkable scroll, "4Q521," was found in Cave Four. This scroll declares that the Messiah will display supernatural powers identical to those described in the Gospels:

> The heavens and the earth will obey his Messiah, the sea and all that is in them. He will not turn aside from the commandment of the Holy Ones. Take strength in his mighty work all ye who seek the Lord. Will ye not find the Lord in this, all ye who wait for him with hope in your hearts? Surely the Lord will seek out the pious, and will call the righteous by name. His spirit will hover over the poor; by his might will he restore the faithful. He will glorify the pious on the throne of the eternal kingdom. He will release the captives, make the blind see, raise up the down trodden. Forever I will cleave to him against the powerful and I will trust in his loving kindness and in his goodness forever. His holy Messiah will not be slow in coming. And as for the wonders that are not the work of the Lord, when he, that is the Messiah, comes then he will heal the sick, resurrect the dead, and to the poor announce glad tidings. He will lead the holy ones, he will shepherd them. He will do all of it.

The messianic parallels between this scroll and the teachings of the New Testament are astonishing. This two-thousand-year-old Jewish Essene document from Qumran reveals a number of prophecies about the coming Messiah that are virtually identical to Christian teachings about Jesus Christ as detailed in the four Gospels.

1. The Messiah is divinely supernatural, not just a man like Moses — "The heavens and the earth will obey his Messiah" (Psalm 110:1–7; Ephesians 1:20–22).

2. He is righteous — "He will not turn aside from the commandment of the Holy Ones" (Isaiah 53:9).

3. He will rule forever — "The throne of the eternal kingdom" (Isaiah 9:6–7; Revelation 21:3–5).

4. He will act as the High Priest in the Year of Jubilee — "He will release the captives" (Isaiah 61:1; Luke 4:18).

5. He will miraculously heal the blind — "Make the blind see" (Isaiah 42:7; John 9:25–33).

6. The Messiah will supernaturally heal the sick and resurrect the dead — "He will heal the sick, resurrect the dead" (Isaiah 35:5–6; Matthew 11:4–6).

7. He will come from heaven with a heavenly army — "He will lead the holy ones" (Deuteronomy 33:2; Revelation 19:14–15).

Recently Hebrew scholars Michael Wise and James Tabor wrote an article that appeared in *Biblical Archæology Review* (Nov./Dec. 1992) analyzing this text:

> Our Qumran text, 4Q521, is, astonishingly, quite close to this Christian concept of the Messiah. Our text speaks not only of a single Messianic figure . . . but it also describes him in extremely exalted terms, quite like the Christian view of Jesus as a cosmic agent. That there was, in fact, an expectation of a single Messianic figure at Qumran is really not so surprising. A reexamination of the Qumran literature on this subject leads one to question the two Messiah theory. As a matter of fact, only once in any Dead Sea Scroll text is the idea of two Messiahs stated unambiguously. . . .
>
> In short, there is not much evidence in the previously published scrolls that straightforwardly supports a putative doctrine of two Messiahs. . . . So the text that is the subject of this article (4Q521) is, in speaking of a single Messiah, more the rule than the exception...The Messiah of our text is thus much closer to the Christian Messiah, in this regard, than in any previously published text and requires us to reexamine the previously, rather restricted, views of Messianic expectations at Qumran.
>
> There is no doubt that the Qumran community had faith in the ultimate victory of such a Messiah over all evil. However, a closer reading of these texts reveals an additional theme, equally dominant — that of an initial, though temporary, triumph of the wicked over righteousness. That is, there was the belief among the Qumran community that the Messiah would suffer initial defeat, but that he would ultimately triumph in the end of days.[4]

Other New Testament Quotes Identified in
the Dead Sea Scrolls

In 1971, a Spanish biblical scholar named Jose O'Callaghan studied some of the small fragments of scrolls discovered in Cave Seven at Qumran. These fragments were quite small, containing only brief portions of each verse. After almost two thousand years, the elements and insects have significantly damaged these manuscripts. In some cases only small fragments containing parts of a verse on three or four lines remain. O'Callaghan was looking for correspondences between these fragments of Greek Dead Sea scrolls and the Septuagint (the Greek translation of the Hebrew Old Testament that was widely used by Jesus and the apostles).

One day, O'Callaghan carefully examined several small scroll fragments located in a photo page in *The Discoveries of the Judean Desert of Jordan*. To his surprise, he noticed that several fragments did not fit any Old Testament text. They were listed as "Fragments not identified." However, O'Callaghan discovered that these Greek language fragments bore an uncanny resemblance to several verses in the Greek New Testament. He read the Greek word "beget" and a word that appeared to be "Gennesaret," a word for the Sea of Galilee. The fragment, Scroll 7Q5, containing "Gennesaret" seems to be a quotation from the passage in Mark 6:52, 53, that refers to Jesus' feeding of the five thousand: "For they considered not the miracle of the loaves: for their heart was hardened. And when they had passed over, they came into the land of Gennesaret, and drew to the shore." *(See picture 3 in photo section.)*

If these texts prove to be Gospel writings, they would be the earliest New Testament texts ever discovered. The *New York Times* remarked, "If O'Callaghan's theory is accepted, it would prove that at least one of the Gospels, that of St. Mark, was written only a few years after the death of Jesus." The *Los Angeles Times*, in an article entitled, "Nine New Testament fragments dated A.D. 50 to A.D. 100 have been discovered in a Dead Sea Cave," stated that "if validated, [they] constitute the most sensational biblical trove uncovered in recent times."

Altogether, Dr. Jose O'Callaghan ultimately identified eight different scroll fragments from Cave Seven that appear to be quotations from New Testament passages. He suggests that the other fragments may be portions of the following seven verses from the Gospels and from Paul's epistles:

"For the earth bringeth forth fruit of herself . . ." (Mark 4:28).

"And he saw them toiling in rowing . . ." (Mark 6:48).

"And Jesus answering said unto them, Render to Cæsar . . ." (Mark 12:17).

"And when they had eaten enough, they lightened the ship . . ." (Acts 27:38).

"And not only so, but we also joy in God through our Lord Jesus Christ . . ." (Romans 5:11–12).

"And without controversy great is the mystery of godliness . . ." (1 Timothy 3:16).

"For if any be a hearer of the word, and not a doer . . ." (James 1:23–24).

As one example of O'Callaghan's study, he examined a small scroll fragment, known as "7Q5," that contained only twenty Greek letters on five lines of text. Many of the thousands of Hebrew Old Testament scroll fragments that were successfully identified by other scholars at the Qumran site are equally small. Another scroll scholar, Professor Carsten Thiede, agrees with O'Callaghan that portions of the Mark 6:52–53 passage appear in this scroll fragment. While other scroll scholars disagree with the identification of this fragment as a verse from the New Testament, they do admit that almost all of the scrolls found in Cave Seven were written in the period between 50 B.C., and A.D. 50, which is consistent with the time of the writing of the Gospel of Mark.

Naturally, as with other matters connected with the controversial Dead Sea Scrolls, many scholars disagreed with O'Callaghan's conclusions. The debate still continues almost thirty years later. At this stage we cannot be certain that O'Callaghan's conclusions are correct. More work needs to be done. However, the recent publication of the discovery of Scroll "4Q246," with its reference to "the Son of God" as found in Luke 1:32 and verse 35, provides strong support for the possibility that these fragments are related to these New Testament passages. In addition, I have great hope that the new archeological exploration of additional caves recently discovered at Qumran by my friend Gary Collett may provide new evidence of additional New Testament references. Many of these mysteries will be solved when the rest of the unpublished scrolls are finally made available to all scholars. The new dig at Qumran may also uncover additional scrolls that will help us understand more clearly the Messianic beliefs of this group of religious men and women who lived at this desert site during the time when Jesus walked the earth.

When we consider the amount of evidence in the Dead Sea Scrolls that confirms the Gospel record about Jesus of Nazareth, we can be confident that God has not left us in darkness concerning the truthfulness of the life and teaching of His Son, Jesus Christ.

Notes

1. Eusebius, *Ecclesiastical History* (A.D. 325).
2. Robert Eisenman, *The Dead Sea Scrolls and the First Christians* (Rockport: Element Books, Inc., 1996).
3. Geza Vermes, *The Dead Sea Scrolls in English* (London: Penguin Books, 1987).
4. Michael Wise and James Tabor, *Biblical Archæology Review* Nov–Dec. 1992: 60–61.

4

The Date of Christ's Nativity, Ministry, and Crucifixion

In establishing the historical existence of an individual, we must attempt to attribute specific dates to that individual's birth and death. There is much evidence to support that Jesus of Nazareth was born around 1 B.C. and ministered to his disciples from A.D. 28 until his death in A.D. 32.

The Date of Christ's Birth

Our current system of numbering years (e.g., A.D. 1999) was developed in the sixth century by a Ukrainian monk named Dionysius Exignus (Dennis the Short). He calculated that the birth of Christ occurred in the Roman year 754. The Romans calculated their calendar from the time when Romulus and Remus allegedly founded the city of Rome. Dionysius computed the new year beginning January 1 of the year following Christ's birth, as recorded by Luke, as the year A.D. 1 of his new calendar (Anno Domini — "year of our Lord"). He based this calculation on the historical records available to him in the Vatican Library in Rome and on the chronological statements of the historian Luke (3:1–2). In A.D. 315, the Christian historian Eusebius appealed to existing Roman government records in the Imperial Archives (regarding the census of the Roman governor Cyrenius and Cæsar Augustus) to prove that Jesus Christ was born in Bethlehem when Joseph and Mary went there to be enrolled in the imperial census. "And it came to pass in those days, that there went out a decree from Cæsar Augustus, that all the world should be taxed. And this taxing was first made when Cyrenius was governor of Syria. And all went to be taxed, every one into his own city" (Luke 2:1–3).

Some modern critics have asserted that there is no evidence that Rome ever required its citizens to return to their historic birthplace to be taxed as described by Luke. However, the historical evidence reveals that during the reign of Ceasar Augustus such census taking did occur. The ancient Oxyrhunchus papyrus and another papyrus (number 904) held in the collections of the British Museum definitely compel all Roman citizens to return to their places of birth for the purpose of census-taking, exactly as recorded in the Gospel of Luke. The papyrus states: "Because of the approaching census it is necessary that all those residing for any cause away from their homes should at once prepare to return to their own governments in order that they may complete the family registration of the enrollment. . . ."

Justin Martyr, a famous early Church writer from North Africa (A.D. 110–165), also stated that official Roman census records were still available in his day to prove the truth of Christ's prophesied birth in Bethlehem.[1] Therefore, it is probable that the monk, Dionysius, had access to accurate historical records in Rome to determine that the birth of Christ occurred in the year 1 B.C. (there is no "year 0").

Scholars discovered evidence several hundred years ago that influenced them to adjust the date of Christ's nativity back to 7 B.C. or 4 B.C. One piece of evidence to support this adjustment was the date of the rule of the governor of Syria, Cyrenius (who administered the taxation in Luke 2:1–3). Cyreni apparently ruled from 7 B.C.–4 B.C. according to the available historical records. However, more recent archeological evidence has now proven that Cyrenius was governor of Syria during two different periods.The first period of rule was from 4 B.C.–1 B.C.

This fact is also supported by Sir Robert Anderson, the head of Scotland Yard in 1895:

> In his Roman history, Mr. Merivale . . . says (vol. iv, page 457), 'A remarkable light has been thrown upon the point by the demonstration, as it seems to be, of Augustus Zumpt in his second volume of *Commentationes Epigraphicæ*, that Quirinus (the Cyrenius of St. Luke II) was first governor of Syria from the close of A.U. 750 (B.C. 4)–753 (B.C. 1).'[2]

Therefore, there is no contradiction with the time of Cyrenius's first Syrian governorship (4 B.C.–1 B.C.) and the census recorded in Luke 2:1–3 occurring during the year 1 B.C., as indicated by the early Christian Gospels.

The dating of King Herod's death (which followed Christ's birth) was another factor that caused scholars to adjust the date of Christ's birth back to 4 B.C. The Jewish historian, Flavius Josephus, recorded that Herod died just before Passover in the same year that there was an eclipse of the moon. Astronomers knew of a partial lunar eclipse that was visible in Jerusalem on March 13, 4 B.C.; therefore, many scholars concluded that Herod's death and Christ's birth must have occurred in 4 B.C.

However, additional astronomical evidence has recently revealed that the date of King Herod's death could be as late as 1 B.C. or A.D. 1, allowing Christ's birth to have occurred in 1 B.C. We now know that a full (not a partial) lunar eclipse was visible in Jerusalem on January 9, 1 B.C., which could well be the one referred to by Josephus in his *Antiquities of the Jews* (book xvii, chapter 6). New astronomical discoveries reveal that several eclipses of the moon were visible in Jerusalem during the nine years from 5 B.C.–A.D. 4: March 23, 5 B.C.; September 15, 5 B.C.; March 12, 4 B.C.; and January 9, 1 B.C.[3]

In light of these discoveries, Christ's nativity could have occurred as early as 4 B.C. or as late as 1 B.C. The weight of evidence leans toward the fall of 1 B.C., which agrees with the understanding and tradition of the early Church.

The traditional date of Christ's birth, which was set as Christmas, December 25, is almost certainly an error. Around A.D. 320, the Church, under the direction of the first Christian Roman emperor, Constantine, adopted the date of December 25 to officially celebrate Jesus' nativity. Apparently, the reason for picking December 25 was to replace Saturnalia, an already existing pagan festival that honored the sun. The information given in Luke 2:8 about the "shepherds abiding in the field, keeping watch over the flock by night," indicates that Christ's birth could not have been in late December because the cold weather would force the flocks and the shepherds to take shelter inside during that season.

The Scriptures give a hint that the actual date of Christ's birth could have been the fifteenth day of Tishri, on the Feast of Tabernacles, which occurs in our months of September and October. The Gospel of John (1:14) states, "And the Word was made flesh, and tabernacled [dwelt] among us." John would certainly be in a position to know Jesus' birthday, and it is probable that he is hinting at the Feast of Tabernacles as the actual date of His birth by using the unusual Greek word "tabernacled" to describe Christ's birth. To give a parallel example, it would be as if a man told you that his child "Christmassed" with them, indicating his wife gave birth on December 25. The fact that some forty other key events in the history of Israel have occurred on biblical anniversaries of annual feast days suggest a high probability that the birth of the Jewish Messiah would also occur on a significant feast date, in this case the Feast of Tabernacles, 1 B.C.[4]

The eight-day-long Feast of Tabernacles was one of three annual feasts on which all Jewish males were required to go to the Temple in Jerusalem to worship. This would cause a huge pilgrimage and thus a temporary increase in the population in the small town of Bethlehem only five miles south of Jerusalem. This would account for the fact that "there was no room in the inn" in Bethlehem on the night of Christ's birth.

The Date of Christ's Ministry and His Crucifixion

In all of the New Testament the clearest, most definitive chronological statement is found in the beginning verses of Luke (3:1–2), which describe precisely the year in which Jesus' cousin John the Baptist began his ministry. Luke recorded that the commencement of Christ's teaching ministry started with His baptism (Luke 3:21–22), and that Jesus, when He began His ministry, "was about thirty years of age" (Luke 3:23, RSV).

Luke's chronological statement is this:

Now in the fifteenth year of the reign of Tiberius Cæsar, Pontius Pilate being governor of Judæa, and Herod being tetrarch of Galilee, and his brother Philip tetrarch of Ituræa and of the region of Trachonitis, and Lysanias the tetrarch of Abilene, Annas and Caiaphas being the high priests, the word of God came unto John the son of Zacharias in the wilderness. (Luke 3:1–2)

The Roman emperor, Tiberius Cæsar, ascended his throne as emperor on the nineteenth day of August, A.D. 14 — a date as well known in Luke's day as the date of the assassination of President John F. Kennedy is known in our day. Therefore, the fifteenth year of Tiberius Cæsar's reign began on the nineteenth day of August, A.D. 28. Historical records confirm that all of the officials named in the statement by Luke (3:1–2) ruled their territories in the year A.D. 28. It is almost certain that Christ's ministry began in the fall of A.D. 28, shortly after John the Baptist began his own ministry. John was six months older than Jesus. The rabbis taught that a man could become a teacher at the age of thirty (Numbers 4:23).

Many Bible commentators have assigned possible earlier dates for the commencement of Christ's ministry, from A.D. 24 to A.D. 27. The reason they ignore the clear date of A.D. 28, described with such precision by the gospel historian Luke, is probably due to their previous commitment to an earlier (7 B.C. to 4 B.C.) dating of the nativity of Christ. Since Christ was "about thirty years of age" at the time of his commencement of public ministry, these commentators are forced to ignore Luke's clear historical dating. If Jesus was born 4 B.C., and began His ministry at the age of thirty, then He must have begun teaching around A.D. 26–27. To account for this, they imagine that the first year of the reign of Tiberius Cæsar as emperor refers to A.D. 12, the year that Cæsar Augustus promoted General Tiberius for his victories in Germany, instead of the official coronation of Tiberius Cæsar as Emperor two years later on August 19, A.D. 14, following the death of Cæsar Augustus. They imagine that there was a kind of co-regency of the two emperors during the last two years of the reign of Cæsar Augustus. This adjustment is necessary in their opinion, because that is the only way to escape the clear meaning of Luke 3:1–2 that points to A.D. 28 (fourteen years after Tiberius' coronation).

An analogy of this artificial calculation would be for a historian to count the years of President Johnson's presidency from January 1960, when President Kennedy was inaugurated, instead of from the date of the death of President Kennedy on November 22, 1963, when Vice-President Johnson succeeded the presidency. Such a calculation would be a total distortion of historical dating.

The problem with their interpretation of a co-regency from A.D. 12 is simply that there is not one shred of evidence in any other contemporary historical writing that the reign of Tiberius Cæsar began on any date other than the true date of his reign, August 19, A.D. 14. It is inconceivable that such an accurate historian as Luke, in writing to the Gentile Theophilus (Luke 1:14), would have used such an unclear method of counting. This would have caused Theophilus confusion about the correct date of the beginning of Christ's ministry.

Our conclusion, therefore, is that Christ's public teaching commenced in the fall of A.D. 28, the fourteenth year of Emperor Tiberius' reign. The first Passover of His ministry would have then taken place six months later on the fourteenth of Nisan, A.D. 29 (John 2:12–23).

The apostle John provides further confirmation of this thesis. He records that, during Jesus' attendance at this Passover Feast six months later, Jesus prophesied in the Temple that He would be killed and would rise again in three days. The Jews, not understanding that He was referring to Himself, and not "the Temple," replied to Jesus, "Forty and six years was this temple in building, and wilt thou rear it up in three days?" (John 2:19–20).

The historical records of that time, including *War of the Jews* by Flavius Josephus, tell us that Herod the Great began the restoration of the Temple in 18 B.C. The year of Christ's first Passover of His public ministry, A.D. 29, is exactly forty-six years from the commencement of Herod's restoration program in 18 B.C.

Jesus continued His ministry over a period of approximately three and one-half years. Dr. Pusey, in his excellent book, *The Prophet Daniel*, states, "It seems to me absolutely certain that our Lord's ministry lasted for some period above three years."[5] According to the Gospel of John, Jesus attended at least three Passovers, and if the Feast mentioned in John 5:1 is also a Passover, then it is certain that the crucifixion occurred on the date of His final Passover in A.D. 32. The Feast described in John 5:1 must be either the Feast of Passover or Purim, and since Purim was strictly a social feast celebrating the events described in the book of Esther, it is unlikely that Jesus would go up to Jerusalem specifically for a nonreligious holiday. The evidence supports the contention that this Feast was also a Passover. Thus, Christ's ministry extended from the fall of A.D. 28, for three and one-half years, to His final Passover and crucifixion in A.D. 32.

Notes

1. Justin Martyr, *Apology* chapter 1, verse 34.
2. Sir Robert Anderson, *The Coming Prince* (London: Hodder and Stoughton, 1895) 92.
3. Rev. Samuel Fallows, *Bible Encyclopedia and Scriptural Dictionary* 423.
4. Grant R. Jeffrey, *Armageddon – Appointment With Destiny* (Toronto: Frontier Research Publications, Inc., 1989).
5. E. B. Pussey, *The Prophet Daniel* (Plymouth:The Devonport Society, 1864).

5

Evidence from the Ancient Christian Tombs

For the last one hundred and fifty years, most archeologists and historians have generally assumed that few Christians lived in Palestine during the first three centuries until the time of Emperor Constantine's Edict of Toleration in A.D. 324. Scholars based this view on the fact that little conclusive archeological evidence had been discovered and published to prove that Jewish-Christianity had left any trace of itself in Palestine prior to the introduction of gentile Christians into the Holy Land after A.D. 325. Naturally, following the conversion of Emperor Constantine there was an explosive growth of gentile Christianity in Palestine and the commencement of a massive church building program after his mother, Queen Helena, visited in A.D. 326.

However, the New Testament clearly reveals that a large number of Jews eagerly accepted the new faith in Jesus as the true Messiah in the first decades following the resurrection of Christ. Luke's book of Acts recounts the dramatic growth of the early Church, despite the active opposition to the new faith from both Roman and Jewish authorities.

Then they that gladly received his word were baptized: and the same day there were added unto them about three thousand souls. And they continued steadfastly in the apostles' doctrine and fellowship, and in breaking of bread, and in prayers. And fear came upon every soul: and many wonders and signs were done by the apostles. And all that believed were together, and had all things common; And sold their possessions and goods, and parted them to all men, as every man had need. And they, continuing daily with one accord in the temple, and breaking bread from house to house, did eat their meat with gladness and singleness of heart, Praising God, and having favour with all the people. And the Lord added to the church daily such as should be saved. (Acts 2:41–47)

In another passage Luke speaks about the continuing growth of the first-century Church in that, "Howbeit many of them which heard the word believed; and the number of the men was about five thousand" (Acts 4:4). Luke also states, "And when they heard it, they glorified the Lord, and said unto him, Thou seest, brother, how many thousands of Jews there are which believe; and they are all zealous of the law" (Acts 21:20). These statements describe a vibrant and growing Church in Palestine that would inevitably have left some historical and archeological evidence if these New Testament statements are correct. The greatest historian of the early Church, Eusebius, writing around A.D. 325, quotes the words of the historian Hegesippus, who was a contempory witness of the New Testament Church, having been born at the time Jesus began His public ministry. Hegesippus wrote about the growing concerns of the leaders of the Jews about the enthusiastic response of the Jewish people to the claims of Christ as preached by James, the brother of Christ. These religious leaders complained, "They have gone astray after Jesus in the belief that He is the Christ." According to Hegesippus, the Jewish leaders approached James, as the leader of the Jerusalem Church, and complained, "Since therefore many even of the ruling class believed, there was an uproar among the Jews and Scribes and Pharisees, who said there was a danger that the entire people would expect Jesus as the Christ."[1]

In light of the historical evidence that a significant group of Jewish believers in Christ existed during the first and following centuries, it is extremely likely that they would have left some archeological evidence of their existence, such as tombs and churches.

The Discovery of Early Jewish Christian Tombs

On November 27, 1873, French archeologist Charles Clermont-Ganneau, the scholar who rescued the famous Moabite Stone inscription, wrote a report from Jerusalem to the Palestine Exploration Fund in London, England. In this report he told them that he had found a group of Jewish ossuaries from the first century in a newly discovered burial cave near Bethany. To Clermont-Ganneau's amazement, he found that these ancient Jewish stone coffins were inscribed with the names of many Christian individuals mentioned in the New Testament. Despite its obvious significance, this report apparently was not published in any of the major newspapers of the day. As a result, this important discovery was almost lost to history.

Several years ago, while visiting a rare-book dealer in London, I purchased a leather-bound book containing Clermont-Ganneau's archeological report from Palestine that was published in 1874–75 by the Palestine Exploration Fund (P.E.F.). The Palestine Exploration Fund is a private group that was created in England in approximately 1865 to support archeological exploration of the Middle East, and especially Israel. For over a century this group has funded and published the explorations and research of many dedicated archeologists. I became a member of this group several years ago during a research trip to London.

Ossuaries Inscribed with a Cross and the Name of Jesus

In the 1874–75 *Palestine Exploration Fund Journal* Professor Clermont-Ganneau recorded that in the spring of 1873 an Arab sheik, Effendi Abu Saud, accidently discovered a large cave beneath his house. He fell through a hole in the stone floor of his basement while constructing his house on the eastern slopes of the Mount of Olives, near the road to ancient Bethany. The archeologist Clermont-Ganneau was called to investigate. The cave proved to be an ancient necropolis, a large burial catacomb that contained thirty limestone coffins and a number of terra-cotta vases filling this ancient family-sepulchral cave carved out of limestone at Bat'n el-Hawa. The Jews buried their dead either in the ground, or, more commonly, in a rock tomb. The family would return several years after a death, clean the bones of the skeleton, and then re-bury the bones in a stone ossuary, usually forty inches long, twenty inches wide, and twenty-five inches high. The lids of these ossuaries are triangular, semicircular, or rectangular with either plain sides or ornamentation consisting of a motif using a geometric rose pattern as illustrated in the photo showing the ossuary of Caiaphas the High Priest. Greek or Hebrew inscriptions containing the name and identification of the deceased were often painted or engraved with an iron pointer on the sides or on the lids of the ossuaries.

Clermont-Ganneau noted: "Several, not only Greek, but also Hebrew, are accompanied by crosses, which leave no doubt of the religion of the persons whose remains were preserved in them; others present a sign of a cruniform appearance. . . ."[2]

The archeologist reported that a number of these ossuaries were also inscribed with a cross or the Hebrew name ישוע *Jesus*, indicating that these deceased Jews from the first century were some of the first early Christians to follow Christ. Although Clermont-Ganneau was unable to take photographs, he did take impressions, or "squeezes," by carefully covering the inscription with a special, very fine, wet cloth soaked in plaster of paris, which retained the impression of the engraved letters or symbols when dried. These squeezes provided a faithful copy of the ornamented surfaces as well as the inscription.

Clermont-Ganneau described his discovery in the P.E.F. Report for 1874:

> This catacomb on the Mount of Olives belonged apparently to one of the earliest families which joined the new religion of Christianity. In this group of sarcophagi some of which have the Christian symbol and some have not, we are, so to speak, [witnessing the] actual unfolding of Christianity. Personally I think that many of the Hebrew-speaking people whose remains are contained in these ossuaries were among the first followers of Christ. . . . The appearance of Christianity at the very gates of Jerusalem is, in my opinion, extraordinary and unprecedented. Somehow the new [Christian] doctrine must have made its way into the Jewish system. . . . The cave on the Mount of Offence belonged apparently to one of the earliest families which

joined the new religion. In this group of sarcophagi [ossuaries], some of which have the Christian symbol and some have not, we are, so to speak, assisting at an actual unfolding of Christianity. The association of the sign of the cross with names written in Hebrew constitutes alone a valuable fact.

Perhaps 'Judah the Scribe,' and even 'Simeon the Priest (Cohen)' belonged to the new religion. In this case Simeon might very well be the second Bishop of Jerusalem.[3]

List of Hebrew and Greek Christian Ossuary Inscriptions

The 1874 P.E.F. Report contained a list of the following inscriptions that Clermont-Ganneau found on ossuaries scattered throughout the necropolis. His French draftsman, A. Lecomte, carefully copied the inscriptions that were engraved into the sides or tops of the ossuaries. The list and information that follows is taken directly from his official report on the discovery:

In Hebrew:

1. *Salome, wife of Judah.* "Engraved in very small characters . . . a cruciform sign." (The name and cross were found on both the ossuary and the lid).

2. *Judah, with the cross + .* Perhaps the husband of Salome.

3. *Judah the Scribe.* On another face of the sarcophagus, *Judah, son of Eleazar the Scribe.*

4. *Simeon the Priest* (Cohen).

5. *Martha, daughter of Pasach.* Perhaps the name is Jewish as well as Christian.

6. *Eleazar, son of Nathalu.* The form *Nathai* for Nathan is not uncommon.

7. *Salamtsion, daughter of Simeon the Priest.* The name of the woman, Salam Sion, is of the greatest interest. It is the name Salampsion of Josephus (daughter of Herod).

In Greek:

1. *Jesus.* Twice repeated, with the cross +.

2. *Nathaniel.* Accompanied by a cross.[4]

One of the ossuaries, possibly the one holding the bones of *Simeon the Priest*, contained three or four small instruments in copper or bronze, very oxidized, which consisted of a small bell, mounted with a ring. The Arabs on the dig suggested the bells were a kind of castanet. Clermont-Ganneau thought that the bells might be worn by a Temple priest like *Simeon the Priest* similar to those which hung on the robe of the high priest that are referred to in Exodus 39:25: "And they made bells of pure gold, and put the bells between the pomegranates upon the hem of the robe, round about between the pomegranates." This is also noted in Flavius Josephus' *Antiquities of the Jews* III, vii.

As a Christian, Clermont-Ganneau was amazed to discover the names of "Eleazar" (which is the Hebrew form of the Greek name "Lazarus"), along with the names "Martha," and "Mary" engraved on the sides of three of the ossuaries found in this cave. These significant names from the early Gospel history of the Jewish Christian church in the area surrounding Jerusalem were clearly engraved on the sides of their ossuaries together with the sign of the cross, providing strong evidence that these were Jewish Christian believers. In the Gospel of John we read the touching story of Christ raising his friend Lazarus from the dead. "Now a certain man was sick, Lazarus of Bethany, the town of Mary and her sister Martha" (John 11:1). Clermont-Ganneau noted that this was one of the most important archeological discoveries ever made concerning the origins of the early New Testament Church. The Jewish historian Professor Ory N. Mazar discussed the significance of Clermont-Ganneau's discovery during an interview with the *Jerusalem Christian Review.*[5]

Of particular interest are the inscriptions and dedications found inside the tomb. Clermont-Ganneau, who was a diligent scholar, believed he had discovered a tomb belonging to one of the first families to embrace Jesus' new teachings.[6]

The French archeologist realized that it was highly probable that these tombs belonged to the family of Mary, Martha, and Lazarus, the close friends of Jesus. Clermont-Ganneau wrote,

> What gives additional value to these short inscriptions, is that they furnish a whole series of names found in the Gospels, in their popular and local Syro-Chaldaic forms — the use of bar for ben (son), for instance. The presence of the names of Jesus, written with its common contraction, and Martha, of which we only knew historically that it was

the feminine form of the Aramaic, would alone be sufficient to make this collection important from an exegetic point of view.

By a singular coincidence, which from the first struck me forcibly, these inscriptions, found close to the Bethany road, and very near the site of the village, contain nearly all the names of the personages in the Gospel scenes which belonged to the place: Eleazar (Lazarus), Simon, Martha . . . a host of other coincidences occur at the sight of all these most evangelical names. . . .[7]

Additionally, an Italian scholar, Professor P. Bellarmine Bagatti, discovered another catacomb holding one hundred ossuaries on the western side of the Mount of Olives, opposite the Temple Mount, on the present grounds of the Catholic chapel called Dominus Flevit, which means "The Lord Wept." In the first century, when people were buried with coins over the eyes, the custom was to use newly minted coins. The discovery of coins minted by the Roman Governor Varius Gratus (A.D. 15–16) in the ossuary indicated that these tombs were used for the burial of Jewish Christians before the fall of Jerusalem in A.D. 70. Several of the ossuaries in this cave displayed inscribed names that belonged to a family of Jewish priests buried in the first century of the Christian era. *(See picture 4 in photo section.)*

The Official Guide to Israel, which is produced by Israel's Department of Tourism, states the following:

About seven hundred metres behind Talpiot a tomb was excavated in 1945 and several ossuaries containing human bodies were found. Inscriptions and coins proved that the burial in the tomb took place in the years 41–42. Two ossuaries were found marked with the word "Jesus," and some others have so far been undeciphered. It has therefore been assumed that followers of Jesus had been buried in this tomb. If this assumption proves correct, this tomb would show the earliest historical evidence known about followers of Jesus.[8]

Jesus Christ, The Redeemer

Based on the presence of inscribed crosses and the engraved Hebrew name יֵשׁוּעַ *Jesus*, Professor Bagatti concluded that several of these priests were among the early Jerusalem followers of Jesus. Bagatti found many other ossuaries containing the following names inscribed on their sides, along with the sign of the cross or the name of Jesus: Jonathan, Joseph, Jarius, Judah, Matthias, Menahem, Maria, Martha, Salome, Simon, Zechariah, and Salamzion, which means "greetings to Zion." Many of these names appear in the New Testament records of the early Church at Jerusalem. One ossuary contained a monogrammed, Greek dedication inscription, "Iota, Chi and Beta," which was translated by Professor J. Finegan of the Pacific School of Religion in Berkeley, California, to read: "Jesus Christ, the Redeemer."[9]

The presence of inscriptions on the tombs of Jewish Christians buried before A.D. 70 bearing the dedication "Jesus Christ, the Redeemer" provides powerful evidence that the early Christians, who were eyewitnesses to His ministry, fully acknowledged the "Jesus of history" as identical with the "Christ of faith," who could redeem humanity from their sins because He was truly the Son of God. This recently found archeological evidence argues strongly against the anti-divine theory of liberal historians such as Professor Marcus J. Borg, who wrote *Meeting Jesus Again for the First Time*. Professor Borg wrote,"Jesus never spoke of himself as the Son of God, as one with God, as the light of the world, as the way, the truth, and the life, and so forth." Borg claims the concept of Jesus as Christ and the Son of God was unknown until the end of the first century.[10]

One of the most fascinating ossuaries discovered to date by Bagatti is one that bears a cross and a Hebrew inscription translated as "Manaen, of the sons of Jachin, the Priest." The Old Testament book of Chronicles refers to the family of Jachin as the twenty-first family in the arrangements of twenty-four families of the priestly sons of Aaron, established by King David to provide daily service in the Temple of his son Solomon in Jerusalem: "Now these are the divisions of the sons of Aaron. . . . The one and twentieth to Jachin, the two and twentieth to Gamul" (1 Chronicles 24:1, 17). Luke mentions the name Manaen: "Now there were in the church that was at Antioch certain prophets and teachers; as

Barnabas, and Simeon that was called Niger, and Lucius of Cyrene, and Manaen, which had been brought up with Herod the tetrarch, and Saul" (Acts 13:1). The book of Acts records that a Christian named Manaen was sent to the city of Antioch on a teaching mission with the disciple Barnabas. This teacher had been "brought up with Herod the tetrarch, and Saul" indicating that he was trained with Saul (the apostle Paul) and Herod in Jerusalem earlier in his life. This remarkable ossuary may contain his remains.

Although many scholars previously declared that the cross was not used by early Christians as a symbol until after the Council of Nicea A.D. 325, the evidence from archeological digs has now confirmed that following Christ's resurrection, the first-century Christians often used the cross as a symbol. Jesus Christ himself had instructed them as follows: "Then said Jesus unto his disciples, If any man will come after me, let him deny himself, and take up his cross, and follow me" (Matthew 16:24, Luke 9:23). Archeological confirmation of the early use of the cross by first-century Christians appears in the works of Professor Eleazar Sukenik, Claude Conder, Charles Clermont-Ganneau, Sylvester Salier, and P. B. Bagatti. *(See picture 5 in photo section.)*

The Protestant archeologist Colonel Claude R. Conder, for example, in his book *Syrian Stone-Lore*, described these names on the ossuaries as "apparently Christian": "Lazarus, Simeon, Martha, Jude, etc."[11] In addition, Professor Bagatti indicated in his writings that before A.D. 135 the Jewish-Christian community often used the symbol *Taw* or + on their tombs to proclaim their faith in Jesus. These ossuraries were apparently taken to the Museum of the House of Biblical Studies at The Flagellation for safekeeping. After decades of research, no one has been able to prove that the symbol of the Cross was ever used by any Jewish group other than the followers of Jesus Christ. In fact, early first-century Jews so totally rejected the symbol of the Cross that it is inconceivable that any non-Christian Jewish group would have used such a despised symbol.

Alexander, the Son of Simon of Cyrene

Several years ago archeologists discovered another Jewish Christian ossuary in Jerusalem that bore the inscription, "Alexander, son of Simon of Cyrene," as well as an inscribed cross. Mark referred to this person when he wrote, "Now they compelled a certain man, Simon a Cyrenian, the father of Alexander and Rufus, as he was coming out of the country and passing by, to bear his cross" (Mark 15:21). This discovery reveals the probable tomb of the son of the man who carried the cross of Jesus Christ on His way to His crucifixion.

During the fall of 1945, the famous Jewish archeologist, Professor Eleazar L. Sukenik of Hebrew University, excavated a first-century burial cave discovered near the Jerusalem suburb of Talpiot on the road to Bethlehem, just at the southern end of the Kidron Valley that lies between the Mount of Olives and the Temple Mount. His monumental discovery revealed some of the most important archeological evidence to date about the first years of the growth of Christianity. He found many ossuaries with the sign of the cross, two occurrences of the name "Jesus," Greek inscriptions, and a coin minted in A.D. 41 for King Herod Agrippa I (indicating the tomb was sealed by A.D. 42). Sukenik believed the evidence from these tombs revealed inscriptions that were created by the early disciples of Jesus. The professor declared, "These inscriptions contain almost the whole dictionary of names in the New Testament."[12]

A Woman Named Shappira

One of the most intriguing ossuaries Professor Sukenik discovered was one inscribed with crosses and the name "Shappira." This unusual female name has not been found in Jewish literature of that era, except for the book of Acts. Luke recorded the death of a woman and her husband after having lied to God and the church about a gift they offered to the Lord: "But a certain man named Ananias, with Sapphira his wife, sold a possession . . ." (Acts 5:1, 5–10). The rarity of this name "Sapphira" and the strong evidence that this sepulchre is a Jewish-Christian catacomb from the first century suggests that this may be the resting place of the bones of the woman mentioned in Acts 5:1–10.

A Jewish First-Century Tomb Dedicated to "Jesus the Lord"

Professor Sukenik published his report in the *American Journal of Archæology*. He wrote:

When the ossuary with four crosses on its sides was found

there was not the slightest possible doubt as to the antiquity of the cross [marks], because it was clear that these [ossuaries] had not been touched from the moment they had been placed inside until the day we took them out. . . . I noticed the inscription on one of the ossuaries in which the name 'Jesus' was clearly discernible, followed here not by the usual [second] name, but by a description or an exclamation.[13]

After the name "Jesus," the exclamation or dedication read "y'ho," meaning "Jehovah" or "the Lord." The full inscription on the ossuary reads, "[To] Jesus, the Lord." In light of the A.D. 42 date for the sealing of this tomb, the presence of this dedication to "Jesus, the Lord" attests to the Christians' acceptance of Jesus Christ as God within ten years of the death and resurrection of Jesus in A.D. 32. Christian theologian Professor Alexander Hopkins commented on this important inscription: "The inscription which was hidden for almost 2,000 years and inscribed at least two decades before any part of the New Testament was written . . . bears a personal testimony of faith . . . a message from the past with a very modern meaning for the present."[14]

An Inscription Referring to the Governor Pontius Pilate

Agnostic critics complained during the last two centuries that there was no independent historical evidence confirming the existence of the Roman governor Pontius Pilate who plays such a critical role in the trial and execution of Jesus. However, in 1961 archeologists discovered a remarkable inscription during their excavations at ancient Cæsarea on the shore of the Mediterranean Sea that revealed the name of Pontius Pilate as well as a title concerning a building that was inscribed in honor of the Emperor Tiberius Cæsar.

The Tomb of Caiaphas the High Priest

According to the Gospels, the High Priest Caiaphas played a key role in the critical Sanhedrin trial of Jesus that ultimately led to the crucifixion of Christ by the Roman authorities. For the last two centuries many scholars have complained that there was little independent evidence about Caiaphas except for the writings of the controversial Jewish historian Flavius Josephus in his *Antiquities of the Jews*. However, the Israeli newspaper, the *Jerusalem Post*, reported in 1992 that the Israeli Antiquities Authority had confirmed the remarkable accidental discovery of the first tomb of a High Priest of the Second Temple period. Providentially, my wife Kaye and I were in Jerusalem at the very time that Israeli construction crews inadvertently discovered an unexpected tomb to the immediate south of the capital city in the Jerusalem Forest. According to Israeli law, any archeological site discovered in the course of construction must be kept for the scientists to examine and preserve the site for future generations. However, this site was almost immediately covered by a new highway and sealed forever.

Fortunately, the leader of my film crew in Israel, Dan Setton of Set Productions, learned of the important discovery and immediately called me to ask if I was willing to fund a film production of the discovery. We were able to immediately authorize the expenditure, which resulted in the obtaining of the exclusive film record of the discovery of the highly ornate tomb of the High Priest's family as well as a filmed interview with the Israeli archeologist Professor Zvi Greenhut, who carefully examined the ossuary as well as the skeletons within the stone coffin. Professor Greenhut confirmed that the ossuary contained a coin minted by King Herod Agrippa (A.D. 41–42) within the mouth of one of the women of Caiaphas' family. The ossuary of Caiaphas can be examined at the Israeli Museum in Jerusalem together with the Pontius Pilate inscription. A documentary video about these discoveries, *Archeological Discoveries V-13*, can be ordered using the Order Form at the end of this book. *(See picture 6 in photo section.)*

This is a remarkable discovery because it strongly suggests that the Greek pagan custom of placing a coin within the mouth of the dead to enable the dead to "pay" the pagan god Charon to take them across the mythical River Styx was actually practiced by some among the family of the High Priest Caiaphas. This amazing evidence of the pagan Hellenizing influence within the family of the High Priest of Israel is a fascinating indication that some of Israel's religious leaders and their families had succumbed to these pagan influences during the critical time when Jesus was challenging the religious leaders of the nation to repent and turn to God. This provides powerful evidence that the Gospels' description of the High Priest Caiaphas was a cynical politician, rather than a sincere spiritual leader.

The history of the exploration of the Middle East over the last two centuries has provided evidence of thousands of archeological and historical discoveries that confirm many of the major as well as minor details of the Gospel records about the life, death, and resurrection of Jesus of Nazareth. The years that lie ahead undoubtably will reveal more fascinating discoveries about the birth of Christianity.

Notes

1. Eusebius, *Ecclesiastical History* (A.D. 325).

2. Charles Clermont-Ganneau, *Palestine Exploration Fund Journal* 1872–73.

3. Charles Clermont-Ganneau, *Palestine Exploration Fund Report* (London: 1874).

4. Charles Clermont-Ganneau, *Palestine Exploration Fund Report* (London: 1874).

5. Ory N. Mazar, *Jerusalem Christian Review* vol. 7, issue 8.

6. Ory N. Mazar, *Jerusalem Christian Review* vol. 7, issue 8.

7. Charles Clermont-Ganneau, *Palestine Exploration Fund Report* (London: 1874).

8. *Official Guide To Israel* (Tel-Aviv: 1950) 247.

9. *Jerusalem Christian Review* vol. 7, issue 3.

10. Marcus J. Borg, *Meeting Jesus Again For the First Time* (San Francisco: HarperSanFrancisco, 1994).

11. C. R. Conder, *Syrian Stone-Lore* (London: 1896) 259–260.

12. E. L. Sukenik, *Report of the Congress of Christian Archeology* (Syracuse: 1950).

13. *Jerusalem Christian Review* vol. 7, issue 6.

14. Alexander Hopkins, *Jerusalem Christian Review* vol. 7, issue 6.

6

The Search for the Real Tomb of Jesus

Why should it matter if we know the actual place of the crucifixion of Jesus, or the location of the tomb where they laid His body? The answer is that Christianity is grounded in the historical events that occurred in definite places at definite times. Unlike ancient myths, the Gospels continually appeal to eyewitness accounts. Although we cannot identify the actual location of Golgotha and the empty Tomb of Christ with absolute certainty at the present time, the existing evidence provides a strong case in support of a particular geographical location in Jerusalem.

For almost seventeen hundred years the vast majority of Christians have assumed that the site of Golgotha and the Tomb were located at the site of the ancient Church of the Holy Sepulchre, one of the oldest churches in Christendom. However, questions about the validity of this location were raised by Catholic writer St. Willibald in A.D. 754.[1] St. Willibald identified the apparent contradiction between the geographic location of the Holy Sepulchre in the center of the walled city of Jerusalem, and the biblical description that Jesus was buried outside the city walls, "without the gate." This chapter examines the evidence for Jesus' tomb being in the Holy Sepulchre and the alternative argument for it being in another tomb north of Jerusalem's Damascus Gate, called the Garden Tomb.

The Scriptural Account about Golgotha and the Tomb

The Gospels contain detailed references about the crucifixion of Jesus at Golgotha and His subsequent burial in a nearby tomb, owned by one of His followers, Joseph of Arimathaea:

> Then delivered he him therefore unto them to be crucified. And they took Jesus, and led him away. And he bearing his cross went forth into a place called the place of a skull, which is called in the Hebrew Golgotha: Where they crucified him, and two others with him, on either side one, and Jesus in the midst. And Pilate wrote a title, and put it on the cross. And the writing was, JESUS OF NAZARETH THE KING OF THE JEWS. This title then read many of the Jews: for the place where Jesus was crucified was *nigh to the city*: and it was written in Hebrew, and Greek, and Latin. (John 19:16–20)

> Now in the place where he was crucified there was a garden; and in the garden a new sepulchre, wherein was never man yet laid. There laid they Jesus therefore because of the Jews' preparation day; for the sepulchre was nigh at hand. (John 19:41–42)

> Now when they were going, behold, *some of the watch came into the city*, and showed unto the chief priests all the things that were done. (Matthew 28:11)

> And they compel one Simon a Cyrenian, who passed by, *coming out of the country*, the father of Alexander and Rufus, to bear his cross. (Mark 15:21)

> For the bodies of those beasts, whose blood is brought into the sanctuary by the high priest for sin, are burned without the camp. Wherefore Jesus also, that he might sanctify the people with his own blood, *suffered without the gate*. (Hebrews 13:11–12)

The Building of the Church of the Holy Sepulchre

The Christian historian Eusebius wrote the history of the building of the Church of the Holy Sepulchre by the newly converted Roman emperor Constantine in A.D. 326:

> After these things, the pious emperor addressed himself to another work truly worthy of record, in the province of Palestine. What then was this work? He judged it incumbent on him to render the blessed locality of our Saviour's resurrection an object of attraction and veneration to all. He issued immediate injunctions, therefore, for the erection in that spot of a house of prayer: and this he did, not on the mere natural impulse of his own mind, but being moved in spirit by the Saviour himself.
>
> For it had been in time past the endeavor of impious men (or rather let me say of the whole race of evil spirits through their means) to consign to the darkness of oblivion that divine monument of immortality to which the radiant angel has descended from heaven, and rolled away the stone for those who still had stony hearts, and who supposed that the living One still lay among the dead; and had declared glad tidings to the women also, and removed their stony-hearted unbelief by the conviction that He whom they sought was alive.
>
> This sacred cave, then, certain impious and godless persons had thought to remove entirely from the eyes of men, supposing in their folly that thus they should be able effectually to obscure the truth. Accordingly they brought a quantity of earth from a distance with much labor, and covered the entire spot; then, having raised this to a moderate height, they paved it with stone, concealing the holy cave beneath this massive mound. . . .[2]

Eusebius then described the actual command of Constantine to Bishop Macarius in Jerusalem to build the new church:

> I have no greater care than how I may best adorn with a splendid structure that sacred spot, which, under Divine direction, I have disencumbered as it were of the heavy

weight of foul idol worship; a spot which has been accounted holy from the beginning in God's judgment, but which now appears holier still, since it has brought to light a clear assurance of our Saviour's passion.

It will be well, therefore, for your sagacity to make such arrangements and provision of all things needful for the work, that not only the church itself as a whole may surpass all others whatsoever in beauty, but that the details of the building may be of such a kind that the fairest structures in any city of the empire may be excelled by this.[3]

An anonymous French traveller, called the Pilgrim from Bordeaux, went to the Holy Land to visit the Church of the Holy Sepulchre in A.D. 333. He described it as follows:

As you leave there and pass through the Wall of Zion towards the gate of Neapolis (now called Damascus Gate) . . . on your left is the hillock Golgotha where the Lord was crucified, and about a stone's throw from it to the vault where they laid his body and he rose on the third day.[4]

One of the strongest reasons in favor of Jesus' tomb being at the Church of the Holy Sepulchre is that for almost seventeen hundred years it has been endorsed as the genuine site of Calvary by millions of Christians, the Roman Catholic Church, and the Russian and Greek Orthodox Churches. *(See picture 7 in photo section.)*

The Problems with the Holy Sepulchre as the Site of Golgotha

For more than twelve hundred years Christians have puzzled over the fact that the Holy Sepulchre is located in the middle of Jerusalem, even though three Gospels identify Jesus' crucifixion as being outside the walls of the city. Twelve hundred years ago St. Willibald was the first recorded writer to note the contradiction, saying that Golgotha "was formerly outside Jerusalem; but Helena, when she found the Cross, arranged that place so as to be within the City of Jerusalem."[5] Another author, Saewulf, who visited Jerusalem in A.D. 1102, addressed the contradiction by suggesting that the city was rebuilt in such a way that it encompassed the original location that was formerly outside the walls: "We know that our Lord suffered without the gate. But the Emperor Hadrian, who was also called Aelius, rebuilt the city of Jerusalem, and the Temple of the Lord, and added to the city as far as the Tower of David."[6]

The inescapable problem is that the Church of the Holy Sepulchre is located deep within the city of Jerusalem. The apologists for the site being at the Holy Sepulchre explain that the Second Wall that defended Jerusalem from the north and west must have curved inward to the south from the present Damascus Gate to encompass the location of the site occupied by the Holy Sepulchre. One of the biggest problems with this theory is that there is not a single piece of archeological evidence that proves the Second Wall was actually placed to the east of the Holy Sepulchre, thus allowing Golgotha to be "without the wall." (See map of ancient Jerusalem overleaf.)

Military men and historians who understand ancient-city plans of military defense think it highly unlikely that a Roman or Jewish military engineer would build a defensive wall for a city like Jerusalem that would leave a higher area, such as the ground on which the Holy Sepulchre rests outside the wall to the north of a city wall. Such a position for a defensive wall would leave the city at the mercy of its enemies, who would attack from the higher ground. It is inconceivable that the military engineers of Rome would permit a defensive wall to be built in a valley that would allow an enemy to easily attack from a higher position.

R. A. Stewart Macalister, a great scholar who considered this problem, rejected the idea of the Holy Sepulchre as a probable location of Calvary:

> Let me say first, that I hold no brief for the traditional site of Calvary and the Tomb, within the Church of the Holy Sepulchre. I find it hard to believe that the city wall really formed such a restraint angle as is necessary for the authenticity of the church site. And even if so built, such a corner (as everyone who knows oriental cities can easily realize) would rapidly become filled with all manner of offensive rubbish, and would therefore be a most improbable site for the garden of a rich man. A very much stronger chain of record or tradition, than we have any evidence for, must be shown to unite the events of the Crucifixion and entombment with the Empress Helena's expedition, before these objections can be satisfactorily removed.[7]

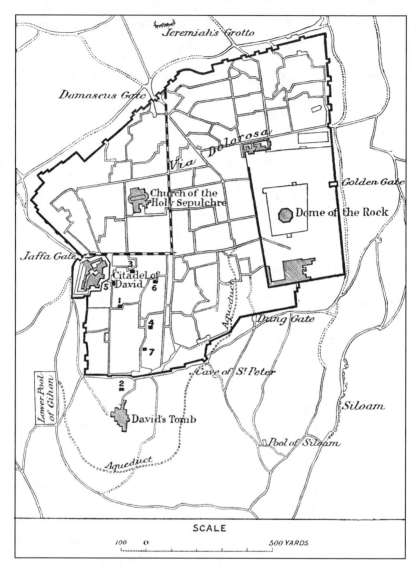

*Map of ancient Jerusalem showing hypothetical position
of the Second Wall.*

Would the Christians in A.D. 325 Remember
the Precise Location of Golgotha?

We have no contemporary evidence that the early Christians during the first two centuries venerated the Tomb or Golgotha as holy places. It was only after the conversion of Emperor Constantine and the building of great basilicas over a number of holy sites (chosen by his mother Queen Helena following her visit to Palestine in A.D. 326) that we see the development of pilgrimage by Christians to visit these important places in the life of Jesus. For example, an early Christian writer, Jerome, wrote in A.D. 385 about the theologian Origen's visit to Palestine "ostensibly to see the holy places" such as Bethlehem and Ascalon, yet makes no mention of him visiting the location of Golgotha.[8]

Jerusalem was literally leveled by the Roman legions following the destruction of the city and the Temple in A.D. 70. Mark recorded Christ's words: "And Jesus answering said unto him, Seest thou these great buildings? there shall not be left one stone upon another, that shall not be thrown down" (Mark 13:2). Sixty-five years after the destruction of Jerusalem in A.D. 70, Emperor Hadrian destroyed Jerusalem again in the Bar Kochba Rebellion of A.D. 135, killing over one million Jewish men, women, and children. Huge numbers of Jews were sold into slavery, and Hadrian ordered that no Jew should be allowed to enter Jerusalem or even come within sight of the city. Hadrian then rebuilt the city and named it Aelia Capitolina. In light of these repeated devastations and the exile of the Jews from the city for many years, it is probable that the transformed geography of the city would make the absolute identification of the site of Golgotha almost impossible.

It is worthwhile to note that Reverend Charles Couasnon, who directed the restoration work on the Holy Sepulchre in the 1970s, has expressed doubts that anyone can prove that this church is the authentic site of Golgotha: "One cannot actually prove that the present site, which has been considered the authentic one since the year 326, is, beyond any doubt, the same as that venerated by the Christian community in apostalic times."[9]

There was a curious tradition within the early Church that the name Golgotha was based on more than the superficial physical resemblance of the cliff wall to the face of a skull. The Greek Christian writer, Origen (A.D.185–253), wrote that there was a Jewish tradition that Golgotha's "place of the skull" referred to the belief that the skull of Adam was actually buried on that site.[10] Bishop Athanasius (A.D. 296–373) wrote that Jesus did not die, "in any other place, but in the Place of a Skull which the Hebrew teachers declare was Adam's sepulchre."[11] Significantly, the Jewish

Christian theologian, Epiphanius (A.D. 321–403), wrote that Christ was crucified, "in no other place than that in which Adam lay buried."[12] Obviously, in light of the thousands of years that had passed and the devastating geological changes brought about by the flood, it is virtually impossible that the Jewish tradition about Adam's skull was based on anything more than an unsupported legend. Christian writers were fascinated with the tradition of Adam's skull and Golgotha because it seemed fitting theologically to them that Jesus Christ, "the second Adam," would die and rise from the dead in the very place where the first Adam, who brought about the fall of man, lay buried.

Others have suggested that the name Golgotha refers to the fact that the execution place was littered with the skulls of execution victims whose bodies were unburied. However, this theory is unlikely because both Jewish and Roman law strictly prohibited leaving bodies or body parts unburied. The *Jerusalem Talmud*, created approximately A.D. 150, revealed that the Jewish Sanhedrin court was in possession of two separate burial places for the bodies of criminals. One burial ground was for those who were strangled, hanged, or decapitated, while the second site was for those who were stoned or burned to death.[13]

One of the most experienced archeologists who examined the holy sites in Jerusalem for many years, British officer and archeological scholar Colonel C. R. Conder, rejected the Holy Sepulchre as the genuine site of Golgotha in his lecture to the Palestine Exploration Fund in its 1886 meeting in London: "I think enough is now known to lead to the conclusion that the traditional site of the Holy Sepulchre must be abandoned and that we are free to accept the site without the walls which Jewish tradition has indicated as the site of Calvary."[14]

Colonel Conder also noted that the large population living in the surburbs to the north of the city would have made an execution site in that immediate neighborhood unlikely. Conder noted,

> The traditional sites are certainly within Agrippa's wall, which was built only eleven years after the crucifixion, to defend the suburb which would probably have taken in those days more than eleven years to attain the extent necessitating a new line of fortification. In this case, whether within or without, the Holy Sepulchre (as fixed by

Constantine) was so close to the second wall that it is impossible to suppose its site not to have been surrounded by houses in the time of Christ, a fact which would be fatal to the authenticity of the site.[15]

Henry Gilman, the American Consul in Jerusalem in the final years of the last century, published his own opinion about the location of Christ's tomb:

I have seen, from time to time, lately, statements to the effect that all recent discoveries have tended to establish the accuracy of the traditional site of the Holy Sepulchre. Nothing can be more contrary to the truth. The recently discovered Roman pavements, in connection with those uncovered two years ago or more, establish the position of Damascus Gate as occupying an ancient site; and the discoveries in general all point to outside the gate as the place of crucifixion.[16]

Reasons Why the Holy Sepulchre May Not Be the Site of Calvary

The problems with the Holy Sepulchre as the site of Calvary can be summarized as follows:

1. There is no evidence that knowledge of the exact location of Calvary was maintained and successfully passed on from generation to generation following the destruction of Jerusalem in A.D. 70 until Queen Helena's visit to Jerusalem in A.D. 326, when the tomb was discovered.

2. The church is located in the middle of the city of Jerusalem, a location that is contradicted by Gospel accounts that describe the site of Calvary as being outside the city walls. Although supporters have claimed the ancient Second Wall "might" have abruptly turned south from the Damascus Gate to cut in a southern direction just east of the church site and then turn west again to allow the site to be "outside the wall," there is no conclusive archeological evidence to prove this assertion.

3. The New Testament states that Jesus "suffered without the gate" (Hebrews 13:12). However, there is no conclusive historical or archeological evidence that there was ever a major gate near the location of the Holy Sepulchre.

4. The Romans crucified victims on major highways to attract large audiences in order to terrorize the population. There is no archeological evidence that any major road ever existed near the Holy Sepulchre site.

5. Placing the Second Wall to the east and then to the south of the site would have exposed the defenders of Jerusalem to grave danger, as the wall would have been built on ground lower than the elevation of the site of the Holy Sepulchre. This would have given an invading army an enormous advantage in attacking the walls from the high ground outside the walls. Military sources are virtually unanimous that no one would choose to place a defensive wall in such a location that would allow an enemy army to penetrate the center of the city.

6. If the Second Wall ran to the east of the site of the Holy Sepulchre, Jersualem would have been compressed between the Holy Sepulchre and the Temple Mount (they were only 800 yards apart).

This is almost inconceivable, considering the estimated population of 50,000 in Jerusalem during the first century. (See the map of ancient Jerusalem)

7. Even if archeological evidence is discovered that proves that the Second Wall ran to the east of the Holy Sepulchre, it would still leave the other problems unanswered. The population of Jerusalem spilled out of the city walls into the northern suburbs during the first century; King Herod Agrippa built a Third Wall to the north of the city to encompass the northern suburbs in A.D. 43, only eleven years after Jesus' death. This population pressure means that there would have been homes built to the immediate north of the Second Wall on the site of the Holy Sepulchre a decade earlier. This growing population would make the area almost impossible to use as a place of execution in A.D. 32.

8. Archeologists have determined that King Herod's palace was located only a few hundred yards from the site of the Holy Sepulchre. It defies common sense to believe that the government of Herod would place a site for executions that close to Herod's home. The sounds of victims screaming, and the stench from bodies left on the crosses, would make it unlikely that they would place an execution site so close to the King's residence.

9. The Holy Sepulchre site does not reveal any evidence that a rolling-stone type door was used to seal the tomb.

An Alternative Theory:
Gordon's Calvary and the Garden Tomb

In 1883 General Charles Gordon, a brilliant English military leader, visited Jerusalem and stayed in a house that overlooked the northern wall of the Old City. Looking out the window of his residence, the general noticed that the hill opposite the wall to the north bore a startling resemblance to a skull. A dedicated Christian, General Gordon commenced a personal investigation that eventually convinced him that the site must be the genuine location of Calvary. Although it turns out that he was not the first to suggest that this site was the true location of Golgotha, General Gordan's fame was so great that his endorsement led many Christians to carefully consider the new evidence in favor of this site. As a result, people began to call the site Gordon's Calvary. Wealthy Christians in England contributed money to the Garden Tomb Association, which was formed to purchase the property that included the Garden Tomb and a strip that extended northwest toward the part of the cliff face that included the skull shape. The Garden Tomb Association bought the site and has preserved and protected it to the present time. Unfortunately, they were unable to purchase the whole area including the cliff face with the skull shape. Today the Jerusalem's main bus terminal sits directly in front of the cliff face of Golgotha, making it difficult for the average visitor to imagine what the site would have looked like in the first century. Fortunately, I have a photograph that was taken in 1890 that shows Golgotha very much as it must have looked two thousand years ago. *(See picture 8 in photo section.)*

One of the strongest reasons for suggesting that the site known as Gordon's Calvary might be the actual location of Golgotha is that this site is outside the ancient and present walls of the Old City of Jerusalem. This present northern city wall was built by the Turks approximately four hundred years ago upon the original Herodian foundation stones built on bedrock that formed his Second Wall. Outside the northern wall, military engineers quarried out massive amounts of limestone to use as building material and in the process they created a huge ditch as a military defence for the city. Any attacking enemy army would be forced to descend into this deep quarry and then attack the very high walls and towers built upon the bedrock on the southern edge of the quarry. Also, the location is not far from the Damascus Gate, which has been proven to be an ancient gate of the Holy City. For more than a century archeologists have seriously considered whether this site might be the true site of Christ's crucifixion.

There is historical evidence that the site of Gordon's Calvary had been considered from as early as the second century as the site of the stoning of the martyr St. Stephen and the prophet Jeremiah before the Temple was destroyed by the Babylonians in 587 B.C. The Church of St. Stephen was built in the third century by the Roman Byzantines to commemorate the martyrdom of St. Stephen, which is believed to have occurred at Jerusalem's place of execution just outside the Damascus Gate.

The Jews have traditionally believed that their ancient prophet Jeremiah was imprisoned and stoned to death by the nobles of Jerusalem in a cistern prison northeast of the Damascus Gate. The remains of this ancient cistern can still be seen. As I have pointed out in a previous book, the archeologists recently discovered the remains of a long narrow tunnel with a very high roof that runs all the way under the Old City of Jerusalem from the Temple Mount to the enormous quarried cave that extends from near the Damascus Gate south toward the Temple. It is believed that this is the ancient tunnel that was used by King Zedekiah to secretly meet with the prophet Jeremiah, discussing with him the will of God. The Bible refers to the king, his family, and his soldiers attempting to escape from the Babylonian army's siege of Jerusalem by secretly following this long tunnel "bewixt the two walls" to a point outside the city walls (Jeremiah 39:4–5; 2 Kings 25:4–5). Very few cities have ever used two places of execution simultaneously. Since the evidence is very strong that this site, known as Gordon's Calvary, was the place of execution of both Jeremiah and St. Stephen, and "the place of stoning," the probability is that the Romans would have used the same place of execution for the crucifixion of Jesus.

Reverend J. E. Hanauer, a respected scholar and a member of the Palestine Exploration Fund, wrote a report about Gordon's Calvary to the *P. E. F . Report* in 1892, describing the site as a "place of stoning" since ancient times. Hanauer wrote,

There exist ancient Christian traditions, dating back to the early part of the second century, and possibly even to Apostolic times, and indicating that 'Gordon's Calvary' was a 'place of stoning.' 'Gordon's Calvary' is the remarkable hillock above the cave called 'Jeremiah's Grotto,' because Jeremiah is said to have written his Lamentations there, and what has been apparently forgotten or overlooked, because he was stoned there.[17]

The ancient Jewish commentary known as the *Mishneh*, which was composed in approximately A.D. 150, contains a passage that describes the "place of stoning" or execution in Jerusalem, called "Beth-has-Sekilah." The site is described as being "far off" from the "Judgment Hall" in the north end of the Temple Mount.[18]

Reverend J. E. Hanauer also described the rites that were held at the Church of the Holy Sepulchre:

Annually, on the 4th of November, the Orthodox (i.e., Greek) Church commemorates the fall of Jerusalem, and during the special Service for the day a portion of an ancient Christian Apocalypse, of the year 136 A.D., and giving an account of the stoning of Jeremiah, is read. The Apocalypse in question is entitled 'The Rest of the Words of Baruch,' and has recently been edited by Professor J. Rendel Harris (Cambridge University Press). In his introduction to the work, Professor Harris says that an 'important tradition concerning Jeremiah is that he was stoned.' This is not an original idea of the Christian Baruch. We find it in the Epistle to the Hebrews. The famous passage, 'they were stoned, they were sawn assunder,' etc., is a summary of the sufferings of the worthies of Faith,' and each statement is based on the history of some real person: it has always been known that 'they were sawn assunder' referred to Isaiah, just as 'stopped the mouths of lions' referred to Daniel, and 'quenched the violence of fire' to the three Hebrew children, but it is not so generally felt that 'they were stoned' belongs to Jeremiah. Yet such is the case, as the Baruch-Jeremiah legend shows; and the Epistle to the Hebrews is therefore one of the early witnesses to the tradition.[19]

The site known as the Garden Tomb is located approximately one hundred yards from Gordon's Calvary. Archeologists know the site was an ancient garden in the distant past. Archeologists have discovered the remains of a wine press as well as a huge underground cistern capable of holding more than two hundred thousand gallons of water. These specifications are consistent with a rich man's garden as described in the Gospels. The Scriptures tell us that the garden and the new tomb were owned by Joseph of Arimathaea, a disciple of Jesus who was also a member of the Jewish religious court known as the Sanhedrin. In the first century the town of Arimathaea was located just five miles north of the site of the Garden Tomb. This would be consistent with a rich man owning a second home in northern Jerusalem, in addition to his home in Arimathaea. It appears that remnants of ritual baths, known as mikvahs, have been found in the garden. This would also be consistent with a religious leader of the Sanhedrin and his need for ritual cleanliness prior to his visits to the Temple.

In 1886 Colonel Claude R. Conder gave an address to the Palestine Exploration Fund meeting in London in which he expressed his conclusion about the tomb of Jesus: "I think enough is now known to lead to the conclusion that the traditional site of the Holy Sepulchre must be abandoned and that we are free to accept the site without the walls which Jewish tradition has indicated as the site of Calvary."[20]

Many Christians have assumed that Jesus was crucified on "Mount Calvary," but Luke calls Calvary "a place": ". . . the place, which is called Calvary . . ."(Luke 23:33), as opposed to a mountain. Three of the Gospels refer to Golgotha as "a place." For example, John 19:17 refers to Golgotha as follows: "And he bearing his cross went forth into a place called the place of a skull, which is called in the Hebrew Golgotha." Major General C. W. Wilson suggests that the reason most people have assumed Calvary was a hill is due to the many paintings that depict the crucifixion scene with three crosses on a hill. There are also several beloved hymns that contain lines such as "on a hill far away stood an old rugged cross," and the "green hill far away." [21]

The first reference to Calvary as being a "mount" occurred in A.D. 333 in a passage by the Pilgrim of Bordeaux. He refers to Calvary as "Monticulus Golgotha," or "little Mount Golgotha."

Two centuries later Golgotha is called a "mount" in the Breviarius (A.D. 530).[22] Archeologist Charles Clermont-Ganneau found several sixth-century Christian tombstones that bore engraved crosses standing on top of a three-lobed or trefoil base. The symbol of a three-lobed, or a trefoil, often symbolized a mountain or hill in ancient Middle Eastern art.[23]

The evidence is quite strong that the Romans would have crucified their victims by placing the cross in holes in the ground at the base of the cliff known as Gordon's Calvary that forms the northern face of the ancient quarry. Such a position would have allowed a large crowd to see the victims anguish and hear their agonized cries because the site is located just outside a major city gate and on the main road that lies north of the city walls connecting Jericho and the road to Jaffa. A Roman writer, Quintillian, described the thinking of the Roman government that motivated the brutal public execution technique known as crucifixion: "Whenever we crucify criminals, very crowded highways are chosen so that many may see it and many may be moved by fear of it; because all punishment does not pertain as much to revenge as to example."[24] Mark's Gospel confirms that Jesus was crucified close to a road. "And they that passed by railed on him, wagging their heads, and saying, Ah, thou that destroyest the temple, and buildest it in three days" (Mark 15:29).

A German architect, Dr. Baurath C. Schick, was hired by Turkish authorities to complete detailed surveys of Jerusalem. He wrote a report to the Palestine Exploration Fund in 1892 reporting his knowledge about the discovery of a tomb only a hundred yards from the site of Gordon's Calvary, but out of direct line of sight because the cliff curves to the north at that point. Schick explained that a Greek native of Jerusalem owned the piece of land to the west of Gordon's Calvary and found this remarkable cave with a cross on the wall when he removed about five feet of earth and rubbish from his property in 1867. The tomb contained a great deal of earth as well as a number of skeletons on the surface. When Dr. Schick examined the tomb he found that its bottom was covered with several feet of dust. This indicated that the tomb was abandoned for many centuries before some Byzantine Christians re-used the empty tomb to bury bodies on top of the earth. The cross painted on the wall in red paint was undoubtedly created in the

Byzantine era rather than in the early centuries. The tomb was approximately 10 feet long, 8 feet wide, and 6 feet 6 inches high. There are three steps that lead down to the area where the body would have been laid. It is obvious that the tomb was not fully finished.[25]

One of the most significant elements of the Garden Tomb is that a stone ledge cut from the bedrock runs parallel to the cliff face direcly in front of the tomb's entrance, as shown in the photograph, that would be consistent with a trough to hold a rolling stone large enough to close the door of the tomb. By actual measurement the width of the stone trough or groove running in front of the Garden Tomb's entrance is precisely the width of the rolling stone that was found in the first-century B.C. Tombs of the Kings discovered in northern Jerusalem. *(See picture 9 in photo section.)*

Objections Against Gordon's Calvary and the Garden Tomb

The problems with these alternative sites can be summarized as follows:

1. While the cliff face at Gordon's Calvary does superficially resemble the face of a skull, some critics note that the name Golgotha, meaning "the place of the skull," does not necessarily mean that the site resembles a skull. The name Golgotha might suggest that the site was associated with a tradition connected to a particular skull. An early Christian theologian, Origen, referred to a traditional belief that Adam had been buried at the site that later became known as Calvary.[26] Another Christian writer, Basil, wrote about the "tradition held in the Church that Adam was buried at Calvaria, which thence took its name."[27] Jerome also referred to this tradition of the burial of Adam's skull at Calvary. [28]

While the origins of the name Golgotha may stem from such a strange Jewish tradition, this would not detract from the fact that the resemblance to a skull might reinforce such an identification. The other details of the location involving its being outside the walls and near a major city gate, with a tomb close by the traditional place of execution, still argue in favor of the site's authenticity.

2. While thousands of churches and pastors visit the site of Gordon's Calvary and the Garden Tomb annually, in demonstration of their belief that the site is genuine, no official denomination

has completely endorsed the site as the authentic location of Golgotha and the empty tomb.

3. Critics who reject the Garden Tomb have stated that the tomb is of a distinctly Byzantine construction, similar to that used by the Greek Orthodox faith in the eighth and ninth centuries. However, a number of experienced archeologists, including Professor Kathleen Kenyon, have stated that the tomb is definitely Jewish and dates back to the time of Christ. Professor Kenyon declared, "The Garden Tomb is a typical Jewish tomb of the first century."[29]

4. Others have pointed out that there is evidence of sockets cut into the stone of the door, indicating that the tomb door once had metal hinges. However, there is no proof that these door hinges were part of the original tomb entrance. As noted earlier, when the tomb was discovered in 1867, there was a red-painted Byzantine cross and numerous skeletons lying on more than five feet of earth. Therefore, the door hinges could easily have been added to close the tomb door in later centuries when Byzantines re-used the tomb for burials, long after the burial of Jesus.

5. Some critics complain that the hill of Gordon's Calvary could not be the genuine site because a cross on the hill would not permit those traveling on the road to hear the voices of those being crucified. However, as I noted earlier, there is no evidence in the Gospel record that the crucifixion took place on the top of the hill. Rather the evidence suggests that the place of crucifixion would have been at the base of the cliff.

The burden of historical and archeological evidence argues persuasively that the Garden Tomb and Skull Hill may be the true site of our Lord's Passion. However, Dr. Baurath Schick's comment in July, 1892 to the Palestine Exploration Fund probably sums up the issue as succinctly as possible: "My conviction is that the question of the real Calvary will never be settled by controversy, but only by excavations."[30]

Unfortunately, despite a century of further archeological investigation, we still cannot be absolutely certain which of the two sites is the true location of Calvary and Jesus of Nazareth's tomb. Hopefully, in the next decade new excavations will conclusively reveal the place of Golgotha to the satisfaction of all those who are searching for the truth about Jesus.

Notes

1. St. Willibald, *Palestine Pilgrims' Texts* vol. 3.
2. Eusebius, *The Nicene and Post Nicene Fathers*, 2nd. series (Grand Rapids: Wm. B. Eerdmans Publishing Co., 1986) 526–528.
3. Eusebius, *The Nicene and Post Nicene Fathers*, 2nd. Series (Grand Rapids: Wm. B. Eerdmans Publishing Co., 1986) 526–528.
4. Pilgrim from Bordeaux, *Palestine Pilgrims' Texts*.
5. St. Willibald, *Palestine Pilgrims' Texts* vol. 3.
6. Claude Conders, *The Holy Sepulchre*, P.E.F.Q.S. (1883).
7. R. A. Stewart Macalister, *Palestine Exploration Fund Statement* 1908: 232–244.
8. Jerome, *Vir. 111* 54P1 23.665.
9. Rev. Charles Couasnon, The Schweich Lectures for 1972 (London: Oxford University Press, 1974).
10. Origen, *Appendix* (III, 1).
11. Athanasius, *Appendix* (III, 2).
12. Epiphanius, *Appendix* (III, 3).
13. *Le Talmud de Jerusalem*, vol. 10, trans. M. Schwab (Paris: 1888).
14. Claude Conder, *Palestine Exploration Fund Statement* Jan. 1887: 20.
15. Claude Conder, "The Holy Sepulchre," *Palestine Exploration Fund* 1883: 73.
16. Henry Gilman, *Palestine Exploration Fund* Jan. 1881.
17. J. E. Hanauer, *Palestine Exploration Fund Statement* 1892.
18. *Mishneh*.
19. J. E. Hanauer, *Palestine Exploration Fund Statement* Oct. 1982: 199.
20. Claude Conder, *Palestine Exploration Fund Statement* Jan. 1887: 20.
21. C. W. Wilson, *Palestine Exploration Fund Statement* 1888.
22. *Palestine Pilgrims' Texts* vol. 2.
23. Charles Clermont-Ganneau, *Palestine Fund Memoirs, Archeological Researches in Palestine* 1: 337.
24. Quintillian, *Declarations* A.D. 90.
25. Dr. Baurath C. Schick, *Palestine Exploration Fund* (1892).
26. Origen, *Series Veteris Interpretation, Commentary on Matthew* (1777) 3: 126.
27. Basil, *In Isaiam* 2 vols. 1:348.
28. Jerome, *Eusebii Pamphili Cæsariensis Onomasticon . . . Græce com Latina*, ed. F. Larson and G. Parthey (Berolini, 1862) 55.

29. William Steuart McBirnie, *The Search For The Tomb of Christ* (Montrose: Acclaimed Books, 1975).

30. Dr. Baurath Schick, *Palestine Exploration Fund Statement* July 1892: 308.

7

The Mysterious Shroud of Turin

Of all the evidence that exists regarding Jesus, the most remarkable and controversial by far is the Shroud of Turin. Millions of Christians believe the Shroud is the burial cloth used by the disciples to wrap the body of Christ following His crucifixion. For centuries people have debated the origin of this ancient piece of faded linen that bears a mysterious image of a crucified man. Despite the reverence millions of believers pay to the Shroud, skeptics reject the claims that this might be the linen burial cloth mentioned in all four of the Gospels. The critics believe that the image on the Shroud is simply the result of a clever medieval artistic forger, which is not so improbable an assumption, given the fact that the medieval period produced thousands of fake relics for the curious and naive religious pilgrims who were easily fooled into believing that someone's old bones might be the mortal remains of one of the apostles or that a piece of the true cross had miraculously survived.

However, even the critics admit that the Shroud of Turin is the most fascinating and controversial of all claimed relics. Despite hundreds of tests no one has been able to successfully explain how the mysterious image of a crucified man could have been produced by a medieval artist on the surface fibers of this linen cloth. After twenty years of testing by some of the world's best scientists, using the most advanced scientific equipment, the mystery of the formation of the image on the Shroud remains unsolved. Over one hundred and fifty thousand hours of detailed scientific testing have only deepened the mystery of how and when the astonishing image of a crucified man was formed on this ancient piece of linen. The Shroud is without doubt the most extensively researched ancient artifact in the history of science. The real question is *Who is the man in the Shroud*? Is this burial cloth a silent witness to the resurrection — the most miraculous event in history? Or is this Shroud evidence of the greatest art forgery known to date?

The modern history of the Shroud of Turin began in 1357 with its first public display in a small wooden church in the forest near the tiny village of Lirey, France. The presentation of the Shroud in the church produced a great deal of interest among the religious inhabitants of the province. Soon great crowds of pilgrims began to appear daily to witness this relic from the distant past that appeared to reveal an astonishing image of the crucified Messiah imprinted on its yellowed linen fibers. Although the earlier history of the Shroud is indeed cloaked in mystery and legend, from 1357 on this curious cloth has captured the attention and the reverence of millions of people throughout the world. Over the centuries the Shroud was often brought forth from its protected silver box to be displayed to the faithful as both a symbol and image of the Savior.

The Biblical Evidence

All four Gospels record the fact that Jesus was buried in a sindone, a linen burial cloth or shroud. This detail of Christ's burial obviously was considered to be very important and worthy of being recorded by the Scriptures. The following passages indicate its importance:

> And when Joseph had taken the body, he wrapped it in a clean linen cloth, And laid it in his own new tomb, which he had hewn out in the rock: and he rolled a great stone to the door of the sepulchre, and departed (Matthew 27:59–60).

> And he bought fine linen, and took him down, and wrapped him in the linen, and laid him in a sepulchre

which was hewn out of a rock, and rolled a stone unto the door of the sepulchre (Mark 15:46).

And he took it down, and wrapped it in linen, and laid it in a sepulchre that was hewn in stone, wherein never man before was laid (Luke 23:53).

Then arose Peter, and ran unto the sepulchre; and stooping down, he beheld the linen clothes laid by themselves, and departed, wondering in himself at that which was come to pass (Luke 24:12).

The disciple John, the author of the Gospel of John, records the scene when Peter and he ran to the tomb after hearing from Mary Magdalene that Christ's body was not there:

And he stooping down, and looking in, saw the linen clothes lying; yet went he not in. Then cometh Simon Peter following him, and went into the sepulchre, and seeth the linen clothes lie, And the napkin, that was about his head, not lying with the linen clothes, but wrapped together in a place by itself. Then went in also that other disciple, which came first to the sepulchre, and he saw, and believed (John 20:5–8).

In this passage John alludes to the fact that there was something remarkable about the burial clothes lying on the floor of the empty tomb that convinced him that Jesus had truly risen from the dead. Is it possible that John saw an image of Christ on the linen burial cloth that proved the truth of His resurrection? Could the mysterious Shroud of Turin be "the clean linen cloth" that Joseph of Arimathaea used to wrap the body of his beloved Jesus of Nazareth when he placed it in his tomb?

A Description of the Shroud of Turin and Its Significance

The Shroud is a sepia-yellow-colored linen cloth fourteen feet long and forty-three inches wide. A hand-sewn seam attached lengthwise was added to the original cloth at some unknown point of time. A faint image of the front and back of a man's body can still be seen on the linen, but the image appears to be formed by a deeper yellowing of some of the surface linen fibers. This subtle image almost melts away as you draw near to the burial cloth. In addition, a number of carmine-or-rust colored stains that appear to be blood stains can be seen on the body image. These stains are consistent with the Gospel's account of the scourging and crucifixion of Jesus. In addition to the image of a man, there are obvious water stains, scorch marks, and diamond-shaped repair patches that are the result of repairs made by nuns after a fire in 1532 that caused the silver box holding the Shroud to melt and burn several holes through the precious cloth.

Many skeptics have assumed that the image was painted on the cloth by a talented but unknown artist during the medieval period, in an era when literally tens of thousands of such relics — alleged pieces of the true cross, bones of the disciples, and even images of Jesus — were found in the monasteries, royal courts, and churches of every nation in Christendom. In fact, when the crusader knights returned from their brutal wars in the Holy Land, they often brought back various relics that they had stolen or purchased at great cost from the churches in the cities and villages of Israel.

The claim that an ancient object such as a linen burial cloth could actually survive throughout twenty centuries of war, pillage, and catastrophe seems almost impossible. However, museums throughout the world contain many examples of cloth that have survived for much longer than the purported age of the burial Shroud of Turin. In fact, there are examples of ancient burial shrouds from Egyptian tombs and Coptic cemeteries that predate the purported age of the Turin cloth by more than a thousand years.

Centuries later, the Shroud was exhibited in Turin in 1898 to celebrate the fiftieth anniversary of the creation of the Italian kingdom. Secondo Pia, an amateur photographer, was given permission to shoot the first photographs ever taken of the Shroud. To his great surprise, the negative of the black and white photograph revealed an extremely life-like image of a tall man with a strong face and striking features and surprising life-like details that could not be seen before. In general, the image revealed an anatomically correct image of a crucified man, whose wounds reflected the wounds suffered by Jesus Christ, as recounted in the Synoptic Gospels. *(See picture 11 in photo section.)*

This intriguing photograph launched the modern period of

scientific examination of the Shroud to determine if it could possibly be the genuine burial cloth of Jesus or simply the result of a brilliant artist's attempt to depict the passion of Christ for the edification of the saints. In 1931, at another exhibition of the Shroud, even more detailed photographs were taken that allowed scientists to carefully examine the image in terms of the medical evidence of the wounds that seemed surprisingly consistent with the Gospels' record of Jesus' crucifixion and modern medical knowledge of human anatomy.

The Medical Evidence of a Crucified Man

The first real scientific examination of the Shroud began in Paris at the Sorbonne University medical school following the release of the photographs created in 1898 by Secondo Pia. Yves Delage, a brilliant professor of comparative anatomy, undertook detailed studies of the physiology of the body image, as well as the evidence of pathology derived from the details of the wounds found in the image of the crucified body. As an atheist, Delage was astonished to find that the image displayed a remarkably accurate anatomic depiction of a dead male, whose body had been both whipped and crucified and showed evidence of rigor mortis. The multiple whip wounds and the resulting blood flow from the scourgings, puncture wounds in the head, spike wounds through the wrists and feet, and a wound in the man's right side were all consistent with the Gospel record of Jesus Christ's crucifixion.

A scientific analysis reveals a naked, well-formed, muscular adult male in his thirties. He has a mustache, full beard, and shoulder-length long hair that appears to be tied back behind the head. Such a hair style and length are consistent with what we know of Jewish customs of the Second Temple period. The body measures approximately 5 foot 10 inches in height, with a weight estimated to be about 175 pounds, which is about average for Jewish males of the first-century, according to recent excavations in Israel. Harvard professor Carleton Coon has described the physical appearance of the man in the Shroud as being "of a physical type found in modern times among Sephardic Jews and noble Arabs".[1]

The image of the body reveals as many as one hundred and twenty wounds, each approximately one and one-half inches long on the back, arms, and shoulders. They appear to be produced by dumbbell-shaped objects and are consistent with wounds formed by the Roman whip, known as the flagrum. The flagrum was a brutal multiple-thonged whip with lead or bone dumbbell-shaped weights attached to the ends of the whip that would tear the skin and flesh. While some critics have pointed out that ancient Jewish law prohibited giving a prisoner more than forty strokes with a whip, Roman law did not limit the number of times prisoners could be whipped. While some critics and skeptics have suggested that Jesus did not die on the cross, the evidence from the Shroud indicates that the man may have been near death from the repeated whippings, even before he suffered the brutality of crucifixion. Scientists have noted that the shoulders appear to be severely bruised and the blood stains from whip wounds are distorted by something having rubbed against the shoulders. This may be explained by the Gospel account that Jesus was forced to carry the cross, which would have produced such bruising. In addition, the various wounds on the knees of the man in the image may reflect what would have happened to Jesus as He stumbled and fell repeatedly while carrying the cross on the way to Golgotha.

Some critics have complained that the evidence from the wounds in the image suggests that the body had not been washed, contrary to ancient Jewish burial practices that required the body to be washed before burial. However, the urgency to bury the body before the commencement of the Sabbath may have prevented the normal washing. A Jewish scholar, Professor Victor Tunkel of London University, has pointed out that Jewish practice would actually have prohibited the washing of a body of a person who was violently killed to ensure that his blood would remain with the body in anticipation of the future bodily resurrection. Even today in Israel ultra-Orthodox religious groups carefully gather the bodily remains and blood of victims of terrorist bombs to bury such items with the body. The fact that the body was unwashed argues that the Shroud is genuine.

Another remarkable aspect of the burial cloth is that the blood flow from the wrist indicates that the spike was placed through the wrist of the man in the Shroud and not through the palm, as we find depicted on countless religious paintings of Christ on the cross. Dr. Pierre Barbet performed numerous experiments with cadavers and amputated arms to demonstrate that a spike through the palm would not hold any body weighing more than 90 pounds. However, by nailing the spike through the opening between the bones in that part of the wrist known as the "Space of Destot," the spike would fully support the weight of an adult male body, exactly as we find in the image on the Shroud.[2]

Israeli archeologists recently discovered an ossuary or stone coffin at Giv'at ha-Mivtar, near Jerusalem, that contained the body of a male who had been crucified. The spike was still in place through both feet, and the spike that held the arms had been placed through the Space of Destot. The legs of the crucified man, specifically the fibula and the right and left tibia, had been broken to hasten his death, exactly as had happened to the two thieves who were crucified on either side of Jesus, according to the Gospel of John.

> The Jews therefore, because it was the preparation, that the bodies should not remain upon the cross on the sabbath day, (for that sabbath day was an high day,) besought Pilate that their legs might be broken, and that they might be taken away. Then came the soldiers, and brake the legs of the first, and of the other which was crucified with him. But when they came to Jesus, and saw that he was dead already, they brake not his legs. (John 19:31–33)

The Shroud's image, however, reveals that the legs of this victim were *not* broken, a fact that agrees with the Gospel account about Christ. One unique characteristic of the Shroud is there is no evidence of any body decomposition. All of the thousands of other burial cloths found in Egypt and North Africa contain stains from body decomposition. The lack of decomposition stains on the Shroud and the fact that the body image shows clear signs of rigor mortis (which would have ended after two days) provides powerful evidence that the body did not decompose in the Shroud, but was separated somehow from it. Significantly, although there are over one hundred and twenty blood stains on the Shroud, there are no blood smears. Experiments with corpses prove that it is impossible to lift a body from a burial cloth without causing blood smears.

That the Shroud image depicts a body in the state of rigor mortis was determined by the fact that all of the limbs appear very stiff, the feet and lower abdomen are distended, and the thumbs are retracted. Doctors and forensic pathologists who have examined the image's anatomical details, the multiple wounds, and the patterns of flow of blood have often remarked that it would be virtually impossible to duplicate perfectly the image of a dead, crucified body in a state of rigor mortis. No medieval artist could have duplicated with such perfection what would happen to a crucified body in death and rigor mortis. Pathologist Robert Bucklin, M.D., a member of the Shroud of Turin Research Project (STURP) team who served as Deputy Medical Examiner of Los Angeles County and who personally examined over twenty-five thousand bodies during his service as a coroner, analyzed the medical details of the Shroud. Bucklin observed, "Each of the different wounds acted in a characteristic fashion. Each bled in a manner which corresponded to the nature of the injury. The blood followed gravity in every instance."[3]

The scalp reveals over thirty separate small wounds covering both the top of the skull and the area around the head, indicating that the crown of thorns was not like the wreath we see in many paintings of the Cross; it was a large mass of thorns that literally covered His head. The large blood loss associated with the scalp wounds is consistent with normal arterial blood loss from scalp puncture-type wounds. Laboratories have tested the rust-colored stains on the cloth and determined they are stains of human blood. Furthermore, the stains reveal red blood corpuscles at the edges of blood clot and a smaller area of clear serum in the center, exactly as would occur with blood stains on cloth. (*See picture 10 in photo section.*)

Another wound, a large oval-shaped wound on the right side of the body, between the fifth and sixth ribs, and measuring approximately 1.75 inches long and less than .5 inches wide, produced the greatest amount of blood flow of all the wounds. There is an indication also of a small amount of secondary bleeding that possibly occurred when the body was laid out on the floor of the tomb. Most medical experts agree that this side wound must have occurred after the body was dead, based on the relatively small amount of blood loss and the obvious separation of the fluid into both blood and clear serum.

Medical opinions differ, however, on the meaning of the Gospel accounts' description of the "water and blood" that flowed from Christ's side. Dr. Barbet suggests that the clear fluid that appeared to be water might have been pericardial fluid. Dr. Moedder suggests that the fluid was from the pleural sac, and Dr. Bucklin suggests that it was serous fluid formed from the blood that settled in the pleural cavity of the chest as a result of the crucifixion. In his new book, entitled *The Last Days of Christ*, a medical specialist from Turin, Italy, Professor Luigi Baima Bollone, suggests that Jesus may have succumbed to a heart attack, a coronary thrombosis caused by the whipping and crucifixion. He suggests that a blood clot may have formed in a coronary artery, obstructing the blood flow and causing a fatal heart attack.

After examining the evidence, Professor Delage of Sorbonne University concluded that the image on the Shroud must have been formed through either direct or indirect contact with an actual cadaver. He said that the image could not have been painted or scorched on the linen. Despite the agnosticism of French universities, Delage, an agnostic himself, had the intellectual courage to admit that the Shroud evidence revealed the correct anatomical features of a crucified man that was perfectly consistent with the Gospels' description of Christ's crucifixion. Delage wrote, "The man of the Shroud is Christ. . . . if instead of Christ, there was a question of some person such as a Sargon, an Achilles or one of the Pharaohs, no one would have thought of making an objection."[4] In the years since Delage's investigation, a large number of medical doctors have come to the same conclusion: the cloth once held the body of a crucified male. *(See picture 12 in photo section.)*

The STURP Investigation

The first detailed scientific examination of the Shroud of Turin occurred between 1969 and 1973, when church authorities chose a team of local Turin scientists to advise them on the best means to preserve the Shroud for future generations. Several of the scientists conducted preliminary studies on the cloth in 1973; however, not much was determined at that time. Several years later, from 1978 to 1981, a properly funded and well-equipped group of twenty-five American scientists conducted the most extensive tests ever performed on a historical artifact. This group of scientists formed The Shroud of Turin Research Project (STURP). The official spokesman of the STURP team was U.S. Air Force officer Dr. Kenneth E.

Stevenson, a friend of mine who has generously shared his unique insights about the continuing Shroud investigation. Ken has personally authored two excellent books on the Shroud of Turin: *Verdict on the Shroud* and *The Shroud and The Controversy*, co-authored with Gary R. Habermas.

As a result of the STURP studies, we know that the linen flax cloth is composed of hand-spun threads woven on a loom in a three-to-one herringbone twill, which was a common weave in antiquity, especially in ancient Syria. However, this type of fabric was not found in Europe in the early medieval period when the Shroud first appeared in 1357. A close examination of the Shroud reveals small amounts of cotton fibers called Asian Gossypum herbaceum, a fact consistent also with a Middle East origin. The presence of cotton fibers may indicate that the Shroud was woven on a hand loom that was also used to weave cotton. If an artist created the Shroud as a forgery, he would have been forced to obtain a unique, ancient linen cloth from the Middle East to use for his painting. *(See picture 13 in photo section.)*

One of the most interesting tests on the Shroud utilized a VP-8 image analyzer, a complex computerized cathode-ray tube device developed by NASA. The image of the man in the Shroud has a two-dimensional appearance to the naked eye. However, the VP-8 reveals a remarkable three-dimensional image that is inexplicable if the image had been produced by an artist. Any photograph or painting analyzed by the VP-8 will be revealed as a two-dimensional image, but the VP-8 reveals that the image of the man in the Shroud was actually produced from a genuine three-dimensional physical body, a fact derived by the varying distances between the different parts of the body and face and the linen cloth as it lay covering the body. *(See picture 14 in photo section.)*

Coins from Pontius Pilate

Another tantalizing piece of evidence appeared when researchers, including my friend Kenneth Stevenson, discovered what appears to be flat coin-shaped objects lying on both eyes. When the scientists used isodensity enhancement equipment, the coins were clearly visible, allowing them to detect individual features. Another researcher, Professor Francis Filas of Loyola University of Chicago, used third-generation enlargements of the 1931 photographs to detect the presence of a coin, known as the lepton, over the right eye. The coin appears to have the letters UCAI printed on it. Filas determined that there were twenty-four points of similarity between the coin image on the eyes and the ancient coin minted by Pilate. Filas claimed that these remarkable similarities of angles, design, and order identified the coin in the Shroud image as "a coin issued by Pontius Pilate between 29 and 32 A.D."[5]

Although some critics speculated that the presence of coins over the eyes was extremely unlikely in light of known Jewish customs, several first-century tombs have been located in past years by archeologists in Israel that contain coins with the skulls. One example of such a tomb belonged to a female relative of the High Priest Caiaphas that was found in the 1990s in southern Jerusalem. Other experiments with filters and polarized light by Professor Alan Whanger, of Duke University, also identified the image as a lepton, a coin that was minted in Palestine during the rule of Pontius Pilate from A.D. 31 to 33. When I was in Jerusalem a few months ago, I purchased a sample of this unusual antique coin, which is illustrated below. While this evidence is fascinating, some of the scientists believe that additional tests must be carried out before we can conclude absolutely that the image on the Shroud of Turin actually reveals these coins. *(See picture 15 in photo section.)*

Blood on the Shroud

The scientists who examined the Shroud in 1978 found clear evidence that the blood stains differ from the rest of the image in that they obviously penetrated the fibers of the linen as a liquid. Examinations with X-ray fluorescence measurements by Professors R. A. Morris and L. A. Schwalbe in 1980 revealed minute iron concentrations only in the areas of visible blood stains. Further tests with reflection spectroscopy revealed the presence of hemoglobin from blood. Professors J. H. Heller and A. D. Adler described twelve different scientific tests that proved conclusively that the Shroud definitely contained blood. They identified heme, protein, bilirubin, and albumin, all elements found in blood.[6] In addition, laboratory tests produced fluorescent antigen-antibody reactions, proving conclusively that the blood on the Shroud is human blood.

The Pollen Evidence

Dr. Max Frei, former director of the Zurich police central scientific laboratory in Switzerland, developed a forensic technique to determine where a defendant had been by the pollen and dust that had collected in his clothes. As a member of the 1973 Turin investigating commission, Frie hoped that his technique could help to settle the issue of the Shroud's origin. If he found only pollen samples from northern Italy and France, the evidence would suggest that the Shroud had been produced by some unknown medieval artist in Europe and that the burial cloth had never left Europe. On the other hand, if he found pollen from the Middle East, that evidence would add to the Shroud's authenticity.

In 1973, Frei lifted samples of microscopic pollen from the surface fibers of the Shroud with the use of adhesive tape. Over the next five years Frei traveled extensively to Turkey and Israel to collect pollen specimens. He planned to publish the results of his investigation in a book about pollen evidence and the Shroud. Unfortunately Frei died in 1983, before his book could be published, but his associate, Professor Heinrich Pfeiffer, published Frei's scientific research after his death. Frei's published pollen analysis identified pollen from fifty-eight plant species, including over a dozen specific species of plants that grow naturally in northern Europe, such as *Fagus Silvatica* (beech) and *Pinus halepensis L.* (pine). The presence of this European pollen is consistent with the exposure of the Shroud to open air on the occasions when it had been on exhibit in France and Italy over the centuries since its first public appearance in Lirey, France in 1357.

However, Dr. Frei also identified pollen from thirteen species of halophyte and desert plants, such as *Tamarix nilotica Bunge,* which the explorer H. B. Tristram found in the southern Negev desert of Israel. These thirteen desert plants are "very characteristic of or exclusive to the Negev and Dead Sea area." Frei also identified pollen from twenty plant species, including *Epimedium pubigerum DC* and *Prunus spartiodes Spa* that are found naturally in the area of southwestern Turkey and the northern part of present-day Syria, where the ancient city of Edessa was located. By far, the most interesting of all the pollen samples that Frei discovered on the shroud were from plants that are found growing *only* in Jerusalem. These include the following six plants:

Bassia muricata Asch
Echinops glaberrimus DC
Fagonla Moills Del.
Hyoscymus aureus L
Onosma sydacum Labil
Zygophyllum dumosum B

As a result of his exhaustive study, Frei concluded that in the past, the Shroud had been exposed to air in France, Italy, Palestine, and Turkey. While some critics of his study suggest that the pollen might have been deposited on the Shroud after being carried on the wind from the Middle East, the large amount of pollen found deposited in the linen fibers of the Shroud makes that theory impossible. Dr. Aharon Horowitz, Israel's most respected pollen specialist, studied Frie's findings and has confirmed that Frie's discovery of pollen species from Israel and Jerusalem provides convincing proof that the Shroud of Turin must have been in Israel at some point prior to 1357. Ultimately, Frei's discovery of pollen from Turkey, Israel, and Jerusalem provides powerful proof that the Shroud of Turin was present in both Jerusalem and Turkey at some point in its history. This pollen study provides compelling evidence that the Shroud is not an artistic creation of some medieval European artist.

Illustration of Fagonia mollis, Del.,
a spring plant found only in the Jerusalem area.

Images of Plants and Herbs on the Shroud

The Gospel of John records that Joseph of Arimathaea and Nicodemus, two of Christ's close followers, quickly buried the body of Jesus after His crucifixion in a tomb that belonged to Joseph. In addition to the specific mention of the linen cloth, the Scriptures record that they placed a large amount of herbs and spices, including myrrh and aloes, around Christ's body, as was the Jewish burial custom: "And there came also Nicodemus, which at the first came to Jesus by night, and brought a mixture of myrrh and aloes, about an hundred pound weight. Then took they the body of Jesus, and wound it in linen clothes with the spices, as the manner of the Jews is to bury" (John 19:39–40).

In addition to the pollen evidence, recent investigators have discovered that the Shroud of Turin contains faint images of a number of plants and herbs that may have been produced on the fibers of the Shroud in the same manner as the image of the crucified man. According to a report about the Shroud by Judy Siegel, published on the Internet and dated April 14, 1997, scientists from Hebrew University in (URL ref.) Jerusalem and Duke University in North Carolina have found images of 28 species of herbs and plants on the Shroud that are grown in Israel, in the area around Jerusalem and Jericho. Remarkably, the majority of the plants are spring flowers that blossom at the very time the Gospels record that the crucifixion of Jesus took place — on Passover. Using special photographic techniques and processes, including ultraviolet scanning, Dr. Alan Whanger, a medical professor at Duke University, was able to enhance the contrast to make the images visible, although they are almost invisible to the naked eye. To his amazement he was able to identify twenty-eight specific species of plants and flowers on the cloth, especially in the area surrounding the face of the crucified man. The authoritative book on plants in Israel, *Flora Palæstina,* allowed Dr. Whanger and his wife Mary to carefully compare each plant image with the detailed drawings in the book to identify each specific flower and herb.

Professor Avinoam Danin of Hebrew University also examined the images of the flowering plants on the Shroud. In a 1997 lecture to his biology students, Danin, a recognized expert on the plant life of Israel, confirmed that the Whangers' identifications were correct and that the images on the Shroud are identical to 28 native species of plants found in Israel. While admitting that he could not be sure that the Shroud of Turin was associated with Jesus of Nazareth, Danin stated, "But this evidence backs up the possibility that it is genuine, and there is no doubt that it comes from the Land of Israel."

The Latest Scientific Evidence from Israel

Two Israeli scientists announced on June 8, 1999 that they had discovered conclusive botanical evidence that the Shroud of Turin originated in ancient Israel. The article by Jack Katzenel of the *Associated Press*, on June 15, 1999, quoted Professor Avinoam Danin, a botanist, and Professor Uri Baruch, a pollen expert with the Israeli Antiquities Authority. Professors Danin and Baruch announced the results of their re-examination of the pollen grains found on the Shroud of Turin at a special session on June 15, 1999 of the 7th International Conference of the Israel Society for Ecology and Environmental Quality Sciences being held in Jerusalem.

The researchers announced that their careful re-examination of pollen grains and photos that were previously collected by scientists during the 1973 and 1978 investigations revealed images of plants on the Shroud. Their examination of several sets of photographs taken in 1898, 1930, and 1978 revealed a clear image of a cluster of thorny thistle tumbleweed (*Goundelia tournefortii*). This plant species, which grows only in Israel, also provides the greatest amount of pollen that was previously detected by Frei within the fibers of the Shroud. Scholars believe that this plant contained the type of thistle that was used by the Roman soldiers to make a crown of thorns that produced the scalp wounds on Jesus' head that are visible on the burial cloth. Another plant species apparent on the cloth is called Rock Rose (*Cistus creticus*), a plant found everywhere in the Middle East. The photographs also reveal images of the leaves of the bean caper plant called *Zygophyllum dumosum*, which grows only in Israel, Jordan, and the Sinai desert. The identical pollen, plant images, and blood stains are on the Sudarium, the face napkin (John 20:7), in Oviedo, Spain, that is known to exist since A.D. 760. Baruch announced: "These plants lead us to state that the Shroud of Turin existed before the 8th century; that it originated in the vicinity of Jerusalem; and that the assemblage of plants became part of the Shroud in the spring

March–April." Danin declared that these flowers "could have been picked up fresh in the fields. A few of the species could be found in the markets of Jerusalem in the spring."[7]

The Dirt on the Shroud

Professor Ray Rogers, one of the STURP team members, took a sample of what appeared to be dirt from the area of the image of the heel on the Shroud. He lifted the particles with some adhesive tape and gave it to a scientist friend, Dr. Joseph Kohlbeck, to test its chemical composition or "fingerprint." Dr. Kohlbeck identified the particles of dirt as limestone or calcium carbonate, the most prevalent form of rock in Jerusalem. Laboratories can now test samples of rock to determine their precise chemical composition and often locate the area from which the sample originated. Dr. Eugenia Nitowski, an Israeli scientist specializing in the geology of the rocks found in the ancient tombs of Jerusalem, provided Kohlbeck with samples of rock particles that are found on the floor of first-century tombs in Jerusalem. Kohlbeck determined that both of the limestone samples, from the Shroud and the Jerusalem tombs, were composed of a type of limestone called aragonite and trace quantities of strontium and iron.

Even more impressive evidence was produced at the Enrico Fermi Institute at the University of Chicago, where Dr. Ricardo Levi-Setti examined both limestone samples using a highly accurate scanning ion microprobe. The measurements revealed an astonishing similarity between the chemical signatures of each sample. Dr. John Heller wrote of this discovery:

> What could be more logical than to find dirt on the foot of a man who has walked without shoes? Obviously no one was crucified wearing shoes or sandals, so he was barefoot before they nailed him to the cross. There is not enough dirt to be seen visually, so it follows that no forger would have put it there, because artists aren't likely to add things that cannot be seen. . . .[8]

While this test does not prove that the dirt on the Shroud came from the Jerusalem area, it is almost impossible to believe that a medieval artist would have gone to the trouble to collect precisely the right kind of microscopic dirt from Jerusalem to place on the

1. Entrance to Cave 4, Dead Sea Caves

2. The Isaiah Scroll

Scroll 7Q5 - Cave 7 - Dead Sea Scrolls
Professor J. O'Callaghan & C. Thiede

"for they [the disciples] did not
understand about the loaves,
but their hearts were hardened.
And when they had crossed over,
they came to land at Genessaret
and moored the boat."
Mark 6:52-53

3. Text of Mark 6:52-53

4. Cave with Jewish Christian Ossuaries at Dominus Flevit

5. The Author at entrance to Burial Cave at Dominus Flevit

6. The Ossuary of Caiaphus the High Priest

7. The Church of the Holy Sepulchre

8. An 1890 Photograph of Golgotha

9. The Garden Tomb. Note the trough below the door for the rolling stone.

10. Close-up view of Shroud fibers showing bloodstains

11. The Face of the Man in the Shroud

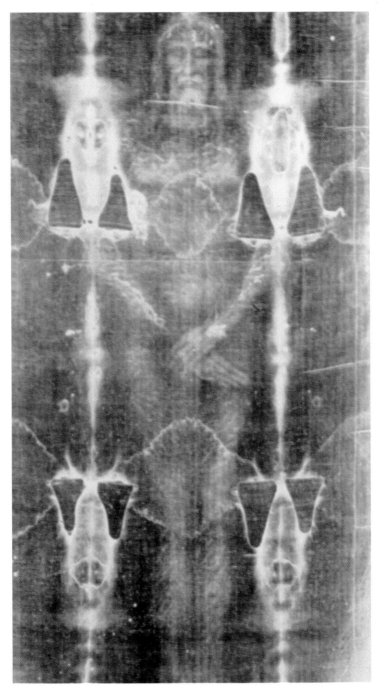

12. The complete Shroud of Turin. - Front View

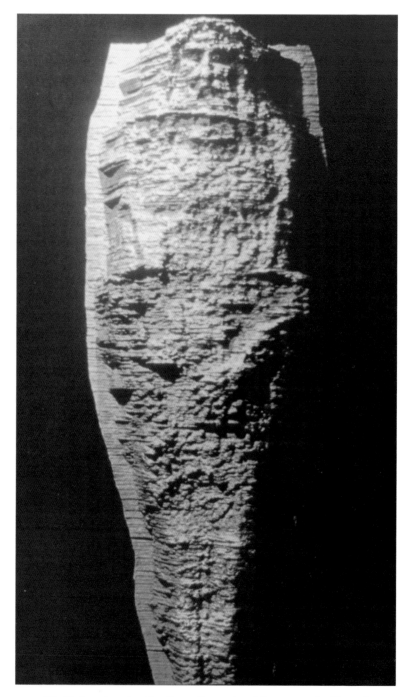

*13. Statue showing the three-dimensional image on the Shroud
as demonstrated by the VP-8 Image Analyzer*

14. The STURP Team

15. The Pontius Pilate Lepton Coin, A.D. 31

All Shroud photographs courtesy of Dr. Kenneth E. Stevenson

*16. Image of the Face of the Man in the Shroud
showing the Blood Stains*

*17. Early Church Painting of Jesus that is remarkably
similar to the image on the Shroud
(St. Catherine's Monastery, Sinai – 6th century)*

18. The Author and his wife, Kaye, at Capurnum where archeologists found the house of Peter

Shroud so it would be discovered by scientists using sophisticated technology six centuries later.

Evidence That the Shroud Might Be a Medieval Painting

Although no one has convincingly provided an explanation of how a medieval artist could have produced the image on the Shroud, Dr. Walter McCrone, a chemical microscopist, argued that the image must have been a forgery because he claimed that he had detected the presence of minute amounts of iron oxide (F_2O_3), an ingredient of paint, on the surface of the linen cloth. McCrone has stated, "It is an absolute fact that the Shroud is a painting." However, despite repeated tests, the other investigators could not find any evidence of the F_2O_3 on the Shroud. It is possible that McCrone's trace chemical evidence of iron is actually a chemical component of the blood that has been proven to exist on the linen. A fatal problem with McCrone's theory is that F_2O_3 was only produced as a paint ingredient in the last two centuries and therefore could not have been available to a medieval artist. All of the other scientists maintain that the body image could not be produced by paint or dye because the image is actually formed by the subtle darker yellow shade of millions of microscopic surface linen fibers that differentiate the image portion from the rest of the fibers in the background cloth. Interestingly, the actual image does not penetrate the surface fibers as would inevitably happen if an artist used paint, dye, or vapor to form the image. Only the fibers on the surface of the Shroud are darkened.

The STURP team did find minute random particles of paint on various nonimage portions of the Shroud. These paint particles may have fallen on the cloth at various times over the centuries when it was exhibited in churches. Even while they performed their experiments, the scientists often noticed that microscopic fragments of paint would fall from the centuries-old painted plaster ceiling of the church. Moreover, the history of the Shroud reveals that dozens of copies of the image were painted by various artists over the centuries. Because of the perceived holiness and sanctity of the Shroud image, historical records reveal that the newly painted image was often laid on top of the original Shroud of Turin to impart its holiness to the copy. It is obvious that particles of newly created painting could easily have attached themselves to the original linen cloth. However, all careful investigators have concluded that there is no evidence that the image of the man is formed by any kind of paint or dye. The image is actually composed of millions of slightly discolored linen fibers. These fibers are less than one-tenth the width of a human hair, causing the image to be composed of millions of randomly distributed picture elements, much like the pixels on a computer screen or the half-tone dots that form an image on a newspaper page. Some experts have speculated that it would have taken an incredibly accurate laser to form such precise picture elements, but that technology is only available today, and was not available six centuries ago.

Any in-depth examination of medieval art reveals that the level of medical sophistication of the artists at that time was quite rudimentary. Artists had little understanding of anatomy or how blood actually flowed from wounds. Despite the claims of various critics that the Shroud is the result of a medieval forgery, no one has ever convincingly demonstrated how such an image could have been produced. The image has probably faded over the centuries.

Additionally, the image on the linen cloth is an image of a naked man, although his hands cover the front of his body. The paintings and statues of Christ from the earliest centuries have always depicted Jesus as modestly covered with a cloth wrapped around his waist. It is extremely unlikely that any medieval artist would have chosen to produce an image of the Savior without clothes when no other artist had done so.

The late Bishop John A. T. Robinson, a famous New Testament scholar and noted skeptic, began his research on the Shroud in disbelief. However, the force of the accumulated scientific evidence finally convinced him that the Shroud of Turin was the genuine burial cloth of Jesus Christ. Robinson later wrote,

> It would not affect my faith, but it would affect my unbelief. For if in the recognition of the face and the hands and the feet and all the other wounds we, like those who knew him best, are led to say, 'It is the Lord!' (John 21:7), then perhaps we shall have to learn to count ourselves also among those who have 'seen and believed!' But that, as St. John makes clear, brings with it no special blessing (John 20:29), but rather special responsibility (John 17:18–21).[9]

The Controversy Over the 1988 Carbon-Dating Results

Ever since the scientific examination of the Shroud by the STURP team in 1978, many people suggested that carbon dating the linen cloth would provide definitive evidence, proving whether the Shroud was created in the first century, when Christ lived, or in the thirteenth century, when it was first displayed in France. Professor Willard F. Libby, a scientist who worked on the first atomic bomb, developed a technique to measure the remaining amount of carbon 14 in a sample artifact. Carbon 14 ceases to be added to any biological object after it dies, and scientists know that radioactive carbon 14 decays in a precisely dated half-life of five thousand seven hundred and thirty years. In other words, after an object dies, radioactive carbon 14 begins to decay or disappear. Precise measurements of the proportion of carbon 14 atoms that remain in the sample, compared to the normal nonradioactive carbon 12 atoms, allow scientists to determine the approximate age of the sample. For many years the custodians of the Shroud refused to allow radioactive testing because early carbon 14 testing required the destruction of an unacceptably large portion of the linen cloth. However, in the early 1980s, Dr. Harry Gove developed an ingenious radioactive technique, called accelerator mass spectrometry, that used a much smaller testing sample. Finally, in 1988, church authorities allowed three well-respected laboratories to test the fiber from the Shroud. To the amazement of many, the three labs quickly announced that the Shroud's linen fiber was grown between A.D. 1260 and 1390, a date indicating that the Shroud must be the work of a medieval artist.

While the media and the public generally assume that carbon dating is absolutely accurate and reliable, archeologists who constantly work with carbon dating know that laboratories routinely produce estimated dates that are wildly inaccurate and contradictory. Many critics of the 1988 carbon 14 testing have alleged that the fourteen scientific protocols that were established before the testing to ensure that the radioactive tests would be carried out correctly and without fraud were violated by the three teams who tested the Shroud fibers. Many of the investigators are demanding that additional tests be conducted to verify or overthrow the earlier test results. Other scientists theorize that the fire that damaged the Shroud in 1532 would have produced carbon, which could easily throw off the proportions of carbon atoms and thereby produce a more recent apparent date.

The Bioplastic Coating and
the Re-evaluation of the Carbon 14 Dating

Dr. Stephen J. Mattingly, professor of microbiology, and Dr. Leoncio A. Garza-Valdes of the University of Texas at San Antonio recently discovered that virtually all ancient objects, whether solid or fabric, are coated with an almost invisible coating composed of "bioplastic" material that is formed gradually over the years from bacteria and fungus. Mattingly is the president of the Texas branch of the American Society for Microbiology. Garza-Valdes is a medical doctor in San Antonio, as well as an archeologist who is acknowledged for his expertise in pre-Colombian artifacts.

In the early 1980s Garza-Valdes discovered that "biogenic varnishes" composed of bacteria and fungus had accumulated on an ancient Mayan-carved jade known as the Itzamna Tun. Several art connoisseurs from New York had suggested that this jade object, one of Garza-Valdes' most precious Incan artifacts, was actually a fake because of the presence of a clear varnish that coated the surface of the jade. Garza-Valdes knew that the jade was ancient because of the location where it was originally found. However, carbon dating of the jade piece suggested a much more recent date than Garza-Valdes knew was possible. Using an electron microscope, he discovered that the plastic-like coating was actually produced as a byproduct of the growth of bacteria and fungi. The Itzamna Tun's bioplastic coating produced a false carbon date that was six hundred years younger than the known date of the artifact.

After the results of the carbon dating of the Shroud, Garza-Valdes theorized that the Shroud's fibers may have been contaminated by the same bioplastic coating that he had previously observed on other ancient artifacts from Mexican jade to the linen wrappings on Egyptian mummies. During a trip to Turin, Italy in 1993, Garza-Valdes obtained a sample of the precious Shroud fibers from Giovanni Riggi di Numana, the trusted scientist who had been appointed by Cardinal Anastasio Ballestrero to cut the official Shroud samples for the carbon dating in the 1988 test.

The scientific team examined the samples of fibers through the use of optical and electron microscopes. In addition, they used sophisticated techniques to both view and photograph the fibers using high magnification and special dyes and lighting. After they sliced the fibers to reveal cross-sections of the underlying fiber and the bioplastic coating, they used a special enzyme process to cleanse the bioplastic contamination from the fiber samples.

Their surprising research, as reported in *Science News* (Vol. 147), demonstrated that up to 60 percent of the fiber samples' weight is composed of this bioplastic coating. The results were consistent with tests performed on other ancient fabrics, including linen wrappings from Egpytian mummies, in which startling discrepancies of as many as one thousand years were found between the radioactive date of the bones and flesh of mummified remains and the linen wrappings that composed the mummy's outer casing.

Scientific examination of the Shroud's fabric through the technique of mass spectroscopy and infrared spectroscopy reveals that the fiber samples used in the 1988 carbon dating by the three laboratories were not pure cellulose, which is the chemical that constitutes flax linen. Rather, the scientists in San Antonio discovered that the fiber samples tested by the labs contained numerous biological microbes. Interestingly, the microbes were of a kind that grew quite readily in natron, a well-known bleaching agent that other tests suggest may have been used to clean the burial cloth in past centuries.

Professors Mattingly and Garza-Valdes have suggested that the original carbon-dating tests were unable to distinguish between the linen's cellulose and the surface varnish, composed of the bacteria microbes and their bioplastic coating, which naturally would be of much more recent origin than the underlying fibers of the Shroud. Garza-Valdes wrote about the original 1988 radioactive testing: "What you are reporting is the age of the mixture, not the age of the linen." The professor concluded that the Shroud of Turin must be centuries older than the medieval date suggested by the 1988 carbon dating results. The San Antonio researchers hope to obtain another Shroud fiber sample and clean it with a special enzyme solution designed to clean away the bioplastic coating and any other contaminants from the underlying cellulose fibers. Then the scientists can accurately carbon date the glucose of the linen fibers. Professor Mattingly commented, "If we can isolate the glucose, that will be the answer."

Significantly, Garza-Valdes' new hypothesis is being taken seriously by microbiologists and archeologists alike. Dr. Harry E. Gove, a leading carbon-dating expert and co-inventor of accelerator mass spectrometry, has admitted that the original 1988 radioactive tests to carbon date the Shroud were flawed because the fibers contained contamination from the bioplastic coating. Gove agrees that the fibers of the Shroud must now be cleansed of the bacteria before an authoritative test can be conducted to determine the true date of the artifact. Gove said, "This is not a crazy idea.... A swing of 1,000 years would be a big change, but it's not wildly out of the question, and the issue needs to be resolved."

If the Shroud of Turin is the genuine burial cloth of Jesus, then its physical evidence confirms the authenticity of many details of the Gospel accounts as genuine history. If genuine, the Shroud will have a powerful impact on biblical studies because it confirms that Jesus truly died on the cross and rose from the dead. The evidence from the Shroud totally contradicts the allegorical school of scriptural interpretation that suggests that the Gospels are only symbolic and spiritual. The Shroud provides a powerful confirmation of the Gospel record of the scourging and crucifixion of Jesus Christ. In contradiction to the theory of many liberals that the early Church simply invented the tradition of the empty tomb, the evidence from the Shroud indicates that the body of the crucified man did not remain covered by the burial cloth for long. Furthermore, the Shroud reveals that the crucified man did not remain in the tomb to decompose as do the bodies of all other men, but that, somehow, this Body left the tomb, exactly as the Scriptures record.

The History of the Shroud

The French knight Sir Geoffrey II de Charny personally presented the Shroud to the small church in Lirey, France, in 1357. It was displayed for the faithful pilgrims for a number of years. The French chronicles record that Sir Geoffrey was the "wisest and bravest knight of them all" at the historic Battle of Poitiers. Unfortunately, Geoffrey de Charny never revealed where the Shroud came from, nor how such a priceless possession had ever come into the possession of this poor knight. A sixteenth-century manuscript suggests that the Shroud was given to Sir Geoffrey de Charny by King Phillip VI of France as a gift for his military service. This is unlikely because, if it were true, this fact would have been raised later in defence of the Shroud's authenticity. Ultimately, after the death of Sir Geoffrey, his widow, Margaurite, transferred the Shroud to the royal family of the powerful House of Savoy in 1452. They protected and occasionally exhibited the linen cloth over the following centuries, primarily on the occasion of royal weddings. Finally, when the last owner of the Shroud, the exiled King Umberto II of Italy, was dying in Portugal in 1983, Pope John Paul II visited him and convinced him to transfer the ownership of the Shroud to the Vatican.

Many critics have pointed out that the Shroud's history began mysteriously in 1357 and that there is no convincing historical trace of its existence before then. Some critics refer to a controversial document discovered a century ago that appears to be a copy of a letter sent by the local Bishop d'Arcis to the pope that purports to discredit the Shroud as a production of an artist and suggests that the relic should not be displayed in public because it was not genuine. Bishop d'Arcis supposedly wrote about "a certain cloth, cunningly painted. . . ." However, the authenticity of this manuscript is in serious doubt because the document is not actually signed by the bishop; nor is there any confirmation from the 14th century that there was any controversy surrounding the exhibition of the Shroud. Papal documents from a few years after the date of the d'Arcis document refer to the de Charny family, the Lirey chapel, and its religious relics in favorable terms that give no indication that there was any controversy concerning the Shroud.

Where Was the Shroud Before 1357?

While the history of the Shroud in Europe from 1357 to the present is relatively clear, the location and history of the linen cloth in the centuries from the time of Christ until it appeared in the possession of de Charny in France is uncertain. If the Shroud of Turin is genuine, where has it been hidden during the first millennium of the Christian era? How could such a precious religious object have survived for thirteen centuries without some reference to it being recorded?

The Cloth of Edessa

A brilliant English writer, Ian Wilson, completed an historical investigation of the history of the Shroud of Turin suggesting the possibility that the linen cloth was treasured as a relic of the church in the city of Edessa (modern Urfa) in ancient Syria and later in Constantinople. Bishop Eusebius, the well-respected historian of the early church wrote in his *Ecclesiastical History*, approximately A.D. 325, that a king of the city kingdom of Edessa on the southeastern border region of Turkey, Toparch Abgar, sent a letter to Jesus and requested that He come and heal him of a deadly disease. This king, Abgar V, ruled the city from A.D. 13 until his death in A.D. 50. According to Eusebius, after the death of Jesus a disciple of Christ visited the king and healed him. This is the story in the words of Eusebius as copied by him from the historical archives of the royal court of Edessa:

> After His resurrection and ascent into heaven, Thomas, one of the twelve apostles, was moved by inspiration to send Thaddæus, himself in the list of Christ's seventy disciples, to Edessa as preacher and evangelist of the teaching about Christ. Through him every word of our Saviour's promise was fulfilled.

> Written evidence of these things is available, taken from the Record Office at Edessa, at that time the royal capital in the public documents there, embracing early history and also the events of Abgar's time, this record is found preserved from then till now; and the most satisfactory course is to listen to the actual letters, which I have extracted from the archives and translated word for word from the Syriac as follows:

Copy of the Letter by Abgar the Toparch to Jesus

Abgar Ukkama the Toparch to Jesus, Who has appeared as a gracious Saviour in the region of Jerusalem — greeting.

I have heard about You and about the cures you perform without drugs or herbs. If report is true, you make the blind see again and the lame walk about; you cleanse lepers, expel unclean spirits and demons, cure those suffering from chronic and painful diseases, and raise the dead. When I heard all this about you, I concluded that one of two things must be true — either you are God and came down from heaven to do these things, or you are God's Son doing them. Accordingly I am writing to beg you to come to me, whatever the inconvenience, and cure the disorder from which I suffer. I may add that I understand the Jews are treating you with contempt and desire to injure you: my city is very small, but highly esteemed, adequate for both of us.

Jesus' Reply to Toparch Abgar

Happy are you who believed in me without having seen me. For it is written of me that those who have seen me will not believe in me, and that those who have not seen will believe and live. As to your request that I should come to you, I must complete all that I was sent to do here, and on completing it must at once be taken up to the One who sent me. When I have been taken up I will send you one of my disciples to cure your disorder and bring life to you and those with you.

To these letters is subjoined the following in Syriac:

After Jesus was taken up, Judas, also known as Thomas, sent to him as an apostle. Thaddæus, one of the Seventy, who came and stayed with Tobias, son of Tobias. When his arrival was announced [and he had been made conspicuous by the wonders he performed], Abgar was told: 'An apostle has come here from Jesus, as He promised you in His letter.' Then Thaddæus began in the power of God to cure every disease and weakness, to the astonishment of everyone.

In light of the proven reliability of Eusebius as an historian and the fact that anyone could check the public archives to verify Eusebius' statement, it is very probable that these historical records actually existed at that time. Although Eusebius's history does not mention a cloth with an image on it, early church traditions describe a linen cloth bearing the image of Christ's face having been brought to the king of Edessa to bring about his healing. History reveals that this city became a stronghold of the early Christian faith in the centuries following Abgar. There are numerous ancient church paintings and even images on coins that depict the face of Jesus on a cloth being displayed in ancient Edessa. However, after a few centuries the cloth disappeared. Then, during a severe flood that overwhelmed the city walls in A.D. 544, the damaged stones over a city gate revealed a hidden vault that contained a mysterious cloth bearing the image of Jesus. Throughout the Middle East and Europe there are numerous paintings that depict this cloth that became known as the Mandylion, a word derived from an Arab root meaning "veil" or "kerchief." Edessa proudly displayed the cloth with Christ's face for many years on public occasions until the Muslim armies conquered the area in the seventh century.

Could the image of Christ's face on the Mandylion cloth be related to the Shroud of Turin, which contains an image of the full body of Jesus? The investigators in 1978 noticed that the Shroud of Turin has been folded in four sections for many centuries, as indicated by the strong permanent creases in the linen cloth. Ian Wilson pointed out that the Shroud would only reveal the face of Christ if it was folded in four. Is it possible that the early followers of Christ folded the linen cloth in four to conceal the fact that the linen was actually a burial cloth? The Jews and Gentiles would naturally have considered any burial cloth as ritually unclean; therefore the cloth may have been arranged to reveal only the face of Jesus to avoid this problem. The ancient paintings of the cloth of Edessa indicate that it was encased in a silver frame that enclosed the face in an oval.

There is a fascinating historical reference to a whole body image on the burial cloth of Christ from Edessa, as opposed to an image of the face alone. This reference is found in a manuscript dated A.D. 1211, entitled *Otia Imperialia* by the English writer Gervase of Tilbury:

> The story is passed down from archives of ancient authority that the Lord prostrated himself with his entire body on whitest linen, and so by divine power there was impressed on the linen a most beautiful imprint of not only the face, but the entire body of the Lord.

In A.D. 944 the Byzantine Emperor Romanus sent his large

army to Edessa and demanded that the Muslim emir (governor) surrender the relic that was still found in the city. After negotiations the emir handed over the cloth and the triumphant Christian army returned with its precious treasure on the Feast of the Assumption, August 15, 944 and presented it to the royal family. The cloth was carried round the massive walls of Constantinople the next day to symbolize Christ's supernatural defence of the capital of Byzantium. Interestingly, to this day, the Greek Orthodox Church still celebrates August 16 as the special "Feast of the Holy Face." The linen cloth was listed in the royal records of Constantinople among the other relics of Christendom by Nicholas Mesarites, the curator of the imperial collection. A manuscript states the collection included, "the burial shroud of Christ: these are of linen. They are of cheap and easy to find materials, still smelling of myrrh and defying decay since they wrapped the outlineless, fragrant-with-myrrh, naked body after the Passion."[10]

This cryptic reference to "outlineless" may refer to the image of the full body of the man seen in the Shroud of Turin. Furthermore, Mesarites' reference to the image of the body being naked provides powerful evidence that this burial cloth in the royal collection may be the same Shroud that is now in Turin.

There is another reference to the burial cloth in Constantinople containing an image of the full body of Christ that links the Edessa cloth to the Shroud of Turin that is found in a book entitled *Ecclesiastical History* by the medieval monk historian Ordericus Vitalis:

> Abgar reigned as toparch of Edessa. To him the Lord Jesus sent . . . a most precious cloth, with which he wiped the sweat from his face, and on which shone the Savior's features, miraculously reproduced. This displayed to those who gazed upon it the likeness and proportions of the body of the Lord.[11]

From A.D. 944 till the Fourth Crusade in 1203, the linen cloth was displayed annually on August 16. When the European knights came to Constantinople on their way to invade the Holy Land, the nervous Greeks made them camp outside the city walls in fear of what their fellow Christian soldiers might do if they were actually to enter the wealthy city in force. However, individual knights were allowed to enter the city gates and wander the streets as tourists. One of these knights, Robert de Clari, who entered the city in the fall of 1203, describes viewing the burial shroud of Christ, revealing the whole body, which he saw displayed in the famous Church of St. Mary at Blachernæ. Robert de Clari reported:

> There was another church which was called My Lady of St. Mary at Blachernæ, where there was the sydoine [Shroud] in which our Lord had been wrapped, which every Friday raised itself upright, so that one could see the figure of Our Lord on it.[12]

Unfortunately, the Greeks' fears about the French crusaders were soon realized. A few months later, when the Greek emperor failed to pay the French mercenaries their promised fee, the Crusader army besieged the imperial city and broke through the gates. During the confusion of several days of looting, the precious burial cloth of Christ disappeared from the church, probably stolen with many other precious relics. Robert de Clari went looking for the linen shroud when the looting finally stopped, but there was no trace of the relic to be found in the city: "And no one, either Greek or French, ever knew what became of this sydoine after the city was taken."[12]

Unfortunately, the historical trail grows cold at this point. Did some knight take the relic home to France as part of his war booty? Ian Wilson has found historical evidence that one of the ancestors of Margaurite, the wife of Geoffrey de Charny, was a knight who fought at Constantinople during the Fourth Crusade. Is it possible that the Shroud was passed down for one hundred and fifty years through this knight's family and thus finally came into the possession of Sir Geoffrey de Charny around 1357? Perhaps additional historical evidence will be found in the future that will establish a firm connection between the burial cloth of Edessa shown in Constantinople in 1204 and the Shroud that was displayed by de Charny in 1357.

The Earliest Paintings of Jesus

Numerous paintings of Jesus Christ from the earliest centuries of the Christian era reveal a remarkable similarity to the image of the man on the Shroud of Turin. Many viewers of the Shroud have described the unsettling feeling of "deja vu," the feeling that they have seen this curious image somewhere before. The reason for this feeling is that there is an uncanny resemblance between the face in the Shroud and many of the paintings of Christ that are found in churches and monastries throughout the Middle East and Europe. It is important to remember that the Gospels do not provide any description of the physical appearance of Christ. The only ancient document that describes our Lord's appearance is a fraudulent letter that was purportedly written to the Roman Senate by Publius Lentulus, the supposed proconsul of Judea who preceded Pilate. In his letter Lentulus claims that Jesus of Nazareth was "tall and comely, of reverent countenance . . . his hair the color of chestnut." However, historians universally reject this historical evidence because the Roman archives do not list any Publius Lentulus as proconsul of Judea at that time.

The writings of the early Church Fathers reveal nothing but speculation about Christ's physical appearance. The respected writer of the early Church, Justin Martyr, described Jesus as follows: "He appeared without beauty as the Scripture proclaimed."[13] Justin's comments are actually a theological reference to the prophet Isaiah's prediction that the Messiah would be disfigured at His death. The prophet Isaiah wrote, "He hath no form nor comeliness; and when we shall see him, there is no beauty that we should desire him" (Isaiah 53:2). Another early Church writer Clement, Bishop of Alexandria, wrote about Jesus' face "not displaying the beauty of flesh"[14] in reference to Isaiah's prophecy about Christ's disfigurement. *(See picture 17 in photo section.)*

Where did the religious artists following the sixth century of the Christian era find their inspiration and specific knowledge to create their detailed images of Jesus? Religious paintings from the sixth century on, including the fresco *Christ Pantocrator* from Daphni, Greece, reveal a bearded man with a face that closely resembles the image of the man in the Shroud of Turin. A Christ Pantocrator icon that was found in the St. Catherines Monastery in the Sinai Peninsula from the sixth century remarkably duplicates the precise physical details of the man in the Shroud. Dr. Alan Whanger from the STURP team developed a new polaroid projection technique that allows the precise comparison of small details in two photo images. Whanger demonstrated one hundred and seventy points of congruence or identity between the Shroud image and the face on the St. Catherines' icon. This amount of congruence between images is far more than is required in a court of law to prove that two separate images are identical.

The similarities between the images include a curious V-shaped feature on the bridge of his nose, a streak that runs across his forehead, an area that is without hair between his lower lip and the top of his beard, a distinctive part that appears in both his hair and beard, and rather heavily accented eyes. Various ancient paintings and coins reveal these similarities including: a surviving painted copy of the Mandylion cloth that was displayed in Constantinople before the city was ransacked in 1204; a wall painting of Christ in a small catacomb in Rome's Trastevere district that was sealed in A.D. 820; a gold coin, dated approximately A.D. 692, that was minted by Emperor Justinian II. The emperor, who ruled twice from A.D. 685 until A.D. 695 and again from A.D. 705 to A.D. 711, ordered his mint to create the first coins known to bear an engraved likeness of Jesus Christ. The image of Jesus on the coin reveals a remarkable likeness to — and, in fact, appears to be directly derived from — the image on the Shroud of Turin.

Conclusion:
Fascinating Evidence, But More Testing Is Necessary

As we conclude this overview of the controversial evidence about the Shroud of Turin, we are left with several distinct possibilities. First, no one had conclusively shown how an unknown medieval artist could possibly produce such an astonishingly accurate image of a crucified man. It appears that such a work of art would be far beyond the capabilities of any modern artist, let alone a medieval one. Second, despite tens of thousands of hours of testing and lab work, no one has found conclusive proof that the Shroud is a fraud. Third, many items of evidence — including the limestone dirt from the heel area, the human blood, the images of Jerusalem plants, an ancient Roman coin of Pilate, and the pollen from the Jerusalem area of Israel — combine to make a powerful argument that, at the very least, the Shroud must be a genuine, ancient burial cloth from Israel. Moreover, the remarkable concurrence of details found in the Shroud image that reveal the medical and pathological characteristics of a crucified man, together with the unique history of what happened to Jesus of Nazareth during His crucifixion, provide powerful evidence that the burial cloth is His.

Three Logical Possibilities

Ultimately, when we consider the totality of the evidence about the Shroud, there are only three logical possibilities:

1. Some unrecognized, fourteenth century artistic genius, using unknown but astonishingly advanced techniques, created a work of art that reveals knowledge of remarkably accurate medical details about a crucified body that no one else in the medieval period apparently knew. This artist somehow would have to obtain herbs and microscopic grains of pollen from dozens of species of plants that grow only in Israel and around Jerusalem to place on the Shroud cloth, despite the fact that no one would be able to see the evidence that indicates an Israeli origin. He somehow creates the world's first and only negative artistic image that will not be revealed until centuries later. In addition, he would have had to obtain an almost invisible amount of limestone dirt from the Jerusalem area and two ancient Palestinian coins minted by Pontius Pilate, even though no one would discover the photographic technique to verify their existence for six more centuries. If some artist forged the image on the Shroud, he did it in such a clever manner that the most extensive scientific examination of an ancient artifact in history has failed to determine how he did it.

2. The image of the man in the Shroud is not Jesus. Nevertheless, some absolutely unprecedented natural chemical or radiation phenomenon produced the image of an unknown crucified man on the Shroud in some manner that cannot be duplicated by modern twentieth-century science.

3. The image of the man in the Shroud is in fact Jesus of Nazareth. The remarkable image was produced by some unknown radiation phenomenon that was associated with the supernatural event known as the resurrection of Christ. Unfortunately, if this is the case, the means by which this unique image appeared on the Shroud may never be determined absolutely by science, due to the divine nature and singular miracle of the resurrection.

At this stage of the investigation, while we await new carbon dating, once the bioplastic coating is removed from the fibers of the linen cloth, the vast majority of evidence strongly suggests that the image on the cloth is actually that of Jesus of Nazareth. If the Shroud ultimately proves to be the true image of the body of Jesus of Nazareth, it would certainly constitute the most powerful evidence of the existence of the historical Christ and especially of His resurrection from the tomb.

The mystery of the resurrection is connected to the mystery of the incarnation of God in human flesh in the form of Jesus of Nazareth. The greatest artist of the Renaissance, Michelangelo, painted the most sublime portraits of Jesus Christ and His apostles in the Cistine Chapel in Rome. As a sincere Christian, Michelangelo observed the hundreds of statues and paintings of the crucified Christ throughout the Vatican and protested against the unremitting concentration on the tragic crucifixion rather than on the glorious resurrection of Christ.

> Why do you keep filling gallery after gallery with endless pictures of the one over-reiterated theme, of Christ in weakness, Christ upon the Cross, Christ dying, most of all Christ hanging dead? Why do you concentrate upon that passing episode, as if that were the last word and the final scene, as if the curtain dropped upon that horror of disaster and defeat? At worst all that lasted for only a few hours. But to the end of unending eternity Christ is alive, Christ rules and reigns and triumphs. The Martyrium, the Anastasis — oh, for a true witness to the Resurrection!"[15]

Michelangelo's protest may be answered by the existence of this mysterious burial cloth. The mysterious Shroud of Turin may constitute a kind of "Fifth Gospel" that testifies directly to the greatest miracle in the life of Jesus of Nazareth — His triumph over death and the grave — and His promise that His resurrection from the dead is a foretaste of the resurrection at the last day that He promises to all those who place their faith and trust in Him.

Notes

1. Robert Wilcox, *Shroud* (New York: Bantam Books, 1978) 130–133.

2. Pierre Barbet, *A Doctor at Calvary* (New York: Image, 1963).

3. Robert Bucklin, "The Medical Aspects of the Crucifixion of Christ," *Sindon* Dec. 1961: 5–11.

4. John Walsh, *The Shroud* (New York: Random House, 1963) 66.

5. Francis L. Filas, *The Dating of the Shroud of Turin from Coins of Pontus Pilate* (1980).

6. J. H. Heller and A. D. Adler, "Blood on the Shroud of Turin," *Applied Optics* 1980: 19:2742–44.

7. Jack Katzenel, "Associated Press," *The Jerusalem Post* 15 June, 1999.

8. John Heller, *Report on the Shroud of Turin* (Boston: Houghton Mifflin, 1983) 112.

9. John Robinson, *The Shroud and the New Testament* (Jennings) 80.

10. A. Heisenber, *Nicholas Mesarites—Die Palasrevolution des Johannes Comnenos* (Wurzburg, 1907) 30.

11. Ordericus Vitalis, *Historia Ecclesistica* part 3, book 9: 8.

12. Robert de Clari, *The Conquest of Constantinople*, trans. E. H. McNeal (New York: Columbia University Press, 1936).

13. Justin Martyr, *Dialogue With Trypho, Ante-nicene Fathers* Chapter 88.

14. Clement of Alexandria, *Pædagogus* 3:1.

15. Robinson and Winward, *The Holy Sepulchre* 116.

8

The Historical Evidence About Jesus

Are the Gospels Historically Accurate?

In the history of the world, no man's life has been as thoroughly examined as has the life of Jesus of Nazareth. The accumulated evidence of the Gospel record is so overwhelming that any unbiased observer who is willing to evaluate Jesus' life without prejudice would surely agree with a statement made by respected scholar Otto Betz in his book, *What Do We Know About Jesus?* that "No serious scholar has ventured to postulate the non-historicity of Jesus."[1] In his book *The New Testament Documents: Are They Reliable?* historian F. F. Bruce wrote, "The historicity of Christ is as axiomatic for an unbiased historian as the historicity of Julius Cæsar."[2]

President Abraham Lincoln, who was an agnostic until he reached the age of forty, reached the same conclusion after he read *The Christian's Defence,* by Dr. James Smith. This brilliant book sought to establish the historical reality of the events in Christ's life. Smith's evidence so convinced Lincoln of the truth about Jesus that he became a genuine Christian. "My doubts scattered to the winds and my reason became convinced by the arguments in support of the inspired and infallible authority of the Old and New

Testaments."[3] Nevertheless, some scholars still maintain that there is little historical evidence about the life of Jesus. For example, the writer Solomon Zeitlin wrote, "Even Paul's epistles have awakened the question, Does he speak of a real historical personage or of an ideal? The main sources for the historicity of Jesus, therefore, are the Gospels." However, Zeitlin also dismisses the Gospels as historical accounts: "So we are right to assume that even the Gospels have no value as witnesses of the historicity of Jesus. The question therefore remains: Are there any historical proofs that Jesus of Nazareth ever existed?"

Another critic, Salomon Reinach, contemptuously refuses "to consider writings founded upon the memory of a collection of illiterates as historical evidence for Jesus." Scholars such as Zeitlin and Reinach also casually dismiss the strong extra-biblical historical evidence from both pagan and Jewish sources that validates the Gospel accounts about Jesus. If liberal scholars applied this same arbitrary criteria in evaluating the historical evidence for the existence of other ancient historical personages, such as Julius Cæsar or Alexander the Great, they would be forced to reject all history as myth.

Reaching the same conclusions as Zeitlin and Reinach, the famous German theologian Rudolf Bultmann declared, "I do indeed think that we can now know almost nothing concerning the life and personality of Jesus." Incredibly Bultmann states, "The early Christian sources show no interest in either, are moreover fragmentary and often legendary; and other sources about Jesus do not exist."[4]

Bultmann proposes the theory of "double dissimilarity." This strange theory states that any Gospel-saying of Jesus that can be found paralleled in either Christian or Jewish sources (first century) must be rejected as "inauthentic" or "invented by Christian editors." The absurdity of this double-dissimilarity argument can be demonstrated by imagining applying the same criteria to quotations by someone like Winston Churchill. Bultmann's criteria would require us to reject as inauthentic any quotation attributed to Churchill that found a parallel in English literature or in any books written by Churchill's biographers or admirers. Bultmann's theory, if applied to other historical personages, would virtually eliminate historical study.

A key point missed by the agnostic and liberal critics of the Gospel record is that the Jews of the first century of the Christian era possessed a unique ability to remember and record the statements of Jesus of Nazareth — a skill virtually absent in today's world. Over the centuries, the religious leaders of Israel developed advanced memory techniques to enable their students to remember in remarkable detail every single statement made by their religious teachers. The Jews' ability to recount verbatim long speeches or teaching would astonish modern teachers. An example of this oral memory technique can be found in the specially trained Maori tribesmen of New Zealand. During their annual festivals, they recite a rendition of their four thousand-year-old tribal history — a ritual that lasts for several days.

When Jewish historian Joseph Klausner examined the historical record regarding Jesus in his book *Jesus of Nazareth,* he concluded that, "In his ethical code there is a sublimity, distinctiveness and originality in form unparalleled in any other Hebrew ethical code; neither is there any parallel to the remarkable art of his parables."[5] Given Jesus' originality of thought, the unique forms of speech He used, and the impact He had on the lives of His disciples, it should be obvious that those of His followers entrusted by God to record the words and deeds of His life did so from detailed and precise recollections.

In his recent book, *A Marginal Jew: Rethinking the Historical Jesus,* scholar John P. Meier wrote about the historical evidence that has survived about Jesus of Nazareth:

> When we look for statements about Jesus from non canonical writings of the 1st or 2nd century A.D., we are at first disappointed by the lack of references. We have to remember that Jews and pagans of this period, if they were at all aware of a new religious phenomenon on the horizon, would be more aware of the nascent group called Christianity than of its putative founder Jesus. Some of these writers, at least, had direct or indirect contact with Christians; none of them had had contact with the Christ Christians worshiped. This simply reminds us that Jesus was a marginal Jew leading a marginal movement in a marginal province of a vast Roman Empire. The wonder is that any learned Jew or pagan would have known or referred to

him at all in the 1st or early 2nd century. Surprisingly, there are a number of possible references to Jesus, though most are riddled with problems of authenticity and interpretation."[6]

In addition to the contemporary archeologists, scholars, and historians who confirm that Jesus Christ existed, there are also a number of ancient historians who have recorded excerpts and events from Jesus' life. These secular historians, although they did not accept Jesus as the Son of God, did acknowledge his life, death, and teaching.

The following pages include a number of Roman and pagan historical manuscript records from the early centuries of this era about the life and influence of Jesus Christ; these documents have survived for almost two thousand years.

Cornelius Tacitus, Governor of Asia

Cornelius Tacitus was a Roman historian and governor of Asia (Turkey) in A.D. 112. He was a personal friend of the historian Pliny the Younger. In his *Annals*, written after A.D. 64, Tacitus referred to Emperor Nero's persecution of the Christians, justified by Nero's false accusation that the Christians had burned the city of Rome. This monstrous lie was intended to cover the truth that the evil emperor himself had ordered the capital set on fire. Tacitus wrote in the *Annals of Imperial Rome*:

> To suppress therefore the common rumor, Nero procured others to be accused, and inflicted exquisite punishments upon those people, who were in abhorrence for their crimes, and were commonly known as Christians. They had their denomination from Christus [Christ], who in the reign of Tiberius was put to death as a criminal by the procurator Pontius Pilate. This pernicious superstition, though checked for a while, broke out again, and spread, not only over Judea, the source of this evil, but reached the city [Rome] also.[7]

Tacitus, a Roman government official and historian with access to the government archives of Rome, confirms many of the historical details in the Gospels and the books of Acts and Romans. He confirms that Jesus was executed as a criminal under the authority of Pontius Pilate, who ruled Judea under the reign of Emperor Tiberius. He confirms also that the Christians, who began in Judea and spread throughout the empire, derived their worship and religion from the person known as Christ. He verified the explosive growth of this new religion within thirty-two years of Jesus' crucifixion, despite the fact that its founder suffered the death penalty as a criminal. Additionally, Tacitus confirms that the Christians were despised, hated, and falsely accused of crimes, yet they rapidly grew to become a vast multitude in Rome itself (*Annals XV* 44). The reason Tacitus and many other Romans hated the Christians is because the Christians refused to worship the pagan gods and Emperor Nero himself.

Suetonius, Roman Historian

Caius Suetonius was the official historian of Rome during the reign of both Emperor Trajan and Adrian. He was also a friend of Pliny the Younger, who referred to Suetonius in several of his letters. In the *Lives of the First Twelve Cæsars,* in the section on the Emperor Claudius (who ruled from A.D. 41 to 54), Suetonius writes that the Christians caused disturbances in Rome that led to their being banished from the city. He says that Claudius "banished the Jews from Rome, who were continually making disturbances, Chrestus being their leader."[8] Suetonius identifies the sect of Jewish Christians as being derived from "the instigation of Chrestus," which was his curious spelling of the name Christ in his *Life of Claudius,* written in A.D. 125. This statement proves that a significant number of Christians lived in Rome before A.D. 54, only two decades after Jesus. This passage confirms Luke's statement (in the book of Acts) that the Jews were exiled from Rome during the reign of Claudius. The apostle Paul found, "a certain Jew named Aquila, born in Pontus, lately come from Italy, with his wife Priscilla; (because Claudius had commanded all Jews to depart from Rome). And came unto them" (Acts 18:2).

Suetonius also wrote about the persecution of Christians during the reign of Nero: "The Christians were punished; a sort of men of a new and magical superstition." His criticism of the early Church affirms that Christianity was a "new" religion that had recently appeared (in confirmation of the Gospels and the book of Acts). Furthermore, his reference to "magical superstition" confirms that the Christians were known to perform miracles and healings. The new faith of Christianity was based on the resurrection of their Messiah Jesus of Nazareth, a fact that would certainly qualify as a "magical superstition" to a pagan Roman historian.

Pliny the Younger

Caius Plinius Secundus, known as Pliny the Younger, was born near Milan, Italy in A.D. 62. The historian Pliny, a close friend of Tacitus, served as a consul during the reign of emperor Trajan and was later appointed governor of the Roman provinces of Pontus and Bithynia (Turkey) in the period A.D. 101–110. He wrote to the emperor to request specific instructions about the interrogation of the Christians whom he was persecuting. In his *Epistles X 96*, he states that these Christian believers would not worship Emperor Trajan, nor would they curse their leader, Jesus Christ, even under extreme torture. Pliny wrote that the Christians were

> in the habit of meeting on a certain fixed day before it was light, when they sang in alternate verse a hymn to Christ as to a god, and bound themselves to a solemn oath, not to any wicked deeds, but never to commit any fraud, theft, adultery, never to falsify their word, not to deny a trust when they should be called upon to deliver it up.[9]

Pliny described the Christians as people who loved the truth at any cost. They were willing to die as martyrs rather than deny their faith in Jesus as the Son of God.

Lucian of Samosata

Lucian lived in Samosata in Syria during the reign of Emperor Adrian in the century following Christ. In the later years of his life he served as a government official in Alexandria, Egypt. In a book entitled *The Passing Peregrinus*, Lucian wrote the history of a well-known Greek traveller named Proteus, who was forced to flee his country after committing several crimes. Travelling the world under the name Peregrinus, he met some followers of Jesus in the early Church. Lucian wrote,

> At which time he learned the wonderful doctrine of the Christians, by conversing with their priests and scribes near Palestine ... they spoke of him as a god, and took him

for a lawgiver, and honored him with the title of master. . . . They still worship that great man who was crucified in Palestine, because he introduced into the world this new religion. . . . Moreover their first lawgiver has taught them, that they are all brethren, when once they turned, and renounced the gods of the Greeks, and worship that master of theirs who was crucified, and engage to live according to his laws.[10]

Lucian has provided independent confirmation of many historical facts that are mentioned in the Gospels, including the fact that Jesus was crucified, that Jesus was considered a lawgiver, that He was worshipped as God, and that His followers committed to follow Christ's laws.

The Letter from Mara Bar-Serapion

A Syrian named Mara Bar-Serapion wrote a curious letter from prison during the first century. The letter was written to his son, Serapion, to encourage him to follow the example of various esteemed teachers of past ages. This letter is listed as Syriac Manuscript number 14,658 in the British Museum:

What advantage did the Athenians gain from putting Socrates to death? Famine and plague came upon them as a judgment for their crime. What advantage did the men of Samos gain from burning Pythagoras? In a moment their land was covered with sand. What advantage did the Jews gain from executing their wise King? It was just after that that their kingdom was abolished. God justly avenged these three wise men: the Athenians died of hunger; the Samians were overwhelmed by the sea; the Jews, ruined and driven from their land, live in complete dispersion. But Socrates did not die for good; he lived on in the statue of Hera. Nor did the wise King die for good; he lived on in the teaching which he had given.[11]

The historical value of this Mar Bar-Serapion letter is that it provides strong independent pagan corroboration that Jesus was considered to be the "King" of the Jews. This letter may refer to a Gospel statement about the written sign that was placed above the cross: "And set up over his head his accusation written, This is

Jesus The King Of The Jews" (Matthew 27:37). The writer of the letter also states that Jesus was executed illegally by the Jews, who then suffered the judgments of God for their misdeeds, a probable reference to the well-known tragic destruction of Judea and Jerusalem by the legions of Rome in A.D. 70. The writer obviously held Jesus in great esteem, saying that His teachings "lived on" after His death. In addition, Mara Bar-Serapion refers to Jesus as "a wise and virtuous man." As a pagan, Mara Bar-Serapion considered Jesus to be a great philosopher, together with Socrates and Pythagoras.

Thallus, Julius Africanus, and Phlegon

A very early confirmation of the crucifixion of Jesus is found in the writings of the pagan historian Thallus, in his *Third History*. This account from the middle of the first century is significant because it may have been written close to the time when the Synoptic Gospels were being composed by Matthew, Mark, and Luke. In addition, it is one of the earliest historical records of an event connected with the crucifixion — the supernatural darkness. Supernatural darkness covered the land during the three hours Jesus hung on the cross. Matthew recorded this event in his Gospel: "Now from the sixth hour there was darkness over all the land unto the ninth hour" (Matthew 27:45). The supernatural darkness was also recorded in Mark 15:33 and Luke 23:45.

Thallus wrote his book in A.D. 52, only twenty years after the resurrection of Christ. Thallus wrote that darkness totally covered the land at the time of the Passover in A.D. 32. Julius Africanus, a North African Christian teacher writing in A.D. 215, mentions Thallus' account of the event:

> As to [Jesus'] works severally, and His cures affected upon body and soul, and the mysteries of His doctrine, and the resurrection from the dead, these have been most authoritatively set forth by His disciples and apostles before us. On the whole world there pressed a most fearful darkness; and the rocks were rent by an earthquake, and many places in Judea and other districts were thrown down. This darkness, Thallus, in the third book of his History, calls as appears to me without reason, an eclipse of the sun. For the Hebrews celebrate the passover on the 14th day according to the moon, and the passion of our Saviour falls on the day

before the passover; but an eclipse of the sun takes place only when the moon comes under the sun."[12]

Julius Africanus explained that Thallus' theory was unreasonable because an eclipse of the sun cannot occur at the same time there is a full moon. The moon is almost diametrically opposite the sun during a full moon, which would make a solar eclipse impossible at that time. This historical reference by the pagan historian Thallus confirms the Gospel account regarding the miraculous darkness that covered the earth when Jesus was dying on the cross.

There are other ancient historical references to the supernatural darkness that occurred at the death of Christ. Modern astronomers confirm that Julius Africanus was right in his conclusion that a normal eclipse could not possibly occur at the time of a full moon, which did occur at the time of the Jewish Passover. The high priest carefully calculated the position of the full moon to the smallest degree because their whole Jewish liturgical calendar, especially Passover, depended on determining the precise lunar position. There are two important points here. First, the pagan Syrian historian Thallus, who was alive at the time of Jesus' death, confirms that darkness covered the earth at the very time recorded by the Gospels. Secondly, the fact that there was a full moon present makes it certain that this darkness was not an eclipse, but rather that it was a supernatural event.

Another remarkable historical reference to this supernatural darkness is found in the manuscript of another pagan historical writer from Lydia named Phlegon, a man who was granted freedom by the Emperor Adrian. In approximately A.D. 138, Phlegon noted the astonishing fact that this "great and extraordinary eclipse of the sun distinguished among all that had happened" occurred "in the fourth year of the two hundred and second olympiad," which was the nineteenth year of the reign of Tiberius Cæsar as emperor of Rome. In his *Chronicle* (A.D. 300), the Christian historian Eusebius quoted from Phlegon's sixteen-volume *Collection of Olympiads and Chronicles* as follows:

All which things agree with what happened at the time of our Saviour's passion. And so writes Phlegon, an excellent compiler of the Olympiads in his thirteenth book, saying: 'In the fourth year of the two hundred and second olympiad there was a great and extraordinary eclipse of the sun, distinguished among all that had happened before. At the sixth hour the day was turned into dark night, so that the stars in the heavens were seen, and there was an earthquake in Bithynia which overthrew many houses in the city of Nice.' So writes the above named author.[13]

Furthermore, Phlegon indicated that the darkness that covered the earth began at the sixth hour, which is equivalent to our noon hour — precisely the same hour recorded in Matthew 27:45.

The Christian writer Tertullian wrote that the event of supernatural darkness was recorded in the Roman archives and that the record could still be consulted: "At the same time at noonday there was a great darkness. They thought it to be an eclipse, who did not know that this also was foretold concerning Christ. And some have denied it, not knowing the cause of such darkness. And yet you have that remarkable event recorded in your archives." The martyr Lucian wrote also that the public archives contained a record of this supernatural event: "Look into your annals; there you will find that in the time of Pilate, when Christ suffered, the sun was obscured, and the light of the day was interrupted with darkness."

A Roman Government Inscription
from the Reign of Emperor Nero

In my research I found a fascinating report of an inscription that was discovered in the ruins of Marquofiæ in the Roman province of Lusitania (ancient Portugal) that is clearly dated to the reign of Emperor Nero who died in A.D. 68. This inscription reads as follows:

NERONI. CL. CAIS AUG. PONT. MAX.

OB PROVINC. LATRONIB

ET. HIS. QUI. NOVAM

GENERI. HUM SUPER

STITION. INCULCAB

PURGATAM.

The translation reads:

TO NERO CLAUDIUS CAESAR, AUGUSTUS, HIGH PRIEST,

FOR CLEARING THE PROVINCE

OF ROBBERS, AND THOSE WHO TAUGHT MANKIND

A NEW SUPERSTITION.

This inscription almost certainly refers to the new faith of Christianity because this was the only popular new religion that appeared throughout the Roman empire during the reign of Nero. While Nero's persecution fell upon the Roman Christians, a number of early Church writers (including Tertullian) affirm that the persecution was carried out throughout the provinces as well. The Roman accusation that the early Christians taught "a new superstition" was related to the Gospel's claim that Jesus had risen from the dead and that He was the Son of God. If this inscription is genuine, it represents the earliest pagan inscription that refers to the new faith of Christianity as having had an impact throughout the empire only thirty-five years after the death and resurrection of Jesus.

The Christian Writer Hegesippus

In A.D. 325, Eusebius, a historian of the early church, wrote about the persecution of the Christians by the Roman emperors in his book *Ecclesiastical History*. He quotes Hegesippus, another Church historian, about an interview with the descendants of the brothers and sisters of Jesus of Nazareth. Speaking of Cæsar Domitian, who ruled from A.D. 81–A.D. 96, he wrote:

> The same emperor ordered the execution of all who were of David's line, and there is an old and firm tradition that a group of heretics accused the descendants of Jude — the brother, humanly speaking, of the Saviour — on the ground that they were of David's line and related to Christ Himself.

This is stated by Hegesippus in so many words:

> And there still survived of the Lord's family the grandsons of Jude, who was said to be His brother, humanly speaking. These were informed against as being of David's line, and brought by the evocatus [veteran] before Domitian Cæsar, who was as afraid of the advent of Christ as Herod had been. Domitian asked them whether they were descended from David, and they admitted it. Then he asked them what property they owned and what funds they had at their disposal. They replied that they had only 9,000 denarii [$5,000] between them, half belonging to each; this, they said, was not available in cash, but was the estimated

value of only twenty-five acres of land, from which they raised the money to pay their taxes and the wherewithal to support themselves by their own toil.

Then, the writer continues, they showed him their hands, putting forward as proof of their toil the hardness of their bodies and the calluses impressed on their hands by incessant labour. When asked about Christ and His Kingdom — what it was like, and where and when it would appear — they explained that it was not of this world or anywhere on earth but angelic and in heaven, and would be established at the end.[14]

The Gospel record is clear that Mary and Joseph did have additional children after the virgin birth of Jesus:

And when he was come into his own country, he taught them in their synagogue, insomuch that they were astonished, and said, Whence hath this man this wisdom, and these mighty works? Is not this the carpenter's son? is not his mother called Mary? and his brethren, James, and Joses, and Simon, and Judas? And his sisters, are they not all with us? Whence then hath this man all these things? (Matthew 13:54–56)

The Crucifixion of Jesus

Both the Gospels and the writings of the Jewish historian Flavius Josephus record that Jesus was crucified by Roman soldiers after a religious trial by the Jewish Sanhedrin court and a capital trial in front of the Roman procurator Pontius Pilate. Luke says of this event: "And when they were come to the place, which is called Calvary, there they crucified him, and the malefactors, one on the right hand, and the other on the left" (Luke 23:33). Josephus wrote, "Upon an indictment by leading members of our society, Pilate sentenced him to the cross" (*Antiquites of the Jews*).

Crucifixion was the cruelest form of execution ever developed by diabolical minds to dehumanize victims and prolong their sufferings for as long as several days until death finally ended their agony. Crucifixion was first developed by the Scythians of southern Russia and later used by the Assyrians and Carthoginians of North Africa. The Roman empire probably adopted this brutal form of execution from their constant enemies, the Carthoginians. Even the blood-thirsty Romans were so appalled by this horrific punishment that they utilized it only against slaves or foreign enemies. Roman citizens were legally immune from crucifixion, which explains why the apostle Paul, as a Roman citizen, was beheaded as opposed to being crucified like Peter.[15] During the slave revolt of 71 B.C., led by Spartacus, the Romans crucified six thousand slaves on the roads outside Rome in order to place fear in the hearts of the slave population throughout the empire. During the final months of the terrible siege of Jerusalem in A.D. 70, the Roman legions daily crucified hundreds of Jewish citizens who attempted to escape the horrific famine.

The Gospel record of Christ's crucifixion mentions the Roman practice of breaking the legs of the victims to hasten death. However, the Gospel of John asserts that the legs of Jesus were not broken because He had died already. John states, "But when they came to Jesus, and saw that he was dead already, they brake not his legs" (John 19:33). Several German theologians had cast doubt on the historical accuracy of this account because they felt that John created this imaginary detail to show that Jesus fulfilled the Old Testament prophecies about the Messiah as a type of the Passover Lamb, of which God commanded, "neither shall ye break a bone thereof" (Exodus 12:46). King David had directly predicted this event: "He keepeth all his bones: not one of them is broken" (Psalm 34:20). However, a recent archeological discovery in Israel of a skeleton of a crucified man confirms the practice reported by the Gospel writer John.

Although very few skeletons of crucifixion victims have been found, Israeli archeologists have discovered an ossuary at the excavations at Giv'at ha-Mivtar, near Jerusalem, that contained the skeleton of one man who had been crucified. The ossuary, which was inscribed with the name of the victim, "Jehohanan," included two heel bones that were transfixed by a single spike six and one-half inches long. Interestingly, the heel bones contained minute particles of olive wood, which could be the remnant of a foot support used by the victim to push himself upward to enable his distended diaphragm to take in air.

Significantly the leg bones of the victim were crushed by a violent blow that would have made it impossible for the criminal to continue raising himself up. This would have caused him to drown quickly, due to the accumulated fluid in his lungs. The scientist who examined the bones, Dr. Nicu Haas, said that the evidence from the fractured bones suggests that the blows were delivered while the victim was still alive. Haas wrote, "This direct, deliberate blow may be attributed to the final 'coup de grace.'"[16]

The great German philosopher and writer of the last century, Goethe, expressed his opinion of the Gospels. "I esteem the Gospels to be thoroughly genuine, for there shines forth from them the reflected splendor of a sublimity, proceeding from the person of Jesus Christ, of so divine a kind as only the divine could ever have manifested upon earth."[17]

Did Jesus Actually Exist?

The brilliant American philosopher and writer, Ralph Waldo Emerson, wrote about the overwhelming influence of Jesus on our history, "The name of Jesus is not so much written as plowed into the history of the world."

In light of the wealth of historical evidence about Christ, it is surprising that there are learned professors and authors who seriously deny that Jesus of Nazareth ever lived. However, numerous books have appeared in the last two hundred years that have made this assertion, in spite of the ample biblical and nonbiblical evidence referred to in this book. For example, Professor John Allegro of Manchester University wrote a book entitled *The Sacred Mushroom and the Cross* in 1970 which suggested that the earliest Christians were actually a secret cult group that used sacred mushrooms and utilized the name "Jesus" as a code word to avoid letting outsiders know about their activities.[18] Not surprisingly, Allegro's thesis was criticized immediately by almost every major historical scholar. For example, *The Times* newspaper of London, UK, printed a letter signed by fifteen scholars in Semitic languages who dismissed his conclusion stating that it was "not based on any philological or other evidence that they can regard as scholarly."

Another scholar, Professor G. A. Wells of Birkbeck College, London, has produced three books in the last decade that deny that the Jesus of the Gospels existed. Wells argues that the first New Testament statements about Jesus were created by the apostle Paul who didn't know any details about the historical Jesus. The professor suggests that the Gospels were written much later (at some point before A.D. 120) and represent a basic fabrication of stories about an imaginary Jesus.

As this book demonstrates, there is powerful historical evidence that confirms many of the details of the life and death of Jesus both in the historically reliable Gospels and numerous nonbiblical sources. C. S. Lewis addressed the question of the historical accuracy of John's gospel:

> I have been reading poems, romances, vision literature, legends, myths all my life. I know what they are like. I know that none of them is like this. Of this text there are only two possible views. Either this is reportage — though it may no doubt contain errors — pretty close to the facts; nearly as close as Boswell. Or else, some unknown writer in the second century, without known predecessors or successors, suddenly anticipated the whole technique of modern, novelistic, realistic narrative. If it is untrue, it must be narrative of that kind. The reader who doesn't see this simply has not learned to read.[19]

Nicholas Sherwin-White commented on the authenticity of the historical statements of the Gospel writers in his book *Roman Society and Roman Law in the New Testament*:

> . . . it can be maintained that those who had a passionate interest in the story of Christ, even if their interest in events was parabolical and didactic rather than historical, would not be led by that very fact to pervert and utterly destroy the historical kernel of their material."[20]

The Martyrdom of the apostles

Most of our information about the deaths of the apostles is derived from early church traditions. While ancient tradition is unreliable as to small details, it seldom contains outright inventions. Eusebius wrote, "The apostles and disciples of the Savior scattered over the whole world, preached the Gospel everywhere." The Church historian Schumacher researched the lives of the apostles and recounted the history of their martyrdom:

• Matthew suffered martyrdom in Ethiopia, killed by a sword wound.

• Mark died in Alexandria, Egypt, after being dragged by horses through the streets until dead.

• Luke was hanged in Greece, as a result of his tremendous preaching to the lost.

• John faced martyrdom when he was boiled in a huge basin of boiling oil during a wave of persecution in Rome. However, he was miraculously delivered from death. John was then sentenced to the mines in the prison island of Patmos. He wrote his prophetic book of Revelation on Patmos. The apostle John was later freed and returned to serve as Bishop of Edessa in modern Turkey. He died as an old man, the only apostle to die peacefully.

• Peter was crucified upside down on an X-shaped cross, according to church tradition because he told his tormentors that he felt unworthy to die in the same position that Jesus Christ had died. The tradition of the early Church recorded that as Peter was being led to his crucifixion he was heard to say, "None but Christ, none but Christ."

• James the Just, the leader of the Church in Jerusalem, was dropped more than a hundred feet down from the southeast pinnacle of the Temple when he refused to deny his faith in Christ. When they discovered that James survived the fall, his enemies beat James to death with a fuller's club. This was the same pinnacle where Satan had taken Jesus during the Temptation.

• James the Greater, a son of Zebedee, was a fisherman by trade when Jesus called him to a lifetime of ministry. As a strong leader of the Church , James was ultimately beheaded at Jerusalem. The Roman officer who guarded James watched in amazement as James defended his faith at his trial. Later, the officer walked beside James to the place of execution. Overcome by conviction, he declared his new faith to the judge and knelt beside him as James was beheaded for being a Christian.

• Bartholomew, also known as Nathanael, was a missionary to Asia, in present day Turkey. Bartholomew was martyred for his preaching in Armenia when he was flayed to death by a whip.

• Andrew was crucified on an X-shaped cross in Patras, Greece, after being whipped severely by seven soldiers. The soldiers tied Andrew's body to the cross with cords to prolong his agony. His followers reported that, when he was led toward the cross, Andrew saluted it in these words: "I have long desired and expected this happy hour. The cross has been consecrated by the body of Christ hanging on it." He continued to preach to his tormentors for two days until he died.

• The apostle Thomas was stabbed with a spear in India during one of his missionary trips to establish the Church in the subcontinent.

• Jude, the brother of Jesus, was killed with arrows when he refused to deny his faith in Christ.

• Matthias, the apostle chosen to replace the traitor Judas Iscariot, was stoned and then beheaded.

• Barnabas, one of the group of seventy disciples, wrote the Epistle of Barnabas. He preached throughout Italy and Cyprus. Barnabas was stoned to death at Salonica.

• The apostle Paul was tortured and then beheaded by the Emperor Nero at Rome in A.D. 67. Paul endured a lengthy imprisonment, which allowed him to write his many epistles to the churches he had formed throughout the Roman empire. These letters, which taught many of the foundational doctrines of Christianity, form a large portion of the New Testament.

Although not every detail can be verified historically, the universal belief of the early Christian writers was that each of the apostles had faced martyrdom faithfully without denying the resurrection of Jesus Christ. Polycarp, another great leader of the early church, was martyred at the age of eighty-six by being burned alive before an audience of thousands in the amphitheater in the city of Smyrna. When the Roman governor demanded that the aged bishop deny his faith in Jesus and worship the emperor, Polycarp refused the invitation to blaspheme Christ and deny his faith with these timeless words: "Eighty and six years have I served Him, and He never did me wrong; and how can I now blaspheme my King who has saved me?"

Henry G. Bosch described the enormous influence of Jesus of Nazareth on the course of Western history, philosophy, theology, and society. Bosch wrote,

> Socrates taught for forty years, Plato for fifty, Aristotle for forty, and Jesus for only three. Yet the influence of Christ's three-year ministry infinitely transcends the impact left by the combined one hundred and thirty years of teaching from these men who were among the greatest philosophers of all antiquity; yet, some of the finest paintings of Raphæl,

Michelangelo, and Leonardo da Vinci received their inspiration from Him.

Jesus wrote no poetry; but Dante, Milton, and scores of the world's greatest poets were inspired by Him. Jesus composed no music; still Haydn, Handel, Beethoven, Bach, and Mendelssohn reached their highest perfection of melody in the hymns, symphonies, and oratories they composed in His praise. Every sphere of human greatness has been enriched by this humble Carpenter of Nazareth.[21]

Notes

1. Otto Betz, *What Do We Know About Jesus?* (Philadelphia: Westminster Press, 1968).

2. F. F. Bruce, *The New Testament Documents: Are They Reliable?* (Downers Grove: Inter-Varsity Press, 1972).

3. Sir Lionel Luckhoo, *Evidence Irrefutable Which Can Change Your Lives.*

4. Rudolf Bultmann, *Jesus and the Word* (New York: Charles Scribner's Sons, 1958) 8.

5. Joseph Klausner, *Jesus of Nazareth* (New York: Macmillan Company, 1926).

6. John P. Meier, *A Marginal Jew: Rethinking the Historical Jesus* (New York: Doubleday, 1994).

7. Cornelius Tacitus, *Annals of Imperial Rome* 15:44.

8. Suetonius, *Lives of the First Twelve Cæsars: Life of Claudius.*

9. Pliny the Younger, *Epistles* 10: 96.

10. Lucian of Samosata, *The Passing Peregrinus.*

11. Mara Bar-Serapion, *Syriac Manuscript # 14,658* (British Museum).

12. Julius Africanus, *Extant Writings 18, Ante-Nicene Fathers* vol. 6.

13. Eusebius, *Chronicon* (A.D. 328).

14. Eusebeus, *Ecclesiastical History* (A.D. 325).

15. Tillemont, *Memoires* 1:324.

16. N. Haas, "Anthropological Observations on the Skeletal Remains from Giv'at ha-Mivtar," *Israel Exploration Journal* 20, 1970: 38–39.

17. Goethe, *Conversations With Eckermann* 3:371.

18. John Allegro, *The Sacred Mushroom and the Cross* (1970).

19. Ian Wilson, *Jesus: The Evidence* (San Francisco: Harper and Row Publishers, 1984) 49.

20. Nicholas Sherwin-White, *Roman Society and Roman Law in the New Testament* (Oxford: Oxford University Press, 1963).

21. Henry G. Bosch, *The Son of Man in Myth and History* (Philadelphia: Westminster Press, 1967).

9

Evidence from Jewish Sources

Many scholars believe that the absence of significant references to Jesus in the Jewish Talmud suggests that Jesus never existed. As we study what Talmudic material does exist about Jesus, it is important to keep in mind that the Talmud contains very little information about individuals who lived during the Second Temple period, from the Babylonian Captivity in 606 B.C. to the burning of the Temple in 70 A.D. Despite the tremendous importance of the Maccabbean Rebellion against the Syrians in 168–165 B.C., there is no reference in the Talmud to the name of the Rebellion's Jewish hero, Judas Maccabeus. Also, despite the conclusive historical evidence for the life of the apostle Paul and the aggressive missionary journeys he undertook to preach in the Jewish synagogues of the Roman world, the Talmud never mentions Paul. The great Jewish scholar Ginzberg discovered also that the Talmud does not contain one single quotation from the great number of Jewish "apocalyptic writings" that are known to exist. If the Talmud, despite its huge volume of writings, covering a six hundred-year period, does not mention Judas Maccabeus, the apostle Paul, or a single quotation from the Jewish apocalyptic writings, we should not be surprised that there is so little material about the life of Jesus. The miracle is that there exists any material at all about Jesus in the Talmud.

In recent years, scholars have discovered evidence that much of the material about Jesus Christ originally found in the Talmud may have been censored and removed during the Middle Ages in an attempt to eliminate inflammatory passages about Jesus that had been used as a pretext to assault Jewish ghettos in Europe. This censored material included both positive and negative comments about Jesus, but even the negative comments are helpful in terms of establishing the historical truth of the life of Christ. Fortunately, some of this material about Jesus escaped the censors and remains available in existing copies of the Talmud. It is essential to examine whatever precious material escaped the censors and survives to this day.

The Babylonian Talmud (Babli or Baraitha) is a comprehensive commentary on the Jewish Law that was written in Babylon (present-day Iraq) over a period of six hundred years (100 B.C.–A.D. 499). A second collection of writings was written by another group of Jewish scholars who remained in Tiberias, Israel, after the Roman destruction of the Temple in A.D. 70. These writings became known as the Jerusalem (*Yerushalmi*) or Palestinian Talmud. The Talmud contains two layers of rabbinic tradition, the Mishneh, which was completed in A.D. 220, and the Gemara, which was finished in A.D. 425, when the Tiberias Talmud school at the Sea of Galilee finally closed. The teachers and rabbis of the Mishneh were known as Tannaim and this period of scholarship became known as the Tannaitic Period. Within the Mishneh, there are several divisions, including the Baraitha and Tosefta (a compilation of sayings), the Midrashim, and Halachic (religious legislation), and Haggadic (inspirational) materials, including elaborations on the Passover.

A Jewish Reference to the Crucifixion of Jesus
Sanhedrin Text 43a. Babylonian Talmud — Baraitha

It has been taught (in a Baraitha): On the eve of Passover they hanged Yeshu, the Nazarene. And an announcer went out, in front of him, for forty days (saying): 'Yeshu, the Nazarene, is going to be stoned, because he practised sorcery and enticed and led Israel astray. Anyone who knows anything in his favour, let him come and plead in his behalf.' But, not having found anything in his favour, they hanged him on the eve of Passover.[1]

This reference is from the Munich manuscript of the Babylonian Talmud, which was translated in A.D. 1343.

This Jewish Talmudic account from the second century confirms the Gospel history of the trial and crucifixion of Yeshu (Hebrew for Jesus) in a number of important points. It identifies the time of Jesus' crucifixion ("hanging") with the Passover Feast. A manuscript copy of this text from Florence, Italy, written in A.D. 1176, also mentions the detail that he was hanged "on the eve of the Sabbath." This statement agrees with the gospel of Mark 15:42–43, which says: "And now when the even was come, because it was the preparation, that is, the day before the Sabbath, Joseph of Arimathaea, an honorable counsellor, which also waited for the kingdom of God, came and went in boldly unto Pilate and craved the body of Jesus." This passage on the trial and death of Jesus appears in an introduction to a discussion of Mishneh law regarding the responsibility to search for evidence of both guilt and innocence prior to the execution of a sentence of death following a trial verdict.

The name *Yeshu*, which is a short form for *Yehoshua* (Joshua), was used during the Tannaitic period of the Talmud to refer to Jesus Christ. Since the Gospels were written and widely distributed in the Greek language, the Greek form *Jesus* was used rather than the Hebrew form, *Joshua*. He is called the "Yeshu, the Nazarene" (the *Hanotzri* in the original Hebrew). This identifies Jesus specifically since He was often referred to as "the Nazarene": "And he came and dwelt in a city called Nazareth: that it might be fulfilled which was spoken by the prophets, He shall be called a Nazarene" (Matthew 2:23). The Talmud passage refers to the fact that he was accused specifically of "sorcery." This would be consistent with the account in Matthew 12:22–29 where Jesus is accused of sorcery by the Pharisees after He miraculously cast a demon out of the man who was blind and dumb.

The reference in the accusation to the fear of the Jewish leaders that Jesus "enticed and led Israel astray" is confirmed by John 11:47–48: "Then gathered the chief priests and the Pharisees a council, and said, What do we? For this man doeth many miracles. If we let him thus alone, all men will believe on him: and the

Romans shall come and take away both our place and nation." The mention of an "announcer" calling for witnesses proves that there was a trial before His execution, as all the Gospels record.

Another fascinating feature of this Talmudic passage is the reference "He is going to be stoned," yet the text also declares that Jesus was "hanged...on the eve of Passover." Since the Jewish Sanhedrin law provided for the penalty of death by stoning, it is consistent that the Talmud would recount that they demanded His death by stoning. However, the Roman government of Judea had removed the authority for capital punishment from the Jewish authorities during this period. They could not execute Jesus on their own authority for violating their Jewish religious laws. Pilate told the priests that he saw no crime worthy of death and said, "Take ye him, and judge him according to your law. The Jews therefore said unto him, It is not lawful for us to put any man to death: That the saying of Jesus might be fulfilled, which he spake, signifying what death he should die" (John 18:31–32).

Their problem was resolved by switching the accusation against Jesus from the religious sphere to the political one, where Roman law and inclination leaned toward instant crucifixion for anyone who attempted political revolt against the empire. The trial shifted to accusations such as, "Art thou the King of the Jews?" Finally, Pontius Pilate was convinced to exercise the ultimate Roman authority by ordering Jesus' death by crucifixion.

A Jewish Reference to Five Disciples of Jesus
Sanhedrin Text 43a. — Babylonian Talmud — Baraitha

"Our rabbis taught (in a Baraitha): Yeshu had five disciples — Mattai, Nakkai, Netzer, Buni, and Todah."[2]

In this second section, which follows the selection above, the Talmud names five of the twelve disciples of Jesus. Here is Talmudic confirmation that Jesus chose specific men of Israel to be His disciples. While we cannot determine at this time the specific source that prompted the Talmudic writer to concentrate on only these five disciples, we can identify those who were referred to in this short Talmudic list. *Mattai* is almost certainly Matthew; *Todah* is likely Thaddeus; *Nakkai* may be Luke; *Netzer* may be Andrew; and *Buni* is possibly John or Nicodemus. The fact that only five disciples are listed does not contradict the Gospel accounts of the twelve major disciples or the additional seventy disciples who were later sent out by Jesus. Possibly the rabbis were only aware of the names of a few of the most prominent ones.

One additional Talmudic reference in Tosefta — Hullin II, 22–23 refers to a Rabbi Elazare ben Damah, who was offered healing by a man named Jacob "in the name of Yeshu."[3] This passage indicates that healing in the name of Jesus was a practice that was recognized in the Talmud during the first few centuries of the Christian era. This, of course, is confirmed in detail by all of the New Testament documents.

Another reference in Baraitha — B. Abodah Zarah 16b, 17a and Tosefta — Hullin II, 24 states that Rabbi Eliezer, a famous Jewish scholar of the day, had an encounter with one of the disciples of Jesus, who was named "Jacob,"[4] in which he was impressed favorably by some of Jesus' teaching. The writer Joseph Klausner makes an interesting case in his book *Jesus of Nazareth* that this "Jacob" was none other than James, the brother of Jesus, and that the event occurred in approximately A.D. 60.[5] Regardless of who this disciple was, the Talmudic passage confirms that Jesus' teaching was received with interest by some Jewish rabbis at a very early date.

Early Jewish Evidence for the Virgin Birth

The Gospels record that Jesus was supernaturally conceived in Mary's womb so that the Christ Child would be "born of a virgin." Although the details of the Talmudic stories about the birth of Jesus are untrue, they provide a confirmation of the miraculous nature of His birth nevertheless. In the Talmudic account Jesus is referred to as "Yeshu, son of Panthera." This is a negative comment that suggests that Mary had an illicit relationship with a Roman legionnaire named Panthera. Hugh Schonfield, a Jewish writer, claimed that Rabbi Shimeon ben Azzai said, "I found a genealogical scroll in Jerusalem, and therein was written, 'so-and-so, bastard son of an adulteress.'"[6] That a Talmudic writer thought it necessary to include these comments indicates that there was something unusual about the birth of the child Jesus that demanded an explanation. If Jesus had been born to Joseph and Mary in a normal fashion, there would have been no need to create such stories. A person who has rejected the biblical truth of the miracle of the virgin birth would have to come up with another more natural explanation such as we see in the above reference.

Another point of interest on this subject is that Islamic references to Jesus in the Koran refer also to Jesus as the "son of Mary."[7] This is quite unusual in that the Arabs and Jews both normally identified people as the "son of (the father)." The reference to Jesus, the son of Mary, acknowledges that Joseph, while the legal father of Jesus, was not the biological father. In other passages the Koran acknowledges specifically that Jesus was miraculously born of a virgin.

Earliest Christian Pictorial Representations of Christ

The oldest known painting of Jesus was located in the tombs in the Catacomb of Priscilla at Rome, which was dated approximately A.D. 150. It is possible that a painting this close to the time of Jesus was based in part on the artist's reconstruction of the descriptions of people who had remembered the accounts of eyewitnesses to the life of Christ.[8] This discovery was documented in Professor Jack Finegan's book, *Light From The Ancient Past*. The next oldest representation of Christ was discovered in a church in Dura-Europos in Syria and was created approximately A.D. 225.

Evidence from Flavius Josephus' Writings

Flavius Josephus, a Jewish historian living during the first century, wrote about Jesus in a controversial passage in his famous book, *Antiquities of the Jews*:

> Now there was about this time Jesus, a wise man, if it be lawful to call him a man, for he was a doer of wonderful works, a teacher of such men as receive the truth with pleasure. He drew over to him both many of the Jews, and many of the Gentiles. He was [the] Christ, and when Pilate, at the suggestion of the principal men among us, had condemned him to the cross, those that loved him at the first did not forsake him: for he appeared to them alive again the third day: as the divine prophets had foretold these and ten thousand other wonderful things concerning him. And the tribe of Christians so named from him are not extinct at this day.[9]

Flavius Josephus was a Pharisee and priest who lived in Jerusalem and, later, in Rome. Born in A.D. 37, a few years after the death of Christ, he witnessed the dramatic events leading up to the destruction of Jerusalem and the Temple. He fought as a general of the Jewish rebel forces in Galilee during the war against Rome. Josephus was captured by the Romans at the fall of the city of Jotapata. He then became friends with the Roman general Vespasian as a result of correctly prophesying that the general would become the emperor of Rome. As an historian with access to both Roman and Jewish government records, Josephus described the events in Israel during the turbulent decades of the first century of the Christian era. In A.D. 93, Josephus published his definitive study of the history of the Jewish people called *Antiquities of the Jews*. One of the most fascinating passages in his important history concerned the events in the life, death, and resurrection of Jesus Christ. In addition, Josephus described in great detail the events in the life and martyrdom of John the Baptist and the stoning to death of James, "the brother of Jesus, called Christ" who was the first bishop of Jerusalem.

Josephus' Evidence about James, the Brother of Jesus

In another passage in his *Antiquities of the Jews*, Josephus describes the death of James, the brother of Jesus:

> As therefore Ananus (the High Priest) was of such a disposition, he thought he had now a good opportunity, as Festus (the Roman Procurator) was now dead, and Albinus (the new Procurator) was still on the road; so he assembles a council of judges, and brought before it the brother of Jesus the so-called Christ, whose name was James, together with some others, and having accused them as law-breakers, he delivered them over to be stoned.[10]

While many liberal scholars reject the historicity of the first passage about Jesus Christ, most scholars accept the authenticity of this second passage about James "the brother of Jesus the so-called Christ."

Josephus' Evidence about John the Baptist

Josephus described the death of John the Baptist as follows:

Now, some of the Jews thought that the destruction of Herod's army came from God, and that very justly, as a punishment of what he did against John, that was called the Baptist; for Herod slew him, who was a good man, and commanded the Jews to exercise virtue, both as to righteousness towards one another, and piety towards God, and so to come to baptism; for that the washing [with water] would be acceptable to him, if they made use of it, not in order to the putting away, [or the remission] of some sins [only] but for the purification of the body: supposing still that the soul was thoroughly purified beforehand by righteousness. Now, when [many] there came to crowd about him, for they were greatly moved [or pleased] by hearing his words, Herod, who feared lest the great influence John had over the people might put it into his power and inclination to raise a rebellion [for they seemed ready to do anything he should advise], thought it best, by putting him to death, to prevent any mischief he might cause, and not bring himself into difficulties, by sparing a man who might make him repent of it when it should be too late. Accordingly he was sent a prisoner, out of Herod's suspicious temper, to Macherus (Massada), the castle I before mentioned, and was there put to death.[11]

For three centuries a great debate has raged among biblical scholars regarding the authenticity of the text of Josephus about Jesus of Nazareth. Many liberal scholars believe that this reference to Jesus Christ, to his brother James, and John the Baptist must be interpolations or forgeries by Christian editors in later centuries. In other words, they have concluded that Josephus' reference to Jesus could not possibly be genuine. However, such an assertion of forgery requires significant proof. If scholars had found dozens of ancient copies of Josephus' book that failed to contain this passage, they would have some evidence that this material was not an original passage written by the Jewish historian. Yet none of these scholars can produce a single ancient copy of Josephus' *Antiquities of the Jews* that does not contain this disputed passage on Jesus. In his book *History of the Christian Church*, Phillip Schaff noted that all ancient copies of Josephus' book, including the early Slavonic [Russian] and Arabic language versions, contain the disputed passage about the life of Christ. No one has ever explained how a Christian editor could have altered each of these widely distributed versions during the centuries following their publication. How could someone introduce a new paragraph in the middle of a complete text? Why wouldn't someone have detected this addition to the popular history?

If the events recorded in the Gospels actually occurred, it is only natural that Josephus would mention them at the appropriate place in his narrative of that turbulent century. In fact, it would be surprising if Josephus failed to mention anything at all about the ministry and resurrection of Jesus. While Josephus does refer directly to Jesus, his brother James, and John the Baptist, he is silent about the many other details of Christ's life and ministry described in the four Gospels. Although this may seem unusual, we know that another popular Galilean prophet, Justus of Tiberias, who was born at the time of Jesus' death, was not even mentioned by Josephus. Therefore, the silence of Josephus and other historians regarding other details about the life and ministry of Jesus does not prove that these events did not occur.

In his book *The Historical Reliability of the Gospels*, biblical scholar Craig Blomberg wrote that

> many recent studies of Josephus however, agree that much of the passage closely resembles Josephus' style of writing elsewhere. . . . But most of the passage seems to be authentic and is certainly the most important ancient non-Christian testimony to the life of Jesus which has been preserved." Blomberg concluded his lengthy analysis of the historical evidence for and against Jesus with this statement: "The gospels may therefore be trusted as historically reliable."[12]

In addition, R. C. Stone, in an article in the journal *ZPEG* titled "Josephus," wrote the following:

> The passage concerning Jesus has been regarded by some as a Christian interpolation; but the bulk of the evidence, both external and internal, marks it as genuine. Josephus must have known the main facts about the life and death of Jesus, and his historian's curiosity certainly would lead him to investigate the movement which was gaining

adherents even in high circles. Arnold Toynbee rates him among the five greatest Hellenic historians.[13]

The historical descriptions by Josephus and the Talmudic material provide ample evidence that Jesus of Nazareth lived in the first century of this era. Writing in A.D. 325, Eusebius was aware of the reference to Jesus' ministry and death in the writings of Josephus. He wrote about these texts as additional evidence in support of the Gospels. Many Protestant Christian scholars, including Burkett and Harnack, agree that Josephus' references to Jesus are authentic. However, other scholars suggest that, while the basic Josephus text is accurate, Josephus' affirming statement "He was the Christ" may have been added to his text by Christian editors in the following centuries.

Another famous Christian writer, Origen, who lived in the third century, does not refer to Josephus' famous passage about Jesus as a "wise man." Despite this fact, Origen expressed his astonishment that Josephus would have rejected Jesus' claims to be the Messiah and still express such admiration for Jesus' brother James, who was martyred in A.D. 62. Origen's references to James provide powerful evidence that the original writings of Josephus did contain references to Jesus, long before any hypothetical Christian editor would have been in a position to introduce the disputed passage about Jesus, "a wise man," into his *Antiquities of the Jews*.

The Arab Christian Version of Josephus' Writings

Some scholars believe that an Arab Christian copy of Josephus' writings dating from the tenth century may contain the original text as it was first written by Josephus:

> . . . his disciples . . . reported that he appeared to them three days after his crucifixion and that he was alive; accordingly he was perhaps the Messiah, concerning whom the prophets have recounted wonders.

Both Jewish and Christian scholars now agree that Josephus probably wrote the majority of this passage as it appears here. This conclusion establishes Josephus as an independent source who provides us with powerful evidence about Jesus of Nazareth. A virtual contemporary of Jesus, Josephus lived and wrote in Galilee and Jerusalem, where he would have naturally encountered many individuals (including Temple priests) who were personal eyewitnesses to the significant events in the life of Jesus of Nazareth. Had Josephus had any doubts about the existence of Jesus Christ, he would never have included details of His life in a historical record that would be read widely by both the pagan Romans and the religious Jews of his native land of Israel.

Notes

1. Baraitha, *Sanhedrin Text 43a, Babylonian Talmud.*
2. Baraitha, *Sanhedrin Text 43a, Babylonian Talmud.*
3. *Talmud,* Tosefta – Hullin II, 2–23.
4. Rabbi Eliezer, *Baraitha – B. Abodah Zarah* 16b, 17a and Tosefta – Hullin II, 24.
5. Joseph Klassner, *Jesus of Nazareth* (New York: Macmillan Company, 1926).
6. Hugh Schonfield, *The Passover Plot* (New York: Random House, 1965).
7. Koran.
8. Jack Finegan, *Light From The Ancient Past* (Princeton: Princeton University Press, 1946) 371–408.
9. Flavius Josephus, *Antiquities of the Jews,* bk. XVIII, chap. III, sect. 3.
10. Flavius Josephus, *Antiquities of the Jews,* bk. XX, chap. IX, sect. 1.
11. Flavius Josephus, *Antiquities of the Jews,* bk. XVIII, chap. V, sect. 2.
12. Craig Blomberg, *The Historical Reliability of the Gospels* (Downers Grove: Inter-Varsity Press, 1987).
13. R. C. Stone, *ZPEG* Vol. 3:697.

10

Ancient Jewish Messianic Expectations

The Promise of the Messiah

While the term Messiah (*Moshiach* in Hebrew) was not a proper noun used in the Old Testament, the concept of "the anointed one" was prophesied by each of Israel's prophets. Eventually, the name "Moshiach" became the accepted term for the coming King who would sit on the throne of David.

Dr. Alfred Edersheim, a great Jewish messianic scholar, wrote *The Life and Times of Jesus the Messiah* in 1863.[1] In the appendix he lists 456 Old Testament passages that were interpreted in ancient Jewish writings to apply to the coming Messiah. Seventy-five of these passages are from the five books of Moses (Genesis through Deuteronomy), 243 are from the writings of the prophets, and 138 are from the balance of the Old Testament. Also, Dr. Edersheim details 558 separate quotations from ancient rabbinical writings that apply these Bible passages to the Messiah. The Jews of Christ's day understood that these prophetic passages applied to the Messiah.

Before the burning of the Temple in A.D. 70, the expectations of the Jewish rabbis about the coming Messiah were radically different than the beliefs and expectations that are part of modern

Judaism. The ancient rabbis looked to the clear teachings found in the Tanach (the Old Testament) as well as the detailed rabbinic commentaries on the ancient prophecies found in the Jewish Talmud. The examination of the beliefs of the ancient Jewish sages provides a fascinating confirmation that Jesus of Nazareth fulfilled hundreds of detailed prophecies from the Old Testament. Additionally, the evidence reveals that He appeared at precisely the time predicted by the Old Testament prophets and the ancient Jewish sages. These well-respected and learned sages possessed a powerful and in-depth knowledge of the Jewish Scriptures of the Old Testament. In addition, detailed commentaries on the messianic prophecies were written by their greatest sages in the centuries surrounding the life of Jesus of Nazareth. These Jewish sages possessed a profound knowledge of the Hebrew language and spent their entire life analyzing the most minute details of the prophecies found in the Old Testament that predicted the coming of the Messiah. The supreme importance of the Messiah to the Jewish faith was confirmed in a curious passage found in the Babylonian Talmud: "The world was not created but only for the Messiah."[2]

The Pre-existence of the Messiah

Modern Jewish scholars strongly reject the New Testament teaching that the Messiah (Jesus) has existed from the beginning of time. They usually teach that the Messiah is only a man who will be chosen by God to serve in a divine mission, like Moses the prophet was thirty-five hundred years ago. However, both the Old and New Testament clearly teach that the Messiah will be a supernatural appearance of God on the earth and will possess miraculous powers. The Messiah will demonstrate His righteous rule over the nations of earth forever, following His defeat of the armies of the Antichrist.

Jewish Christian writer Alfred Edersheim described the ancient Jewish understanding of the nature of the coming Messiah:

> Even in strictly Rabbinic documents, the premundane [before the world] if not the eternal existence of the Messiah, appears as a matter of common belief. Such is the view expressed in the *Targum* [Jewish Commentary] on Isaiah 9:6 and on Micah 5:2. But, the *Midrash* on Proverbs 8:9,

expressly mention the Messiah among the seven things created before the world ... 'The name of the Messiah is said to have been created before the world.' The Septuagint version of the Messianic Psalm 72, contains a fascinating commentary on verse 5 and 7 which declares: 'And he shall continue as long as the sun, and before the moon forever ... In his days shall righteousness spring up; and abundance of peace till the moon be removed.' [3]

Edersheim also wrote about the Jewish anticipation of the coming Messiah:

A careful perusal of [the rabbinical] scriptural quotations shows that... such doctrines as the premundane existence of the Messiah; his elevation above Moses and even the angels; his representative character; his cruel sufferings and derision; his violent death, and that for his people; his work on behalf of the living and the dead; his redemption, and restoration of Israel; the opposition of the gentiles; their partial judgment and conversion; the prevalence of his law; the universal blessings of the latter days; and his (the Messiah's) Kingdom — can all clearly be deduced from the unquestioned passages in the ancient rabbinical writings.[4]

The Jewish people have always longed for the appearance of their Messiah. An abundance of ancient Jewish documents demonstrates this hope. The controversy lies in whether or not Jesus of Nazareth fulfilled that expectation. To determine this, one must conduct a careful study of ancient religious and nonreligious Jewish documents that pertained to the Messiah's identity. Once the expectations about the Messiah are understood, an examination of Jesus' life can determine if He fulfilled the prerequisites.

While visiting Israel several months before writing this book, I talked to many Israelis who spoke of the need for Messiah to come to solve the terrible problems Israel and the world face. Bumper stickers in Jerusalem declared, in Hebrew, "We want Moshiach Now." Even in New York City these stickers are now appearing: "We want Messiah now." Every few days a speaker in the Israeli parliament, known as the Knesset, will refer to the coming of the Messiah. *The Jerusalem Post* and other secular newspapers often refer to the need for Messiah to come and lead Israel to "the peace of Jerusalem." A growing number of bookstores in Jerusalem contain books that refer to the Talmudic and biblical teachings about the Messiah. Songs on the radio in Israel often proclaim a longing for the coming of Messiah and the age of redemption. In one of these songs, which refers to Ezekiel's prophecy that the Messiah will open the sealed Eastern Gate, young people sing these words: "O Moshiach, how we want you now. Hurry and open the gates. Please return us to our homeland Yisroel. Ad Mosai, how long must we wait?"

Jewish Anticipation of the Time of the Coming of the Messiah

As his doctoral thesis, Rabbi Abba Hillel Silver wrote a brilliant analysis of Jewish messianic thought over the last two thousand years. The thesis was later published in 1927 as *A History of Messianic Speculation in Israel.* Rabbi Silver illustrates that there was a tremendous explosion of messianic expectation during the first few decades of the first century of the Christian era at the very time that Jesus of Nazareth made His claims to be Israel's true Messiah:

> Prior to the first century the Messianic interest was not excessive, although such great historical events as the conquest of Persia by Alexander, the rule of the Ptolemies and the Seleucides, the persecutions under Antiochus, the revolt of the Maccabees, and the Roman aggression find their mystic-Messianic echo in the apocalyptic writings of the first two pre-Christian centuries. Calculations, however, as to the exact hour of the Messiah's appearance are wanting. . . . The first century, however, especially the generation before the destruction [of the Temple in A.D. 70], witnessed a remarkable outburst of Messianic emotionalism. This is to be attributed, as we shall see, not to an intensification of Roman persecution but to the prevalent belief induced by the popular chronology of that day that the age was on the threshold of the Millennium.

> When Jesus came into Galilee, spreading the gospel of the Kingdom of God and saying the 'time is fulfilled' and 'the kingdom of God is at hand,' he was voicing the opinion

universally held that the year 5000 in the Creation calendar, which is to usher in the sixth millennium — the age of the Kingdom of God — was at hand. It was this chronologic fact which inflamed the Messianic hope of the people rather than Roman persecutions. There is no evidence anywhere to show that the political fortunes of the people in the second quarter of the first century of the common era — the period of many Messianic movements — were in any degree lower than those in the first quarter, in which no Messianic movements are recorded.

Jesus appeared in the procuratorship of Pontius Pilate (26–36 C.E.). The first mention of the appearance of a Messiah in Josephus is in connection with the disturbances during the term of office of the procurator Cuspius Fadus (c. 44 C.E.). It seems likely, therefore, that in the minds of the people the Millennium was to begin around the year 30 C.E.

Be it remembered that it is not the Messiah who brings about the Millennium; it is the inevitable advent of the Millennium which carries along with it the Messiah and his appointed activities. The Messiah was expected around the second quarter of the first century C.E., because the Millennium was at hand. Prior to that time he was not expected, because according to the chronology of the day the Millennium was still considerably removed.[5]

Rabbi Silver's exhaustive research conclusively demonstrates that the ancient Jewish sages understood from the Bible's prophecies that the Messiah was expected to appear in the first few decades of the first century, in the lifetime of the generation that ended with the burning of the Second Temple in A.D. 70.

Talmudic sources contain many traditions and comments about the Messiah. Rabbi Elijah (not the prophet), who lived about two hundred years before Jesus, told his students: "The world will exist six thousand years. The first two thousand years were those of chaos [without the Torah]. The second two thousand years were those under the Torah. The last two thousand years are the Messianic years." This time corresponds with the birth of Christ two thousand years ago.

A Note Regarding the Five Thousand Years

The belief of the Jews of the first century that they were living approximately five thousand years after the creation of Adam and Eve was due to a chronological error in the traditional Jewish account of the duration from Creation till the first century of our era. This misunderstanding of their chronology was widely held by the Pharisees, as demonstrated by the Jewish historian Flavius Josephus in his history of the Jews: "Those *Antiquities* contain the history of 5,000 years, and are taken out of our sacred books."[6] According to the scriptural account of the biblical chronology, it appears that only approximately four thousand years actually transpired from the creation of Adam until the birth of Jesus. The apocryphal book Ezra IV, which was written around the first century, refers to this belief that only five thousand years had elapsed: "And I did so in the seventh year of the sixth week of 5,000 years of the creation, and three months and twelve days."[7]

Jacob's Prophecy of the Messiah — Until Shiloh Comes

God gave the patriarch Jacob a profound prophetic vision, which Jacob shared with his twelve sons just before his death. Genesis 49:1 records this prophecy about the last days: "And Jacob called unto his sons, and said, Gather yourselves together, that I may tell you that which shall befall you in the last days." When Jacob addressed his son Judah he made this declaration: "The sceptre shall not depart from Judah, nor a lawgiver from between his feet, until Shiloh come; and unto him shall the gathering of the people be" (Genesis 49:10). The word "sceptre" refers to the royal power and the name "Shiloh" is a well-known title of the coming Messiah. In the Babylonian Talmud, Rabbi Johanan comments, "The world was created for the sake of the Messiah, what is the Messiah's name? The school of Rabbi Shila said 'his name is Shiloh, for it is written; until Shiloh come.'"[8] In other words, God promised that the tribe of Judah (the kingdom of Judah) will not lose its sovereign right to govern (which naturally includes the right to capital punishment of criminals) before the appearance of Shiloh, the Messiah. A Jewish paraphrase of the Scriptures, known as the Targum Onkelos, revealed a similar interpretation of Genesis 49:10: "The transmission of dominion shall not cease from the house of Judah, nor the scribe from his children's children, forever, until Messiah comes." [9]

During all of the centuries from Solomon until the destruction of the Temple in A.D. 70, Judah retained the ability to run its own courts as a sovereign power. Even during the seventy-year Babylonian Captivity, the Jewish people retained the ability to run their own courts and systems of religious laws under the Persians, the Greek Seleucids, and the early years of Rome's rule over Judea. However, the history of Flavius Josephus (*Antiquities* 17:13) reveals that during the life of Jesus of Nazareth, Israel's Sanhedrin court lost its power to judge capital cases (those involving the death penalty) after the Roman Cæsar Augustus appointed a Roman procurator in A.D. 7 to rule Judea directly. The New Testament confirms that the Sanhedrin had lost its power to command the death penalty, which forced the Sanhedrin to bring Jesus as a prisoner to the Roman procurator Pontius Pilate to have him issue a death sentence: "The Jews therefore said unto him, It is not lawful for us to put any man to death" (John 18:31).

Biblical Documents

Before the Temple was burned in A.D. 70, the ancient rabbis upheld the teachings found in the Tanach (the Old Testament), the prophetic commentaries in the Talmud, and records of other early Jewish writings about the coming Messiah. They understood who this Messiah would be and what He would do. These learned sages possessed a wealth of knowledge from the Jewish Scriptures of the Old Testament, as well as from the detailed commentaries that were written by their colleagues, who were contemporaries of Jesus. They had a profound knowledge of the Hebrew language and spent their entire lives analyzing the most minute details of the Old Testament prophecies that predicted the coming of the Messiah. An examination of the messianic requirements, in comparison with a study of the life of Jesus Christ, provides confirmation that Jesus of Nazareth was precisely who he claimed to be — the Messiah and the Son of God.

Let us now examine several of these prophecies, and their documentation.

The Two Messiahs of Jewish Belief

The Jews are still looking for their Messiah to come. Although the Church has always taught that the Messiah would come twice, once in the first century and again at the end of this age, Jewish teachers have rejected the idea. However, recent Jewish commentaries of the Talmud proclaim two future messiahs. One Messiah, they suggest, will appear before the War of Gog and Magog (the coming Russian-Arab invasion of Israel). He will lead the forces of Israel to victory, as described in Ezekiel, chapters 38–39. He is called *Moshiach Ben Joseph* (Messiah, the son of Joseph). They claim he will be killed in the battle with Russia, thus fulfilling the suffering Messiah prophecies. Then, they suggest that the second Messiah, *Moshiach Ben David* (Messiah, the son of David), will come forth. He will lead Israel into the promised Kingdom and the "age of redemption." This interesting interpretation is their way of dealing with the undeniable and difficult fact that the Scriptures do prophesy two separate comings of the Messiah. The first Messiah will suffer persecution and death; the second Messiah will achieve glorious victory over the enemies of God and Israel. The curious factor here is that this interpretation of two comings of the Messiah is precisely the claim of the New Testament; however, Christians present the evidence that Jesus of Nazareth fulfilled the prophecies of the first Messiah during His First Coming and believe that He will return to redeem both Israel and the Church in the near future, in the Second Coming. Jesus of Nazareth clearly proved himself to be a "Prophet like Moses" and, therefore, fulfilled this qualification of being the Messiah as documented in Chapter 12.

The Messiah in the Prophecy of the
Suffering Servant in Isaiah 53

Isaiah 53 is a powerful prophecy about the "Suffering Messiah." Rabbi Isaac Abarbanel (1437–1508) wrote the following passage about the identity of the Suffering Servant of Isaiah 53:

> The first question is to ascertain to whom this prophecy refers, for the learned among the Nazarenes expound it of the man who was crucified in Jerusalem at the end of the Second Temple, and, who according to them, was the Son of God and took flesh in the virgin's womb, as is stated in

their writings. Jonathan ben Uzziel interprets it in the Targum of the future Messiah; and this is also the opinion of our learned men in the majority of their Midrashim.[10]

A sixteenth-century sage, Rabbi Elijah De Vidas, also commented on Isaiah 53:

> The meaning of 'He was wounded for our transgressions, bruised for our iniquities,' is that since the Messiah bears our iniquities, which produce the effect of his being bruised, it follows that who will not admit that the Messiah thus suffers for our iniquities must endure and suffer them for himself.[11]

Rabbi Moshe Cohen Crispin (14th century) interpreted the prophecy of Isaiah 53 to refer to the coming Messiah, not to the nation of Israel. To defend his position, Crispin wrote that interpreting Isaiah 53 as a reference to the Jewish people "distort[s] the verses of their natural meaning." He goes on to say,

> As then it seemed to me that the doors of the literal interpretation [of Isaiah 53] were shut in their face, and that 'they wearied themselves to find the entrance,' having forsaken the knowledge of our Teachers, and inclined after the 'stubbornness of their own hearts' and of their own opinion, I am pleased to interpret it, in accordance with the teaching of our Rabbis, of the King Messiah, and will be careful, so far as I am able, to adhere to the literal sense: thus possibly, I shall be free from the forced and farfetched interpretations of which others have been guilty. This prophecy was delivered by Isaiah at the divine command for the purpose of making known to us something about the nature of the future Messiah, who is to come and to deliver Israel.[12]

The *Targum of Isaiah*, a commentary on the prophet's writings prior to the second century B.C., contains a fascinating passage that reveals the Jewish sages' understanding of the great prophet's predictions about the Messiah in His role as the Suffering Servant found in Isaiah 53:

> Behold, My servant the Messiah shall prosper; he shall be

exalted and great and very powerful. The Righteous One shall grow up before him, lo, like sprouting plants; and like a tree that sends its roots by the water-courses, so shall the exploits of the holy one multiply in the land which was desperate for him. His appearance shall not be a profane appearance, nor shall the awe of an ignorant person, but his countenance shall radiate with holiness, so that all who see him shall become wise through him. All of us were scattered like sheep . . . but it is the will of God to pardon the sins of all of us on his account . . . Then I will apportion unto him the spoil of great nations . . . because he was ready to suffer martyrdom that the rebellious he might subjugate to the Torah. And he might seek pardon for the sins of many.[13]

This passage from the Jewish Targum, written two thousand years ago, reveals an understanding that the Messiah will be the One who will forgive our sins because of His personal holiness before God as "The Righteous One."

Rabbi Moshe el Sheikh (16th century) wrote about the Suffering Servant in his *Commentaries of the Earlier Prophets:* "Our rabbis with one voice accept and affirm the opinion that the Prophet is speaking of the King Messiah, and we shall ourselves also adhere to the same view."[14]

Although traditional Jewish scholars are inclined to interpret this "Suffering Servant" as Israel, and not as the Messiah, recent Jewish scholars are beginning to change their view. If Isaiah 53 is interpreted as applying to the Messiah, Jesus of Nazareth clearly fulfilled this role.

References to the Messiah in Psalm 22

Psalm 22 describes the Messiah as being the "pierced" one. Many contemporary Jewish rabbis and scholars reject the Christian interpretation that Psalm 22 refers to the Messiah. They suggest that Christian writers have simply created this specific translation themselves because it fits their theology! For example, the Jewish writer Samuel Levine declared,

That verse of 'they pierced my hands and feet,' which seems to point to Jesus, is a mistranslation, according to all of the classical Jewish scholars, who knew Hebrew perfectly. In fact, the Christians have invented a new word in the process, which is still not in the Hebrew dictionary.[15]

It is true that the ancient rabbis probably understood the subtle nuances of their language far better than any Hebrew scholar today, but the evidence is overwhelming that the ancient rabbis translated the word *karv* or *vrak* in Psalm 22 as "pierced," exactly as the Christian translators did centuries later in their King James Bible. This is proved conclusively from the rabbis' translation in the Jewish authorized Greek Septuagint translation of the Hebrew Old Testament (285 B.C.). In addition, the Jewish commentaries on the Old Testament text, known as the *Targums,* written in the same period before the Christian era, translate and interpret the text of Psalm 22 using the word "pierced" exactly as the Christian translators did centuries later.[16]

Another Jewish commentary on Psalm 22, known as *Yakult Shimoni,* revealed the true meaning of "pierced" as follows: ". . . many dogs have surrounded me,' this refers to Haman's sons. 'The assembly of the wicked have enclosed me. They pierced *vrak* (*karv*) my hands and feet.' Rabbi Nehemiah says; 'They pierced my hands and feet in the presence of Ahasuerus.'"[17]

The Babylonian Talmud (Sukkah 52a about Zechariah 12:10) makes an interesting comment about the identity and characteristics of the coming Messiah as one who will be "pierced" and suffer martyrdom. The text reads as follows:

> What is the cause of the mourning? It is well according to him who explains that the cause is the slaying of Messiah, the son of Joseph, since that well agrees with the Scriptural verse, 'And they shall look upon me because they have thrust Him through, and they shall mourn for Him as one mourneth for his only son.'[18]

Psalm 22 predicted that the Messiah to come would be pierced. Jesus of Nazareth was pierced by the spikes through His hands and feet. Also, a Roman soldier's spear pierced His side to prove He was truly dead (John 19:34). In these sufferings, Jesus fulfilled the qualification of a "pierced" Messiah.

Nonbiblical Ancient Jewish Documents

Many of the ancient Jewish writings, not found in the Bible, also indicate Israel's expectation of a Messiah. In some cases, they describe precisely what that Messiah will do, and in others, they simply refer to a coming "savior."

The Writings of Moses Maimonides

Moses Maimonides, known affectionately as Rambam, was the greatest Jewish commentator and scholar of the Middle Ages (approximately A.D. 1200). In the Jewish tradition he is referred to as follows: "From Moses to Moses (Maimonides), there is no one like Moses." In his *Thirteen Principles of Faith,* Moses Maimonides wrote, "I believe with perfect faith in the coming of the Messiah. Even if he delays I will wait every day for him to come."[19]

Rambam's *Mishneh Torah,* a commentary of the first five books of the Bible, describes some facts about the history and Messianic claims of Jesus Christ. This great Rabbi reveals his intellectual struggle to come to terms with apparent contradictions regarding the separate biblical prophecies about the suffering Messiah and the glorified Messiah. The *Mishneh Torah,* composed of fourteen volumes, is the most authoritative Jewish commentary of the Jewish understanding of the Law of God as it related to Israel, the Messiah, and the Temple. The final fourteenth volume, *Hilchot Melachim U'Milchamoteihem (the Laws of Kings and Their Wars)* is about the coming of the Messiah.

Rambam believed that the coming of the Messiah was the key to the restoration of the Temple, the fulfillment of the Torah, and the coming of the messianic age of redemption.

> He [the Messiah] will build the Temple, gather the dispersed of Israel. Then, in his days, all the statutes will return to their previous state. We will offer sacrifices and observe the Sabbatical and Jubilee years, according to all their particulars mentioned by the Torah. (*Halachah* 11:11)[20]

Compare the qualifications of the Messiah, which Rambam enumerated from his study of the Old Testament prophets, with the history of Jesus Christ:

> If a king will arise from the house of David who is learned

in Torah and observant of the mitzvot (commandments), as prescribed by the written law and the oral law, as David, his ancestor was, and will compel all of Israel to walk in [their light] and reinforce the breaches; and fight the wars of God, we may, with assurance, consider Him the Messiah. If he succeeds in the above, builds the Temple in its place, and gathers the dispersed of Israel, he is definitely the Messiah. He will then improve the entire world [motivating] all the nations to serve God together as [Zephaniah 3:9] states: I will make the peoples pure of speech that they all will call upon the Name of God and serve Him with one purpose. (*Halachah* 11:4)[21]

In the first paragraph Rambam describes the first coming of the Messiah; in the second paragraph he described the second coming. Jesus fulfilled the prophecies as the Son of David and astonished His listeners as a teacher of the Torah Law. In His unfolding purpose to accomplish the salvation of all those who would believe in Him, Christ allowed Himself to be sacrificed on the cross after fulfilling this first group of prophecies. His ultimate sacrificial gift to mankind was prophetically anticipated by God's miraculous substitution of the ram to replace Abraham's sacrifice of his son Isaac on Mount Moriah almost two thousand years earlier.

In one fascinating section of his commentary, Rambam deals with the puzzle about the historical Jesus, the problems associated with His partial fulfillment of the Messianic prophecies, and the claims of Christianity.

If he [the Messiah] did not succeed to this degree or he was killed, he surely is not [the redeemer] promised by the Torah. [Rather] he should be considered as all the other proper and complete kings of the Davidic dynasty who died. God only caused him to arise in order to test the many, as [Daniel 11:35] states, and some of the wise men will stumble, to try them, to refine, and to clarify until the appointed time, because the set time is in the future. (*Halachah* 11:4)[22]

Rambam's conclusion, that Jesus' death disqualified Him as the promised Messiah, has been repeated by Jewish scholars for hundreds of years. However, Rambam admits that if the person legitimately fulfills part of the prophecies, but is killed before completing the restoration of the Temple, et cetera, he is to be considered as "all the other proper and complete kings of the Davidic dynasty who died," not as an impostor.

Maimonides then considers the historical evidence he had in his possession about Jesus Christ. As the greatest scholar of his day, he had access to rabbinical literature (which was still available at that time) that dealt with the period before the burning of the Temple in Jerusalem in A.D. 70. This evidence about Jesus had been censored for the last eight hundred years by Jewish and Christian religious authorities during the Middle Ages. During fifteen years of study, I often found references to the existence of censored passages of the *Mishneh Torah* that spoke about the historical reality of Jesus Christ. Whenever I tried to find these sources, I was told they were unavailable or nonexistent; however, my search was finally rewarded in a rabbinical bookstore in the Jewish Quarter of the Old City of Jerusalem in the spring of 1989.

The reasons for censoring this controversial material are unusual and intriguing. Some material refers to Jesus in an unflattering light because of the Talmud's rejection of the Gospels' claims that Jesus was the Messiah. During the terrible centuries of persecution of the Jews by the medieval Church, it was not uncommon for an ignorant, bigoted priest to quote some of these unflattering passages to his angry congregation. He would then lead a furious rampage into Jewish ghettos to burn the "Christ killers." Some of the enlightened leaders of the Church were appalled at this terrible misuse of the Jewish Mishneh and Talmudic commentaries. These leaders met with Jewish rabbinical leaders to discuss ways to prevent recurrences of these evil pogroms and ghetto burnings. The decision to censor all references to Jesus of Nazareth from these Jewish sources was apparently a joint decision made by both the Church and the Jewish leadership. Thus, these controversal Jewish materials in both Christian monasteries and Jewish libraries were censored. Aside from the motive of disarming religious bigots, this decision had an additional benefit for the rabbis by eliminating embarrassing evidence from Jewish sources that concluded that Jesus of Nazareth had fulfilled many of the biblical messianic prophecies. It was simply easier to avoid any mention of Jesus and treat the Gospels as Christian myth.

In 1631, a Jewish Assembly of Elders in eastern Europe published a command of censorship: "We enjoin you under the threat of the great ban to publish in no new edition of the Mishneh or the Gemara anything that refers to Jesus of Nazareth." Once the material was removed from copies in Christian monastery libraries and Jewish rabbinical libraries, most future editions of Maimonides' *Mishneh Torah* would omit these censored passages and signify the omissions by blank spaces or small circles. Eventually, even these indications of censorship were eliminated and replaced with small notes referring to missing material about Jesus as a result of medieval censorship.

Fortunately, several rare copies of this censored material escaped the hands of the religious authorities in Europe. One important existing copy is the Yemenite manuscripts of the *Mishneh Torah* discovered at the tip of the Saudi Arabian peninsula. A portion of this manuscript was included in a book, *Jesus in the Jewish Tradition*, by Rabbi Morris Goldstein (published in 1950). The complete censored portions have now been published in a new, full, fourteen-volume commentary by Rabbi Eliyahu Touger (published by the Maznaim Publishing Corporation, Jerusalem, Israel). The book jacket of the fourteenth volume on the Messiah has the word "CENSORED" over-printed upon it, and the text explains the curious history of these censored portions.

The following is quoted from the censored material from the *Mishneh Torah*:

> Jesus of Nazareth who aspired to be the Messiah and was executed by the court was also [alluded to] in Daniel's prophecies, as (ibid., 11:14) states: 'the vulgar [common] among your people shall exalt themselves in an attempt to fulfill the vision, but they shall stumble.' Can there be a greater stumbling block than [Christianity]? All the prophets spoke of the Messiah as the Redeemer of Israel and its Savior, who would gather their dispersed and strengthen their [observation of] the Mitzvot [the commandments]. By contrast, [Christianity] caused the Jews to be slain by the sword, their remnant to be scattered and humbled, the Torah to be altered and the majority of the world to err and serve a god other than the Lord. Nevertheless, the intent of the Creator of the world is not within the power of man to

comprehend, for His ways are not our ways, nor are His thoughts, our thoughts. [Ultimately,] all the deeds of Jesus of Nazareth and that Ishmælite [Mohammed] who arose after him will only serve to prepare the way for the Messiah's coming and the improvement of the entire world [motivating the nations] to serve God together, as [Zephaniah 3:9] states: I will make the peoples pure of speech that they will all call upon the Name of God and serve Him with one purpose. (Halachah 11:4)[23]

In this censored material Rambam admits that the basic historical account of the Gospels about Jesus' trial and death is correct. He states that Jesus of Nazareth was a legitimate teacher, that He aspired to be the Messiah, and that He was executed by the Sanhedrin court. He declares that He was a legitimate king of Israel in the line of King David and that He was referred to in the prophecies of Daniel. Rambam struggles with the problems posed by the failure of Jesus to establish His kingdom at that time, His death, and the subsequent history of Christianity when the Church persecuted the Jewish people for two thousand years. However, he refers to the mysterious ways of God and believes that ultimately the deeds of Jesus of Nazareth will be used by God to prepare the hearts of men for the Messiah's glorious coming, the establishing of the Messianic Kingdom, and the improvement of the whole world.

Rambam's comment, "Can there be a greater stumbling block than [Christianity]?"[24] is a mysterious echo of what the apostle Paul said, twelve hundred years earlier, about the effect Jesus Christ had upon His people, the Jews: "But we preach Christ crucified, to the Jews a stumbling block and to the Greeks foolishness, but to those who are called, both Jews and Greeks, Christ the power of God and the wisdom of God" (1 Corinthians 1:23, 24). Before Paul, the prophet Isaiah had indicated that, "He shall be for a sanctuary; but for a stone of stumbling and for a rock of offence to both the houses of Israel, for a gin and for a snare to the inhabitants of Jerusalem" (Isaiah 8:14).

Rambam believed that the re-establishment of the Jewish monarchy through the appearance of the Messiah was the key to complete the fulfillment of both the Torah (the books of Moses) and the Mitzvot (the commandments). In his view, as described in Halachah 4:10, "the king's (Messiah's) purpose and intent shall be to elevate the true faith and fill the world with justice, destroying the power of the wicked and waging the wars of God." The coming of the Messiah not only fulfills the prophecies, but it is also the key event that allows Israel to complete the true aim of Torah — the Sanctification of God's Holy Name throughout the world.

In the *Mishneh Torah* Rambam declares the centrality of the Messiah to the future of both Israel and the world:

> He will build the Temple, gather the dispersed of Israel. Then, in his days, (the observance of) all the statutes will return to their previous state. We will offer sacrifices and observe the Sabbatical and Jubilee years, according to all their particulars mentioned by the Torah. (*Halachah* 11:1) [25]

Rambam expected a "Messiah." But he could not accept Jesus of Nazareth as that Messiah because of Jesus' death on the cross.

A Jewish prayer book for the services on Yom Kippur and Rosh Hashanah reveals the following interesting passage about the Messiah:

> Our righteous anointed is departed from us: horror has seized us, and we have none to justify us. He has borne the Yoke of our iniquities, and our transgression, and is wounded because of our transgression. He bears our sins on his shoulders, that we May find pardon for our iniquities. We shall be healed by his wound, at the time that the eternal will create the Messiah as a new creature. O bring him up from the circle of the earth. Raise him up from Seir, to assemble us the second time on mount Lebanon, by the hand of Yinon [a name used to indicate the Messiah].[26]

The Sanhedrin portion of the Talmud includes the following comments regarding the Messiah: "This teaches us that God will burden the Messiah with commandments and sufferings as with millstones" (*Sanhedrin* 93b).

There is a whole discussion in the Talmud about Messiah's name. The several commentators suggested various names and cited scriptural references in support of these messianic names. The disciples of the school of Rabbi Yehuda Ha' Nasi said "*The sick one* is his name," for it is written, "Surely he has borne our sicknesses and carried our sorrows and pains, yet we considered him stricken, smitten, and afflicted of God" (*Sanhedrin* 98b).

A Midrash discussion about the Messiah's suffering reveals the following interesting statement about the Messiah. Rabbi Huna in the name of Rabbi Acha says: "The sufferings are divided into three parts: one for David and the fathers, one for our own generation, and one for the King Messiah, and this is what is written, 'He was wounded for our transgressions.'"[27]

The Birthplace of the Messiah

The belief of the ancient Jewish sages that the Messiah would be born in Bethlehem, the city of David's birth, is derived from Micah's prophecy. The Greek translation of the Old Testament reads as follows: "And thou, Bethlehem, house of Ephrathah, art few in number to be reckoned among the thousands of Judah; yet out of thee shall one come forth to me, to be a ruler of Israel; and his goings forth were from the beginning, even from eternity" (Micah 5:2, Septuagint).

This interpretation is confirmed by many ancient rabbinical sources, including *Pirqe' de Rabbi Eliezer* (chap. 3) and the *Targum of Jonathan*, whose commentary refers directly to Bethlehem as the birthplace of the Messiah:

> And you, O Bethlehem Ephrathah, You who were too before small to be numbered among the thousands of the house of Judah, from You shall come forth Me the Messiah, to exercise dominion over Israel, He whose name was mentioned before, from the days of creation.[28]

The Messiah's Identity as the Revealed Son of God

One of the greatest points of disagreement between Jewish and Christian scholars about the nature of the Messiah is His identity as the Son of God, which is a core tenant of the New Testament. This issue of His divinity is so fundamental that many Jewish critics will admit that the Christian claim that Jesus is the Son of God is the greatest single reason they reject Jesus' claim to be their true Messiah. Many Jewish books about Jesus of Nazareth cite the lack of support in the Old Testament Scriptures or in the writings of the ancient Jewish sages for this Divine identification of the Messiah as the Son of God.

However, a careful examination of the ancient Jewish sources proves conclusively that the greatest and most respected Jewish teachers understood and taught that the Messiah was not simply a man, but that He was truly the Son of God. Passages in the Talmud, the Midrash commentaries, the apocryphal writings, and the recently published Dead Sea Scrolls provide powerful evidence that they expected the Messiah to be the Son of God.

Repeatedly throughout the four Gospels we find Jesus, His disciples, and His enemies declaring that Jesus claimed He was divine. John wrote, "Say ye of him, whom the Father hath sanctified, and sent into the world, Thou blasphemest; because I said, I am the Son of God?" (John 10:36). When Jesus was accused at His trial before the Jewish Sanhedrin court, they asked, "Then said they all, Art thou then the Son of God?" (Luke 22:70). Significantly, Jesus did not deny the charge but answered, "And he said unto them, Ye say that I am." The trial record reveals that the Jewish leadership accepted that His claim to be the Messiah was equivalent to His claim to be "the Son of God." This identification is confirmed by numerous passages, including John 1:49 and Matthew 16:16.

A famous messianic prophecy, Psalm 2:1–8, reveals God the Father speaking to the Messiah, "His anointed," as His "begotten" Son. In this passage God addresses "His anointed" Messiah with these words: "Thou art my Son; this day have I begotten thee" (Psalm 2:7).

Remarkably, a medieval Jewish commentary on this messianic Psalm, known as *Yakult Shemoni*, refers to the crucifixion of the Messiah.

> 'Against God, and his Messiah,' likening them to a robber who stands defiantly behind the palace of the King and says, 'If I shall find the son of the King, I shall lay hold of him, and crucify him, and kill him with cruel death.' But the Holy Spirit mocks at him. 'He that sits in the heavens laughs, Jehovah has them in derision.'[29]

This Jewish commentary, written during the Middle Ages, declares that the gentile nations would be involved in the crucifixion of the Messiah, the "Son of the King."

The Timing of the Coming of the Messiah

The expectation of the Jews for their Messiah was focussed on a specific time when they expected Him to appear. Many Jewish sources discuss this period when they anticipated the Messiah would come.

The Prophet Daniel's Reference to the Time When He Would Appear

Daniel 9:24–27, a detailed prophecy that describes precisely when the Messiah was expected to appear, was a passage of Scripture well known by all religious Jews during the first decades of the first century of this era. Significantly, a widespread anticipation that the appointed time had finally arrived for the long-promised birth of the Messiah was prevalent already when Jesus of Nazareth was born in Bethlehem. The Gospel of Luke records that the "just and devout" Simeon was in the Temple "waiting for the consolation of Israel" when Joseph and Mary brought "the child Jesus" to be blessed. An old holy woman, a prophetess named Anna, was also waiting for a child to be brought to the Temple and she then "spake of him to all them that looked for redemption in Jerusalem" (Luke 2:38).

A Jewish commentary on Daniel 9:24 by Rabbi Malbim, entitled *Mayenei HaYeshuah,* contains a fascinating comment about the Jews' expectation of the nearness of the Messiah's appearance: "If the Jews had repented during this period [Daniel's 70 Weeks of Years equals 490 years] the Messianic king would have come at its termination."[30] The great Jewish sage Nacmonides, known as Ranban, who wrote his celebrated commentaries around A.D. 1300, also said of Daniel's prophetic vision that had the Jewish people not sinned greatly against God during this period, the complete and final messianic redemption would have occurred at the completion of the 490-year period. In addition, Rabbi Moses Abraham Levi acknowledged that the writings of the prophet Daniel reveal the time when the Messiah was expected to appear: "I have examined and searched all the Holy Scriptures and have not found the time for the coming of Messiah clearly fixed, except in the words of Gabriel to the prophet Daniel, which are written in the 9th chapter of the prophecy of Daniel."

During the years before their destruction in A.D. 68, the Jewish

Essene community at Qumran taught that their generation would witness the fulfillment of Daniel's prophecy of the Seventy Weeks concerning the Messiah in their lifetime.

The Babylonian Talmud, written in ancient Iraq by a group of Jewish sages, also contains a reference about the time of Messiah's coming in relation to Daniel's prophecy of the Seventy Weeks. Rabbi Judah wrote about the prevailing belief in the centuries following the burning of the Second Temple in A.D. 70 that the time of Daniel's prophecy was now fulfilled: "These times were over long ago" (*Babylonian Talmud Sanhedrin* 97a and 98b). Since they rejected the Christian claims that Jesus of Nazareth was the true Messiah, who had appeared precisely when Daniel predicted, they were forced to deny that this period was significant.

Naturally, Moses Maimonides rejected the claims of the Christians that Jesus was the Messiah referred to by Daniel's prophecy of the Seventy Weeks. In A.D. 1200 he wrote,

> Daniel has elucidated to us the knowledge of the end times. However, since they are secret, the wise [Jewish sages] have barred the calculation of the days of Messiah's coming so that the untutored populace will not be led astray when they see that the End Times have already come but there is no sign of the Messiah. [31]

In this passage Rambam acknowledges that Daniel's prophecy indicates that the Messiah should have appeared in the first quarter of the first century of this era, the very time when Jesus lived and claimed that He was the Messiah. This obvious conclusion was so dangerous that the Jewish sages prohibited the teaching of Daniel's prophecy to prevent the Jews from considering the possibility that Jesus' claim to be the Messiah might be authentic.

In the *Targum of the Prophets*, in *Tractate Megillah* 3a, which was composed by Rabbi Jonathan ben Uzziel, we read,

> And the (voice from heaven) came forth and exclaimed, who is he that has revealed my secrets to mankind? . . . He further sought to reveal by a Targum the inner meaning of the Hagiographa (a portion of scripture which includes Daniel), but a voice from heaven went forth and said, Enough! What was the reason? — Because the date of the Messiah was foretold in it! [32]

In this important commentary, the writer expresses the knowledge that Daniel's prophecy referred to the coming of the Messiah.

Other Historical References to the Time of the Messiah

The Gospel of Matthew records that the eastern magi, or wise men, came to Jerusalem to visit King Herod. Naturally, they requested information about the birthplace of the new king. When the jealous king Herod inquired of the high priests and scribes, they replied immediately that He would be born in Bethlehem as prophesied by Micah (5:2). This suggests that there was an expectation that the Messiah would appear about that time.

The Jewish historian, Flavius Josephus, refers to a popular messianic calculation, which was well known in the first century, that suggested that the Messiah would appear shortly. He referred to "an ambiguous oracle that was also found in their sacred writings, how about that time, one from their country should become governor of the habitable earth."[33] This reference likely points to Daniel 9:24–27.

Even the pagan Roman writer Tacitus records in his history that there was an authoritative and popular prophetic speculation that suggested a great leader would arise from the East to rule the world: "The majority were deeply impressed with a persuasion that it was contained in the ancient writings of the priests that it would come to pass that at the very time, that the East would renew its strength and they that should go forth from Judea should be rulers of the world."[34] Another Roman historian, Seutonius, wrote, "A firm persuasion had long prevailed through all the East that it was fated for the empire of the world at that time to devolve on someone who should go forth from Judea."[35]

Haggai's Prophecy Indicated the Messiah Would Appear Before the Temple's Destruction in A.D. 70

For thus saith the LORD of hosts; Yet once, it is a little while, and I will shake the heavens, and the earth, and the sea, and the dry land; And I will shake all nations, and the desire of all nations shall come: and I will fill this house with glory, saith the LORD of hosts. The silver is mine, and the gold is mine, saith the LORD of hosts. The glory of this latter house shall be greater than of the former, saith the

LORD of hosts: and in this place will I give peace, saith the LORD of hosts. (Haggai 2:6–9)

The indications of the timing of the Messiah's appearance in this prophecy of Haggai are enumerated below:

1. The desire of nations (a title of the Messiah) will come.
2. God will fill this House (Second Temple 516 B.C. to A.D. 70) with glory.
3. The glory of this Temple will be greater than the First Temple of Solomon.
4. The message is imminent: "It is a little time."

A Midrashic Jewish commentary on Deuteronomy, called *Tractate Debharim Rabba,* discusses Haggai's prophecy and correctly applies this series of predictions to the time of the Messiah's coming. However, a careful analysis of the prophecy indicates that the Messiah must have already come and filled "this latter house" (Second Temple) with glory so that it would be greater than Solomon's Temple, even though the glorious Ark of the Covenant was lost and had never occupied the Second Temple. Since the Second Temple was destroyed by the Roman legions in A.D. 70, it is logical to conclude that the prophecy predicts that the Messiah must have appeared in the Second Temple at some time before its burning. Jesus of Nazareth is the only person in history who claimed to be the true Messiah who appeared in Jerusalem's Second Temple before its destruction by Rome.

In Judaism there is a curious parallel to the Christian warning about date-setting the time of the second coming of the Messiah. The rabbis warned against trying to set absolute times for the coming of the Messiah and Redeemer. Yet, in every age various writers, including the great Maimonides, have calculated possible times when the Messiah might come. This creative spiritual tension includes both a longing for the coming Messiah, as well as a wise repudiation against date-setting. Judaism evolved the theory that the Messiah could come at any time if Israel's repentance ever merited it. However, they also taught that there is a final point of prophesied time beyond which the Messiah would no longer delay his coming. Many Jewish rabbis have taught that the Messiah would come before the conclusion of the six thousand years from Adam.

In a sermon in Barcelona, Rabbi Moses ben Nahman Gerundi,

known as Nachmanides (who lived from A.D. 1195 to A.D. 1270), discussed the Genesis account of the creation in six days as a symbolic prophecy of the great week of God's dealing with mankind. This sermon was quoted by Julius H. Greenstone in his book *The Messiah Idea In Jewish History*. Rabbi Nachmanides stated,

> The Torah is 'a history of humanity written in advance.' He compares the six days of creation with the six millenniums of the world's existence. On the sixth day, animals were created first, and then came man, the animals representing the nations of the earth to whom the Jews are subjected, and man the Messiah, man in the image of God, who will appear during the sixth millennium. The Sabbath represents the seventh millennium, when the life of the future will be inaugurated, and he considers the institutions of the Sabbatical year, the Jubilee year, and the counting of the 'Omer' as other indications that the world will change its present form at the end of six thousand years of its existence.[36]

When Jesus came into Galilee, spreading the gospel of the Kingdom of God and saying the "time is fulfilled" and the "kingdom of God is at hand," he was voicing the virtually universally held opinion that the age of the Kingdom of God was at hand. It was this fact that inflamed the Messianic hope of the people.

Rejection of Jesus as the Messiah

If there was so much proof, why did so many Jews in the first century reject Jesus as their Messiah? The Jews believed that the Messiah, the prophet which Moses spoke about, would come and deliver them from Roman bondage and set up a kingdom where they would be the rulers. Many people in Jerusalem thought Jesus was that deliverer. Many of His disciples shouted praises to God for the mighty works they had seen Jesus do and called out "Hosanna, save us" when He rode into Jerusalem on a donkey. They treated Him like a conquering king. Then when He allowed Himself to be arrested, tried, and crucified, many of the people stopped believing that He was the Promised Prophet. They rejected their Messiah.

Therefore, the promised kingdom was postponed. But God is a

covenant-keeping God and the Lord's promises of a kingdom are still in force for Israel. Paul told the Christians in Rome,

> I do not desire, brethren that you should be ignorant of this mystery, lest you should be wise in your own opinion that blindness in part has happened to Israel until the fullness of the Gentiles has come in. And so all Israel will be saved, as it is written, The Deliverer will come out of Zion, and He will turn away ungodliness from Jacob; for this is My covenant with them, when I take away their sins. . . . For the gifts and the calling of God are irrevocable. (Romans 11:25–27, 29)

Note that Paul tells the Church that the spiritual blindness of Israel is a "mystery" that previously had not been revealed. For thousands of years Israel had been the one nation that looked to God, while the gentile nations generally rejected the light and chose to live in spiritual darkness. Israel and her inspired prophets revealed monotheism — one God who was personally interested in mankind's destiny of Heaven or Hell, the path to salvation, the Ten Commandments, and the written Word. Yet Israel rejected her prophesied Messiah, and the promises of the kingdom of heaven were postponed. A veil of spiritual blindness fell upon the eyes of the Jews, the people who had given spiritual light to the world. As Paul explained, this hardening of Israel's heart ultimately led to the blessing of the gentiles who would believe in Jesus and accept Him as their Lord and Savior.

The Jews rejected Jesus because He failed, in their eyes, to do what they expected their Messiah to do — destroy evil and all their enemies (in this case, the Romans), and establish an eternal kingdom with Israel as the pre-eminent nation in the world. The prophecies in Isaiah 53 and Psalm 22 describe a suffering Messiah who would be persecuted and killed, but the Jews chose to focus on those prophecies of Isaiah 9 and 11 that predicted His glorious victories, not His crucifixion.

The commentaries in the Talmud struggle to understand how the Messianic prophecies of Isaiah 53 and Psalm 22 would be fulfilled with the glorious setting up of the Kingdom of the Messiah. After the Church used these same prophecies to prove the messianic claims of Jesus Christ, the Jews naturally took the position that the prophecies did not refer to the Messiah but, rather, to the travails of the nation of Israel, or some other person.

During a recent research trip to Israel, I searched through several Jewish theological bookstores in the Old City of Jerusalem for some specific material on the Temple and the Messiah. Several times, rabbinical students engaged me in conversation regarding my research. First, they were curious about my genuine interest as a Christian in Israel and in Jewish commentaries on the Bible. Then, invariably, they turned the conversation to Jesus and His claims to be the Jewish Messiah. The words, "He could not have been the promised Messiah because he failed, he was killed as a criminal," were spoken in almost every conversation. They could see that Jesus fulfilled many of the specific Old Testament Messianic prophecies — His being born in Bethlehem, coming out of Egypt, living in Nazareth, being preceded by a messenger, His awesome miraculous powers and tremendous teaching. However, they still felt as their Jewish fathers did two thousand years before: Jesus had failed, he was killed; he could not be the glorified Messiah. The Jews are still looking for their Messiah to come.

Sholern Asch, a Jewish writer, was profoundly moved by his study of the life and teachings of Jesus even though he rejected Christ's claim to be the true Messiah. In contemplation of Jesus' impact on humanity, Asch was moved to write the following:

> Jesus Christ is the outstanding personality of all time. . . . No other teacher — Jewish, Christian, Buddhist, Mohammedan — is still a teacher whose teaching is such a guide post for the world we live in. Other teachers may have something basic for an Oriental, an Arab, or an Occidental; but every act and word of Jesus has value for all of us. He became the Light of the World. Why shouldn't I, a Jew, be proud of that?[37]

Arabic Documents About the Expected Messiah

Arab writings also reflect a strong expectation of the coming Messiah. Their belief is derived from both Old and New Testament writings that were partly accepted and adopted by Mohammed. This longing for the coming of the Messiah, known in the Koran as the "Mahdi," has played a profound role in the history of Islam. All religious Moslems look for the coming of the Redeemer who will set up a kingdom to establish peace and justice for all. The teachings of the Koran of Mohammed incorporate certain parts of the Old Testament, and while they reject the truth of the divine nature of Christ, they do acknowledge the historical Jesus as a legitimate prophet of God. The Islamic writings about Jesus are ambivalent about Jesus' death and resurrection.

It is interesting to note that the Moslems accept Jesus of Nazareth as one of the greatest of the prophets of God, in that the Koran refers to His supernatural virgin birth through Mary and acknowledges also that He performed numerous miracles of healing, while admitting that Mohammed did not perform any miracles.

The Third Book of Sybil

These prophetic books were written by the Jews of Alexandria, Egypt and widely distributed throughout the Mediterranean world during the centuries before Christ, which at that time was under the rule of the Roman Empire. The Roman Senate and emperors often used these sealed prophecies, which were kept under guard in the city archives, to gain wisdom as to proposed courses of action. Among these prophecies, which were primarily derived from the prophetic books of the Old Testament, we find mention of many of the biblical messianic predictions. One included the prediction that "a king would arise from the East who would rule the entire world." This prophecy was so widely known that it played a significant role in the rise to power of Emperor Vespasian, the ruler who defeated the Jewish Rebellion against Rome between A.D. 66 and A.D. 70. Vespasian and his supporters used this prophecy to convince many of his divine right to rule the Empire. Even the writer Flavius Josephus referred to this prediction when he foretold that General Vespasian (a commoner at that time who was not in the Julian family, the family that had produced all the previous Cæsars) would ultimately become Emperor of Rome. This prediction flattered the general and motivated him to save Josephus' life and later promote him.

The Third Book of Sybil predicted that the Jews and all other nations would finally find peace under the reign of the Messiah. God would use the Messiah to end all wars and establish universal righteousness under God's protection. Then all nations will turn to

God's Law, and the Lord will dwell in Zion. An examination of these and other prophecies in the books of Sybil will convince most people that the books are a simple pagan restating of the prophecies of the Bible in a non-Jewish format, which made them well known and acceptable to the gentile nations at that time. It is interesting to see that this pagan publication of the ancient Jewish prophecies from the Old Testament created a situation where the gentile Roman world was made aware of these prophecies and prepared for the claims of Jesus Christ and His disciples. People who would never have been interested in the Jewish prophecies of the small nation of Israel became fascinated by them when they were presented under this more acceptable pagan format.

Notes

1. Alfred Edersheim, *The Life and Times of Jesus the Messiah* (MacDonald Publishing Co., 1883).

2. *Talmud – Sanhedrin* 98b.

3. Alfred Edersheim, *The Life and Times of Jesus the Messiah* (MacDonald Publishing Co., 1883) 164–65.

4. Alfred Edersheim, *The Life and Times of Jesus the Messiah* (MacDonald Publishing Co., 1883) 164–65.

5. Abba Hillel Silver, *A History of Messianic Speculation in Israel* (1927).

6. Flavius Josephus, *Antiquities of the Jews* book 1:1.

7. *Ezra IV* 14:48.

8. *Talmud – Sanhedrin* 98b.

9. Samson H. Levy, *The Messiah: An Aramaic Interpretation; The Messianic Exegesis of the Targum* (Cincinnati: Hebrew Union College Jewish Institute of Religion, 1974) 2.

10. Arthur W. Kac, *The Messianic Hope* (Grand Rapids: Baker House, 1975) 75.

11. Arthur W. Kac, *The Messianic Hope* (Grand Rapids: Baker House, 1975) 76.

12. S. R. Driver, ed., *A Commentary of Rabbi Mosheh Kohen Ibn Crispin of Cordova, The 53rd Chapter of Isaiah According to Jewish Interpreters* (New York: KTAV Publishing House, 1969).

13. *Targum of Isaiah.*

14. Arthur W. Kac, *The Messianic Hope* (Grand Rapids: Baker House, 1975) 76.

15. Samuel Levine, *You Take Jesus, I'll Take God* (Hamoroh Press, 1980) 34.

16. Mark Eastman and Chuck Missler, *The Search for Messiah* (Fountain Valley: Joy Publishing, 1996) 31–33.

17. Arthur W. Kac, *The Messianic Hope* (Grand Rapids: Baker House, 1975).

18. *Babylonian Talmud*, Sukkah 52a.

19. Moses Maimonides, *Hilchot Melachim U'Milchamoteihem* (A.D. 1200).

20. Moses Maimonides, *Hilchot Melachim U'Milchamoteihem* (A.D. 1200).

21. Moses Maimonides, *Hilchot Melachim U'Milchamoteihem* (A.D. 1200).

22. Moses Maimonides, *Hilchot Melachim U'Milchamoteihem* (A.D. 1200).

23. Moses Maimonides, *Hilchot Melachim U'Milchamoteihem* (A.D. 1200).

24. Moses Maimonides, *Hilchot Melachim U'Milchamoteihem* (A.D. 1200).

25. Moses Maimonides, *Hilchot Melachim U'Milchamoteihem* (A.D. 1200).

26. Arthur W. Kac, *The Messianic Hope* (Grand Rapids: Baker House, 1975).

27. Alfred Edersheim, *The Life and Times of Jesus the Messiah* Appendix IX (1883).

28. Samson H. Levy, *The Messiah: An Aramaic Interpretation; The Messianic Exegesis of the Targum* (Cincinnati: Hebrew Union College Jewish Institute of Religion, 1974) 92.

29. Yakult Shemoni.

30. Malbim, *Mayenei HaYeshuah.*

31. Moses Maimonides, *Hilchot Melachim U'Milchamoteihem* (A.D. 1200).

32. Jonathan ben Uzziel, *Targum of the Prophets*, Tractate Megillah 3a.

33. Flavius Josephus, *Wars of the Jews*, Book VI, 5.4.

34. Tacitus, *History*, V.13.

35. Suetonius, *Life of Vespasian, Lives of the Cæsers.*

36. Julius H. Greenstone, *The Messiah Idea In Jewish History* (Philadelphia: The Jewish Publication Society of America, 1948).

37. Sholern Asch, *Christian Herald.*

11

The Genealogy of Jesus: His Legal Right to the Throne of David

The Old Testament prophets stated emphatically that the promised Messiah would descend directly from the line of King David. The prophet Jeremiah declared, "Behold, the days come, saith the LORD, that I will raise unto David a righteous Branch, and a King shall reign and prosper, and shall execute judgment and justice in the earth" (Jeremiah 23:5). Isaiah also foretold the following: "Of the increase of his government and peace there shall be no end, upon the throne of David, and upon his kingdom, to order it, and to establish it with judgment and with justice from henceforth even for ever. The zeal of the LORD of hosts will perform this" (Isaiah 9:7).

Anyone who presented himself as Israel's Messiah without documented proof of his proper lineage from King David would never have been accepted by the Jewish people. Two of the Gospels begin their history of the life of Jesus with a detailed genealogy, proving His right to claim to be the King of Israel. If the Herodian royal line had been overthrown, Jesus of Nazareth was probably the only person who could have proven, with reference to the genealogical records preserved in the Temple in Jerusalem, that He had the right to assume the throne of David. Eusebius recorded in his *Ecclesiastical History* that the Roman Emperor Domitian interviewed the surviving grandsons of Jesus' brother Jude to assure himself that they would not pose a threat by claiming they were Jewish royalty. The relatives demonstrated by their calloused hands that they were only poor farmers.

The Bible gives two different genealogies of Jesus — one in the Gospel of Matthew, the other in the Gospel of Luke. Over the last two thousand years, many Bible students have puzzled over these apparent discrepancies. The difference in the way Matthew and Luke record the lineage of Christ needs to be resolved in order to avoid confusion. In Matthew, Jesus' royal line is traced back to King Solomon, the son of King David. In Luke, His line is traced back to Solomon's elder brother, Prince Nathan, who was also a son of King David.

It is important to note that during Jesus' life, and for two hundred and fifty years thereafter, no one questioned His genealogical right to David's throne. If there was a real (rather than an "apparent") problem in the different accounts of His genealogy as recorded by Matthew and Luke, surely His Jewish enemies would have challenged the accuracy of the Gospel accounts. The Jewish people at the time of Christ had access to the genealogical records, which were available for legal examination in the Temple until A.D. 70. The silence of His critics on this score clearly suggests that they understood the two different accounts of His genealogy as being complementary, not contradictory.

Matthew Records Jesus' Royal Claim Through His Legal Father, Joseph

And Jacob begot Joseph the husband of Mary, of whom was born Jesus who is called Christ.

—Matthew 1:16

The genealogy recorded in the book of Matthew 1:1–17 shows that Jesus had the legal right to the throne of King David through his legal descent from King Solomon, the son of David. Beginning with Abraham, Matthew traces this royal descent all the way from King Solomon to Joseph, the legal father of Jesus. The relationship of

Joseph to Jesus is described accurately in verse 16 as "Joseph, the husband of Mary, of whom was born Jesus."

Jesus attained His legal inheritance of the right to the throne from his legally presumed father (just as though he had been legally adopted by Joseph). If it were not for this need to prove his legal right to the throne of David through Joseph, God could have chosen a virgin who never married to be the mother of Jesus.

Luke Records Jesus' Royal Claim Through His Mother, Mary

And Jesus Himself began to be about thirty years of age, being (as was supposed) the son of Joseph, which was the son of Heli. . . .

— Luke 3:23–24

The historian Luke details Christ's genealogy through Mary, working back all the way to Adam. Both Matthew's and Luke's genealogies are identical from the period between Abraham and King David. However, from David until Jesus, the genealogy of Luke differs from that of Matthew in all but three names. Therefore, Luke must be listing Mary's ancestors, not Joseph's ancestors. Luke records the legal line of descent of Jesus through Prince Nathan, the older brother of Solomon, and a royal son of King David (2 Samuel 12:24), and ends with Heli, the father of Mary, the mother of Jesus.

Another apparent contradiction in Matthew and Luke is the identity of Joseph's father. Matthew 1:16 states, "And Jacob begot Joseph." Luke 3:23 states, "Joseph, which was the son of Heli." Matthew 1:16 identifies Joseph as the natural, "begotten" (biological) son of Jacob. The word "begat" means "to biologically be the father." Yet Luke records that Joseph was the "legal" son of Heli. The solution to this problem is found by understanding that the original Greek word *nomizo* (which Luke uses in 3:23) means "to lay down a thing as law; to hold by custom, or usage; to reckon correctly, take for granted." Luke indicates that Joseph was the "legal" son-in-law of Heli, who was the biological father of Mary. Note that Luke does not say that Heli "begat" Joseph. Since Joseph was known as the natural son of Jacob, as recorded in Matthew, it is clear that Luke's choice of the word *nomizo* (reckoned by custom and law) was intended to emphasize that Joseph was also legally listed in the royal line of descent, as a result of his marriage to Mary.

Since the genealogical records of Israel were lost in the burning of the Temple in August, A.D. 70, no one else is able to provide legal evidence that his ancestry traces back to King David. Therefore, Jesus of Nazareth is the only one who can prove He has a legal right to sit on the throne of David as Israel's Messiah.

Is the Original Hebrew Name of Jesus Yeshua יֵשׁוּעַ or Yeshu יֵשׁוּ?

Some critics claim that the name *Yeshua* יֵשׁוּעַ is not the true name that Jesus of Nazareth used during His lifetime. They claim that *Yeshu* יֵשׁוּ, a name often used by Jews today to refer to Jesus, is the correct name and that *Yeshua* is a recent, manipulative invention used to facilitate the proselytization of Jews. Others have noted that "Jews say *Yeshu* and messianic Jews say Yeshua." Which name is the correct name of Jesus used by the first-century Jews in Israel?

Eliezer Ben-Yehuda was a linguistic genius who recreated the ancient Hebrew language in Palestine in this century. He began with the ancient Hebrew words used in the Bible and in Temple worship and expanded the basic vocabulary with new, modern words based on biblical Hebrew forms and ancient rules of grammar. Ben-Yehuda discusses the name Jesus in the prolegomena to his thesaurus to the Hebrew language, *Thesaurus Totius Hebraitatis*. According to a study on this subject by Professor Kai Kjoer-Hansen in the magazine *Mishkan,* Ben-Yehuda refers to Jesus eight times, using the spelling *Yeshua.* While most Hebrew writings in Israel today use the name *Yeshu,* due to centuries of habit, the historical evidence strongly supports the claim that the original Hebrew name of Jesus was Yeshua יֵשׁוּעַ.[1]

Today most Jews in Israel and those Jews living outside the country believe that *Yeshu* יֵשׁוּ is the true name of Jesus of Nazareth. How did the name *Yeshua* יֵשׁוּעַ become transformed to the shortened form *Yeshu* יֵשׁוּ? The answer is not simple. However, the evidence reveals that the original name of Jesus was clearly Yeshua יֵשׁוּעַ in the first century. As Jewish and rabbinic opposition to Jesus grew, following the first-century expansion of the Church throughout the Roman empire, the changed spelling of the name Jesus began to appear in the rabbinic literature that rejected Christian claims about Jesus of Nazareth. The rabbis changed the name by dropping the final letter ayin ע to render it *Yeshu* ישׁו. Some ancient sources suggest that the shortening of a name was a derogatory gesture. An anti-Jesus type of ancient Jewish literature called *Toledoth Yeshu* reveals that the Jewish authorities purposely changed the name of *Yeshua* ישׁוע to *Yeshu* ישׁו to reflect their rejection of His claims to be their Messiah and the Son of God. The ancient Jewish opponents of Jesus used the expression *Yimach Shemo Uzikhro* ("May his name and memory be blotted out") as a curse, in which the first letter of each of the three words spell *Yeshu* ישׁו. However, most modern Jews who commonly use the name *Yeshu* ישׁו have no knowledge of this possible origin of the name or why the Jews historically chose to call Jesus by that name.

The Evidence that Yeshua was the True Name of Jesus

The great Jewish rabbi Moses Maimonides (A.D. 1200), used the Hebrew name *Yeshua* ישׁוע to refer to Jesus in his *Epistle to Yemen*. He also used this spelling in his monumental fourteen-volume study *Mishneh Torah*, a work that codified all of the religious laws from the Torah. In the volume entitled *The Laws of Kings and Their Wars*, which deals with the qualifications of the true Messiah, Rabbi Maimonides wrote about Jesus of Nazareth and spelled His name twice as *Yeshua* ישׁוע. He wrote, "Jesus of Nazareth who aspired to be the Messiah and was executed by the court was also [alluded to] in Daniel's prophecies. . . ."[2] The Hebrew words "Jesus of Nazareth" were spelled as follows: ישׁוע הנוצרי. As noted in an earlier chapter, most editions of the *Mishneh Torah* have been censored during the last eight hundred years and have had the relevant passages that deal with Jesus of Nazareth removed. However, when the Jews of Yemen flew back to Israel in the 1950s they carried with them uncensored copies of Maimonides' great work that dated back to his original eleventh-century writings. Rabbi Eliyahu Touger translated and edited this volume, which was published by the Maznaim Publishing Corporation in New York and Jerusalem in 1987. Rabbi Touger wrote this footnote: "Though most published texts of the *Mishneh Torah* conclude this chapter with this paragraph, a large portion of the Maimonides' text was censored and left unpublished. We have included the original text, based on the Yemenite manuscripts of *Mishneh Torah* and early uncensored editions."[3]

The original name *Yeshua* was related to the name of Joshua, the son of Nun, whose Hebrew name was spelled *Yehoshua*. It appears that the form *Yeshua* is a short form of the longer name *Yehoshua*, as demonstrated in Nehemiah 8:17, where the biblical writer refers to Joshua using the shortened form *Yeshua*: "And all the congregation of them that were come again out of the captivity made booths, and sat under the booths: for since the days of Jeshua [ישוע] the son of Nun unto that day had not the children of Israel done so. And there was very great gladness" (Nehemiah 8:17). Ezra also refers to a man by the name of "Jozabad the son of Jeshua" and uses the same spelling *Yeshua* ישוע. Therefore, the biblical evidence is clear that the name *Yeshua* ישוע was used in biblical times. In addition, archeologists have found the name *Yeshua* ישוע several times in the ancient Hebrew texts of the Dead Sea Scrolls found at Qumran, including a scroll known as *4QT Testimonium*.[4]

Even more powerful evidence of the use of the name *Yeshua* was provided by the discovery of ossuaries found in a first-century burial cave near Bethany. The coins found in the ossuaries included those of Herod the 1st (A.D. 42), which confirmed a first-century period of burial. The lids or sides of these ossuaries were inscribed with the names of the Jewish Christians who were buried within, as well as the sign of the cross. Several had the name *Yeshua* inscribed in Hebrew on the lids or sides. The Hebrew spelling of Jesus was clearly *Yeshua* ישוע. The report of this discovery by Charles Clermont-Ganneau was published in the *Palestine Exploration Fund* in January 1874.[5] In 1931 Professor E. L. Sukenik, an archeologist, also described the discovery of a first-century ossuary with the name *Yeshua* ישוע.

In light of the evidence we can have confidence that the name *Yeshua* ישוע is the genuine Hebrew name of Jesus of Nazareth. The Greek translation of the Hebrew name *Yeshua* ישוע was rendered *Iesous*, the name used throughout the Greek New Testament. When translated into English, the New Testament *Iesous* became "Jesus," the name that is used by followers of Christ around the world.

Notes

1. Kai Kjaer-Hansen, "Yehoshua, Yeshua, Jesus and Yeshu" *Mishkan* (Jerusalem: Issue 17–18, Jan., 1993).

2. Moses Maimonides, *The Laws of Kings and Their Wars*, Ch. II, 234–235.

3. Moses Maimonides, *The Laws of Kings and Their Wars*, Introduction.

4. Geza Veres, *Dead Sea Scrolls in English, 4QT Testimonium* (London: Penguin Books, 1987).

5. Charles Clermont-Ganneau, *Palestine Exploration Fund Statement* Jan. 1874.

12

Fulfilled Prophecies about Jesus as the Messiah

The Old Testament contains over three hundred prophetic passages that refer to the first coming of Jesus the Messiah. Forty-eight of these prophecies refer specifically to the life, death, and resurrection of Jesus. All of them were published during an eleven-hundred-year period that ended four centuries before Jesus was born in Bethlehem. In this chapter we will discuss seventeen of these prophecies, examine the evidence of their fulfillment, and prove that Jesus of Nazareth was the one who fulfilled them.

The Laws of Probability

The study of statistics includes the theory and laws of mathematical probability. This theory states that if the probability of a single event occurring randomly is one chance in five, and the probability of another event occurring is one chance in ten, then the combined probability that both events will occur together in sequence is five multiplied by ten. Thus, the combined chance of both events occurring in sequence is one chance in fifty. To put this in a perspective we can appreciate, consider the odds when we toss a coin in the air. Since a coin has two sides, the odds are 50 percent (or one chance in two) that you will get "heads." However, suppose that you toss two coins in a row. What are the odds against getting "heads" twice? The answer is only one chance in four. The combined odds are $2 \times 2 = 4$. The odds against you tossing ten coins in a row and getting ten "heads" one after another are so large that it would happen by random chance only once in approximately one thousand attempts. According to the laws of probability, the precise odds against getting ten "heads" in a row are one chance in 1,024. The calculation is as follows:

$$2 \times 2 \times 2 \times 2 \times 2 \times 2 \times 2 \times 2 \times 2 \times 2 = 1,024.$$

Old Testament Predictions about the Coming Messiah

Christians have appealed to the evidence that Jesus of Nazareth fulfilled the hundreds of messianic prophecies in the Old Testament as a powerful argument that He was the true Messiah, the promised Son of God. However, many critics over the centuries have suggested that either these predictions were simply fulfilled in the life of Jesus of Nazareth by chance or that He arranged the events of His life to fulfill these well-known prophecies on purpose in order to fraudulently declare that He was the Messiah. To answer the question of whether Jesus fulfilled these Old Testament predictions by chance or whether He fulfilled them by the will of God, we need to analyze the likelihood of these seventeen prophecies occurring by random chance in the life of one individual.

Consider the odds against the following seventeen prophecies about the life and death of Jesus Christ happening by random chance, keeping in mind that the odds are the same whether we analyze the odds that Jesus fulfilled these prophecies by chance or whether we analyze the odds from the standpoint of whether or not the Old Testament prophets correctly guessed the details about the future life of the Messiah by random chance alone.

Seventeen Prophecies about the Messiah's First Coming

The First Prediction: Probability: 1 chance in 2,400

He would be born in Bethlehem and be descended from the tribe of Judah.

The Old Testament Prediction:
"But thou, Bethlehem Ephratah, though thou be little among the thousands of Judah, yet out of thee shall he come forth unto me

that is to be ruler in Israel; whose goings forth have been from of old, from everlasting." (Micah 5:2)

"The sceptre shall not depart from Judah, nor a lawgiver from between his feet, until Shiloh come; and unto him shall the gathering of the people be." (Genesis 49:10)

The New Testament Fulfillment:

"Now when Jesus was born in Bethlehem of Judæa in the days of Herod the king, behold, there came wise men from the east to Jerusalem." (Matthew 2:1)

There were twelve tribes in ancient Israel from which Jesus could have descended by chance, yet He was born from the tribe of Judah, just as the patriarch Judah had predicted fifteen hundred years earlier (Genesis 49:10). Since there were twelve tribes, the odds were 12 to 1 against Christ being born to the tribe of Judah by chance. In addition, Jesus could have been born in any one of over two thousand villages and towns in the densely populated area allotted to the tribe of Judah during the first century. However, to be conservative, I use the figure of *1 chance in 2,400* to estimate the combined odds against anyone guessing correctly, centuries before Jesus was born, that He would be born in Bethlehem and that He would descend from the tribe of Judah.

The Second Prediction: Probability: 1 chance in 20

A messenger would precede the Messiah.

The Old Testament Prediction:

"The voice of him that crieth in the wilderness, Prepare ye the way of the LORD, make straight in the desert a highway for our God." (Isaiah 40:3)

The New Testament Fulfillment:

"In those days came John the Baptist, preaching in the wilderness of Judea, And saying, Repent ye: for the kingdom of heaven is at hand." (Matthew 3:1, 2)

I estimate the odds as 1 in 20, but, to my knowledge, historical records do not reveal any other king who was preceded by a messenger to herald his arrival. To calculate the combined probability of these first two predictions, we must multiply 2,400 times 20, which equals only *1 chance in 48,000* that Jesus would fulfill both predictions by chance.

The Third Prediction: Probability: 1 chance in 50

He would enter Jerusalem on a colt.

The Old Testament Prediction:

"Rejoice greatly, O daughter of Zion; shout, O daughter of Jerusalem: behold, thy King cometh unto thee: he is just, and having salvation; lowly, and riding upon an ass, and upon a colt the foal of an ass." (Zechariah 9:9)

The New Testament Fulfillment:

"And they brought him to Jesus: and they cast their garments upon the colt, and they set Jesus thereon. And as he went, they spread their clothes in the way. And when he was come nigh, even now at the descent of the mount of Olives, the whole multitude of the disciples began to rejoice and praise God with a loud voice for all the mighty works that they had seen." (Luke 19:35–37)

Of all the kings in history, I do not know of any other who ever entered his capital on a colt, as Jesus did on Palm Sunday, A.D. 32, in fulfillment of this prophecy. The combined odds of the three predictions occurring by chance are 50 × 48,000, which equals only *1 chance in 2,400,000* that the prophets would correctly guess these three predictions centuries before the events occurred. With the addition of every subsequent prediction the laws of probability reveal that the combined odds against anyone fulfilling these multiple prophecies by chance are simply astronomical.

The Fourth Prediction: Probability: 1 chance in 10

He would be betrayed by a friend.

The Old Testament Prediction:

"Yea, mine own familiar friend, in whom I trusted, which did eat of my bread, hath lifted up his heel against me."(Psalm 41:9)

The New Testament Fulfillment:

"And while he yet spake, lo, Judas, one of the twelve, came, and with him a great multitude with swords and staves, from the chief priests and elders of the people. Now he that betrayed him gave them a sign, saying, Whomsoever I shall kiss, that same is he: hold him fast." (Matthew 26:47, 48)

Although it is not that unusual for a king to be betrayed by a close associate, the betrayal of a religious leader by a disciple is rather unusual from an historic standpoint. However, to be conservative, I have assigned the odds of this occurring by chance as only

1 chance in 10. The combined probability for these four predictions (10 × 2,400,000) is now only *1 chance in 24 million.*

The Fifth Prediction:　　　　　　　Probability: 1 chance in 100

His hands and feet would be pierced.

The Old Testament Prediction:
"For dogs have compassed me: the assembly of the wicked have enclosed me: they pierced my hands and my feet." (Psalm 22:16)
The New Testament Fulfillment:
"And when they were come to the place, which is called Calvary, there they crucified him, and the malefactors, one on the right hand, and the other on the left." (Luke 23:33)
　　　　The combined probability of these five predictions (10 × 24 million) is now *1 chance in 2.4 billion.*

The Sixth Prediction:　　　　　　　Probability: 1 chance in 10

His enemies would wound the Messiah.

The Old Testament Prediction:
"For thy Maker is thine husband; the LORD of hosts is his name; and thy Redeemer the Holy One of Israel; The God of the whole earth shall he be called." (Isaiah 54:5)
The New Testament Fulfillment:
"Then released he Barabbas unto them: and when he had scourged Jesus, he delivered him to be crucified." (Matthew 27:26)
　　　　Throughout history most kings who have been murdered were killed quite suddenly. Very few kings were ever subjected to torture, as was Jesus. I estimate that the odds of this occurring by chance were less than 1 chance in 10. The combined odds for the six predictions (10 × 2.4 billion) now rises to *1 chance in 24 billion.*

The Seventh Prediction:　　　　　　Probability: 1 chance in 50

He would be betrayed for thirty pieces of silver.

The Old Testament Prediction:
"And I said unto them, If ye think good, give me my price; and if not, forbear. So they weighed for my price thirty pieces of silver." (Zechariah 11:12)
The New Testament Fulfillment:
"And said unto them, What will ye give me, and I will deliver him

unto you? And they covenanted with him for thirty pieces of silver." (Matthew 26:15)

Consider how impossible it would be for anyone to correctly predict, five hundred years before the event, the exact price of betrayal that would be paid for the death of a future king. I conservatively suggest the odds are 1 chance in 50. The odds (50 × 24 billion) now rise to 1 *chance in 1 trillion, 200 billion*, against all seven predictions occurring in one lifetime.

The Eighth Prediction: Probability: 1 chance in 10

He will be spit upon and beaten.

The Old Testament Prediction:

"I gave my back to the smiters, and my cheeks to them that plucked off the hair: I hid not my face from shame and spitting." (Isaiah 50:6)

The New Testament Fulfillment:

"Then did they spit in his face, and buffeted him; and others smote him with the palms of their hands." (Matthew 26:67)

Although many kings throughout history were killed violently, few were tormented, beaten, and ridiculed. Most kings in history were killed through sudden assassination or during a solemn execution such as Charles the First of England. The odds of these eight predictions (10 × 1 trillion, 200 billion) occurring by chance to one man are now 1 *chance in 12 trillion*.

The Ninth Prediction: Probability: 1 chance in 200

His betrayal money would be thrown in the Temple and then given to buy a potter's field.

The Old Testament Prediction:

"And the LORD said unto me, Cast it unto the potter: a goodly price that I was prised at of them. And I took the thirty pieces of silver, and cast them to the potter in the house of the LORD." (Zechariah 11:13)

The New Testament Fulfillment:

"And he cast down the pieces of silver in the temple, and departed, and went and hanged himself. And the chief priests took the silver pieces, and said, It is not lawful for to put them into the treasury, because it is the price of blood. And they took counsel, and bought with them the potter's field, to bury strangers in." (Matthew 27:5–7)

This complicated prophecy appears to be contradictory at first glance. However, despite its apparent impossibility, every detail of this prophecy was fulfilled. The disciple Judas threw the thirty pieces of silver betrayal money into the Temple. Later the priests used this money to purchase a potter's field to bury strangers, including Judas (who, overcome with guilt, hanged himself). I calculate that the odds against this two-part prediction being fulfilled by chance very conservatively as only 1 chance in 200. However, the combined odds (200 × 12 trillion) against these nine predictions occurring now rise to 1 *chance in 2,400 trillion*.

The Tenth Prediction: Probability: 1 chance in 100
He would be silent before His accusers.
The Old Testament Prediction:
"He was oppressed, and he was afflicted, yet he opened not his mouth: he is brought as a lamb to the slaughter, and as a sheep before her shearers is dumb, so he openeth not his mouth." (Isaiah 53:7)
The New Testament Fulfillment:
"And when he was accused of the chief priests and elders, he answered nothing. Then said Pilate unto him, Hearest thou not how many things they witness against thee? And he answered him to never a word; insomuch that the governor marvelled greatly." (Matthew 27:12–14)

Whenever individuals are accused of a crime, they usually defend themselves, even if they are guilty. Consider this unlikely prediction that a totally innocent man facing a death sentence would stand in silence before His accusers. While I estimate that the odds against this event occurring as only 1 chance in 100, realistically, the odds against this event occurring are actually much higher. The odds against these ten predictions occurring to one person (100 × 2,400 trillion) are now 1 *chance in 24,000 trillion*.

The Eleventh Prediction: Probability: 1 chance in 100
He would be crucified with thieves.
The Old Testament Prediction:
"Therefore will I divide him a portion with the great, and he shall divide the spoil with the strong; because he hath poured out his soul unto death: and he was numbered with the transgressors; and

he bare the sin of many, and made intercession for the transgressors."(Isaiah 53:12)

The New Testament Fulfillment:

"Then were there two thieves crucified with him, one on the right hand, and another on the left." (Matthew 27:38)

The continued multiplication of these probabilities reaches a truly staggering number when we consider the likelihood that all seventeen prophecies occurred by random chance. At the end of this analysis, I will give the final calculation of these incredible odds.

The Twelfth Prediction: Probability: 1 chance in 100

People would gamble for His garments.

The Old Testament Prediction:

"They part my garments among them, and cast lots upon my vesture." (Psalm 22:18)

The New Testament Fulfillment:

"Then the soldiers, when they had crucified Jesus, took his garments, and made four parts, to every soldier a part; and also his coat: now the coat was without seam, woven from the top throughout. They said therefore among themselves, Let us not rend it, but cast lots for it, whose it shall be: that the scripture might be fulfilled, which saith, They parted my raiment among them, and for my vesture they did cast lots. These things therefore the soldiers did." (John 19:23–24)

King David wrote this prophecy that soldiers would gamble to win the garments of a crucified prisoner a thousand years prior to its fulfillment. Notice that this apparently contradictory prophecy contains two distinct elements: 1) the soldiers would divide His garments among them, and 2) they would gamble for His clothing. Both prophecies were fulfilled precisely as recorded in John 19:23–24. I suggest a conservative probability of 1 chance in 100.

The Thirteenth Prediction: Probability: 1 chance in 100

His side would be pierced.

The Old Testament Prediction:

"And I will pour upon the house of David, and upon the inhabitants of Jerusalem, the spirit of grace and of supplications: and they shall look upon me whom they have pierced, and they shall mourn for him, as one mourneth for his only son, and shall be in bitterness for him, as one that is in bitterness for his firstborn." (Zechariah 12:10)

The New Testament Fulfillment:
"But one of the soldiers with a spear pierced his side, and forthwith came there out blood and water." (John 19:34)

The cruelty of the Romans was expressed in the unspeakable pain they inflicted on prisoners who were condemned to lengthy deaths on the cross. However, despite orders to produce a drawn-out death, the Roman centurion was motivated by God to pierce Christ's side with his spear. The blood and water that flowed out of Christ's right side proved that Jesus was already dead before the spear entered Him. The normal Roman custom was to allow the victim of crucifixion to linger in agony for days on the cross. The odds against a soldier plunging a spear into the side of a crucified man on a cross is estimated conservatively as 1 chance in 100.

The Fourteenth Prediction: Probability: 1 chance in 20

None of His bones would be broken.

The Old Testament Prediction:
"He keepeth all his bones: not one of them is broken." (Psalm 34:20)

The New Testament Fulfillment:
"But when they came to Jesus, and saw that he was dead already, they brake not his legs." (John 19:33)

When the Romans crucified a prisoner, the body was placed on the cross in such a manner that the victim could breathe only by painfully lifting his upper body, using the strength of his legs to expand his diaphragm. The Jewish legal authorities in Israel had an agreement with the Roman governor to avoid desecrating the Sabbath; therefore, the Roman soldiers needed to speed up the death of a condemned Jewish prisoner to avoid having the body hang on the cross once the Sabbath had commenced at sundown. The soldiers would break the prisoner's legs with a club, thus preventing him from lifting himself up to breathe. Within minutes the prisoner would die, due to oxygen deprivation and fluid accumulation in his lungs. To avoid desecrating the Sabbath, which was about to begin, the soldiers broke the legs of the two prisoners on either side of Jesus to assure their quick deaths. However, in fulfillment of King David's prophecy, Jesus was already dead; so they did not need to break His legs.

The Fifteenth Prediction: Probability: 1 chance in 10,000
His body would not decay.
The Old Testament Prediction:
"For thou wilt not leave my soul in hell; neither wilt thou suffer thine Holy One to see corruption." (Psalm 16:10)
The New Testament Fulfillment:
"He seeing this before spake of the resurrection of Christ, that his soul was not left in hell, neither his flesh did see corruption."(Acts 2:31)

The odds against anyone dying without suffering body decay, and later rising from the dead, are obviously astronomical. However, I have conservatively estimated the odds against resurrection as only 1 chance in 10,000 because God did resurrect several individuals in the Old Testament, including the Shulammite widow's son who was raised from the dead by the prophet Elisha (2 Kings 4:28–37).

The Sixteenth Prediction: Probability: 1 chance in 100
He would be buried in a rich man's tomb.
The Old Testament Prediction:
"And he made his grave with the wicked, and with the rich in his death; because he had done no violence, neither was any deceit in his mouth." (Isaiah 53:9)
The New Testament Fulfillment:
"When the even was come, there came a rich man of Arimathæ, named Joseph, who also himself was Jesus' disciple: He went to Pilate, and begged the body of Jesus. Then Pilate commanded the body to be delivered. And when Joseph had taken the body, he wrapped it in a clean linen cloth, And laid it in his own new tomb, which he had hewn out in the rock: and he rolled a great stone to the door of the sepulchre, and departed." (Matthew 27:57–60)

The most likely site of the tomb of Jesus is northeast of the Damascus Gate along the northern wall of the Old City of Jerusalem, only a hundred yards from the probable site of Golgotha. The Garden Tomb, discovered in 1867, is located in a large, ancient garden. In the days of Jesus, the garden had a wine press and an underground cistern capable of holding two hundred thousand gallons of water, suggesting that the garden tomb belonged to a wealthy man. A stone trough in front of the tomb door would have held a rolling stone to seal the entrance.

The Seventeenth Prediction: Probability: 1 chance in 1,000
Darkness would cover the earth.

The Old Testament Prediction:
"And it shall come to pass in that day, saith the Lord GOD, that I will cause the sun to go down at noon, and I will darken the earth in the clear day." (Amos 8:9)

The New Testament Fulfillment:
"Now from the sixth hour there was darkness over all the land unto the ninth hour." (Matthew 27:45)

Thallus and Phlegon, two pagan historians who lived in the first century, both reported an unusual darkness that blotted out the sun for three hours during the Passover in the year A.D. 32, the year of Jesus' crucifixion. These reports confirm that the prophecy of Amos and Matthew's historical records are accurate.

This analysis has shown that seventeen detailed prophecies, which were written more than four centuries before the birth of Jesus, were fulfilled with absolute precision during the life, death, and resurrection of Jesus Christ. The question we need to consider is this: What are the chances that all seventeen of these predictions occurred by chance in the life of a single man rather than by the divine plan of God? The combined probability against these seventeen predictions occurring is equal to:

1 chance in 480 billion × 1 billion × 1 trillion
or,
1 chance in 480,000,000,000,000,000,000,000,000,000,000.

In other words, there is only 1 chance in 480 billion × 1 billion × 1 trillion that the Old Testament prophets could have accurately predicted these seventeen specific prophecies. Regardless of the individual estimates for probability we assign to these seventeen separate predictions, we are still confronted with a combined probability so staggering in its magnitude that it is highly improbable that these events occurred by chance to one person. In the unlikely event that you still are not convinced, consider the fact that we have examined only seventeen of the forty-eight major prophecies given in the Old Testament about the promised Messiah.

Some Bible critics, such as Professor Hugh J. Schonfield, have suggested that Jesus of Nazareth, as a rabbi, naturally knew about these predictions and simply arranged the events of His life to fulfill these specific prophecies. But how would you arrange to be born in Bethlehem? How would you manage to be born into the tribe of Judah? How would you make sure that the price of your betrayal would be precisely thirty pieces of silver? How would you arrange to be crucified with thieves? How would a crucified man arrange to have his enemies gamble for his garments? The truth is that, if you could arrange all of these details, you would have to be the Son of God.

The details of Jesus of Nazareth's life and death were foreseen and fulfilled by God alone, and the fulfillment of the Old Testament messianic prophecies establishes Jesus' identity as Israel's promised Messiah.

The Great Messianic Prophecy of Moses

One of the greatest messianic prophecies was delivered to Israel by Moses. To Christians, Moses may appear to be just one of many great men of the Bible. However, to the Jews, Moses occupies a place of supreme importance, much higher even than Abraham, the father of the Jews. For over three thousand years Israel has looked back with reverence to their great prophet Moses, who brought them out of centuries of bondage in Egypt to freedom in the Promised Land. He was a unique leader with outstanding qualities as a prophet, priest, teacher, savior, and lawgiver. None of the other Old Testament prophets or leaders came close to fulfilling so many roles.

Nevertheless, in one of his most important prophecies, Moses declared that in the future God would raise up another Jewish prophet whose life would closely resemble his and be as instrumental to the nation of Israel. The Talmud declares also that "the Messiah must be the greatest of future prophets, as being nearest in spirit to our master Moses." Moses' prophecy is important to Israel in determining the credentials of the coming Messiah.

The LORD thy God will raise up unto thee a Prophet from the midst of thee, of thy brethren, like unto me; unto him ye shall hearken. . . . And the LORD said unto me, They have well spoken that which they have spoken. I will raise them up a Prophet from among their brethren, like unto thee, and will put my words in his mouth; and he shall speak unto them all that I shall command him. And it shall come to pass, that whosoever will not hearken unto my words which he shall speak in my name, I will require it of him. (Deuteronomy 18:15, 17–19)

Moses' prophecy was fulfilled in detail in the life, death, and resurrection of Jesus: "Then those men, when they had seen the sign that Jesus did, said, 'This is truly the Prophet who is to come into the world'" (John 6:14). Throughout the Gospels and the Epistles, we find the claim that Jesus fulfilled these messianic prophecies. For example, when the scribes sent people to question John the Baptist, they asked two specific questions. The first was, "Art thou Elias [Elijah]?" (John 1:21), referring to Malachi's prophecy that Elijah would appear as a messenger before the coming of the Messiah. Jews around the world still set out a cup of wine for Elijah at Passover — the prophesied forerunner of the Messiah. The smallest boy in the family is delegated to open a door to invite Elijah to join the family's Passover Seder, in the hope that this year's Passover will usher in the Prophet Elijah, who will announce that the long-awaited Messiah has come.

Was Jesus Truly the Prophet "Like unto Moses"?

The second question the people asked John was, "Are you the Prophet?" (John 1:21). This question referred to Moses' prophecy that God would send "a Prophet like me." When Philip found Nathanæl, he "said to him, 'We have found Him of whom Moses in the law, and also the prophets, wrote — Jesus of Nazareth, the son of Joseph'" (v. 45). After Jesus miraculously fed the five thousand with loaves and fishes, the people referred to the well-known prophecy of Moses, "This is truly the Prophet who is to come into the world" (John 6:14). In his dying speech, the martyr Stephen referred to Moses' prophecy when he declared that Jesus was the promised Messiah: "This is that Moses who said to the children of Israel, 'The lord your God will raise up for you a Prophet like me from your brethren. Him you shall hear'" (Acts 7:37–38).

Was Jesus' life a true parallel to Moses'? Yes, so much so that no other person in history has come close to fulfilling this prophecy except for Jesus of Nazareth. The last verses of Deuteronomy, written after the death of Joshua, tell us that even Joshua missed the mark: "There has not arisen in Israel a prophet like Moses whom the Lord knew face to face" (34:10).

A comparison of the lives of Moses and Jesus of Nazareth reveals at least fifty elements common to both lives, many of which were beyond the ability of any human to control. Consider the unusual multiple roles that Moses and Jesus both played: prophet, priest, lawgiver, teacher, and a leader of men. Both taught new truths from God, and both confirmed their teaching with miracles. Both spent their early years in Egypt, supernaturally protected from the evil kings who sought their lives. Moses' family initially did not accept his role, but later his brother Aaron and sister Miriam helped him. Jesus' brothers and sisters initially failed to follow Jesus, but later his brother James became the leader in the church in Jerusalem.

Each of them was considered the wisest man of his day. Both confronted demonic powers and successfully subdued them. Moses appointed seventy rulers to rule Israel; Jesus anointed seventy disciples to teach the nations. Moses sent twelve spies to explore Canaan; Jesus sent twelve apostles to reach the world with the Gospel. Both fasted for forty days and faced spiritual crises on mountain tops. Just as Moses stretched his hand over the Red Sea to command it to part to save the Israelites, so Jesus rebuked the Sea of Galilee and quieted the waves to save His disciples. Both of their faces shone with the glory of heaven — Moses on Mount Sinai and Jesus on the Mount of Transfiguration.

While Moses rescued Israel from the dead religion of pagan Egypt, Jesus rescued Israel from the dead letter of the law of tradition. Moses and Christ both cured lepers and proved their spiritual authority through the miracles they performed before many witnesses. Moses conquered Israel's great enemy, the Amalekites, with his upraised arms; Jesus conquered our great enemies of sin and death by His upraised arms on the cross. Moses lifted up the brazen serpent in the wilderness to heal his people; Jesus was lifted up on the cross to heal all believers from their sin.

Despite the spiritual leadership of Moses and Jesus, the Jewish people were ungrateful to both men and rebelled against them.

Both generations that rebelled against the two men sent from God died due to their lack of faith — one generation died in the wilderness of Sinai and the other died in the siege of Jerusalem in A.D. 70. Moses promised that God would send his people another Prophet; Jesus promised His Church that His Father would send another "Comforter," the Holy Spirit.

On the fourteenth day of the month of Nisan, which was the Feast of the Passover, both Moses and Jesus freed all who would trust them. On the seventeenth day, the Feast of Firstfruits, Moses brought about the resurrection of the children of Israel by taking them through the parted Red Sea; on the Feast of Firstfruits, Jesus ensured the resurrection of all believers by becoming the symbolical Firstfruits of resurrection as He arose from the dead. Fifty days after the Jews passed through the Red Sea on the Feast of Pentecost, God gave Israel the gift of the Torah, the Law of God. Fifty days after Christ's resurrection, on the Feast of Pentecost, God gave His Church the great gift of the baptism of the Holy Spirit.

The evidence is compelling that Jesus truly was the prophesied Messiah, the "prophet like unto Moses."

The good news of the New Testament is that we are approaching a time when all Gentiles and Jews throughout the earth will finally see Jesus as the true fulfillment of the Bible's prophecies and humanity will enter into the glorious reign of the Messiah Jesus Christ. The apostle Paul promised that the spiritual "blindness" of Israel would not last forever. When the time arrives for His return to earth "all Israel shall be saved." Paul declared: "And so all Israel shall be saved: as it is written, There shall come out of Sion the Deliverer, and shall turn away ungodliness from Jacob" (Romans 11:26).

Notes

1. Hugh Schonfield, *The Passover Plot* (New York: Random House, 1965).

13

Jesus – The Son of God

"Who Do Men Say That I Am?"

One of the most controversial matters that must be addressed by all serious inquirers about the life of Jesus of Nazareth is the question of His identity. Who did He personally claim to be? Did He actually claim to be the chosen Messiah and the Son of God? Did He truly claim to be Divine as the Gospels and the rest of the New Testament epistles affirm? The question of Jesus' true identity has puzzled serious inquirers for almost two thousand years.

The Gospels reveal a deep mystery concerning the nature of Jesus of Nazareth, beginning with the first prophecy in the New Testament when the angel Gabriel identifies the promised son of Mary as "the Son of God." The Gospel writer Luke recounts the angel's message:

> He shall be great, and shall be called the Son of the Highest: and the Lord God shall give unto him the throne of his father David. . . . And the angel answered and said unto her, The Holy Ghost shall come upon thee, and the power of the Highest shall overshadow thee: therefore also that holy thing which shall be born of thee shall be called the Son of God. (Luke 1:32, 35)

This remarkable declaration confirmed the Old Testament

prophecies that suggested that the Messiah would be far more than a heroic human leader of Israel, such as Moses.

Jesus Christ Declared That He Was Truly God

The theological word "Trinity" is derived from the Latin word *trinitas,* or the word *trinitus,* which means "three in one" or "threefold." This word, Trinity, expresses the clear teaching of the New Testament on the mysterious nature of God, as a Trinity in Unity.

Consider these profound words of Jesus of Nazareth that reveal His authoritative teaching about the mystery of the triune nature of God, known as the Trinity: "Believe me that I am in the Father, and the Father in me: or else believe me for the very works' sake. . . . And I will pray the Father, and he shall give you another Comforter, that he may abide with you for ever" (John 14:11, 16). Jesus affirmed in this verse that He and the Father were one. At the same time, He identified Himself and the Father as two distinct persons, using His own name and that of "the Father." Jesus promised His disciples that the Father would answer His prayers and would send "another Comforter," referring to the Holy Spirit, the third person in the Trinity. If we carefully examine the words of Jesus in the Gospels, we discover that they reveal clearly that He taught that the unity of God was expressed in three distinct manifestations: the Father, the Son, and the Comforter (or the Holy Spirit).

The pages of the Bible reveal a deep mystery concerning the nature of God, beginning with the opening verses of the Scriptures. From the initial verses in the book of Genesis through to the closing promises found in the book of Revelation, there are many inspired statements that affirm that there is only one God. However, it is equally clear that the Word of God constantly affirms, often in the very same verses, that this same God is revealed in three persons or three manifestations. This seeming contradiction has puzzled millions of thoughtful believers over the centuries. The infinite and omnipresent nature of God is far beyond the power of our finite minds to understand perfectly. Despite the difficulties, the mysterious truth of the triune nature of God is taught throughout the Scriptures from Genesis to Revelation and is accepted by all orthodox Christians as truth.

Most Christians and virtually all non-Christians acknowledge that the mystery of the Trinity is the most profound and difficult of all biblical doctrines to understand. As a result of numerous conversations over thirty-five years with both pastors and laymen, I have come to believe that many Christians do not have a clear understanding of the great scriptural truths about the triune nature of God. Unfortunately, many pastors and Bible teachers in our generation have failed to teach this vital doctrine, perhaps because of its obvious difficulty. However, the sad result of this failure is that many Christians are unable to express clearly in either thought or word their personal understanding of the true nature of God as revealed in the Scriptures. Surely, those who truly love Jesus Christ need to come to a full, mature understanding of the great biblical truths regarding His divine and human nature. It is obvious that the only source of true knowledge about Christ's nature must be found in the genuine written revelation of God, the Holy Scriptures. Nevertheless, it is worthwhile to examine the writings of the early Church about the nature of God. In addition, I will share some fascinating and astonishing research about the greatest of the Jewish rabbis, who lived in the years before Jesus was born, who taught in the clearest language possible about the sacred mystery of the Trinity.

While the doctrine of the Trinity is beyond our ability to fully appreciate intellectually, it is not fundamentally contrary to reason. This is a study that needs to be approached with a holy reverence, an open heart, and an obedient spirit.

What does the Bible actually teach about the triune nature of Jesus Christ as the Son of God? The scriptural revelation of the triune nature of God can be succinctly described in two sentences:

> The Bible declares that there is one God who is revealed to us as Father, Son, and Holy Spirit, each of whom has distinct personal attributes; however, there is no division regarding nature, essence, or being. The Gospels and the other New Testament books reveal clearly that Jesus of Nazareth claimed repeatedly that He was God.

These statements sum up every significant point that the Scriptures teach us about the doctrine of the Trinity, as held by orthodox Christian believers in all denominations during the last two thousand years. While the Bible describes this triune or threefold nature by its constant use of the words *Father, Son,* and *Holy Spirit,* the Scriptures also declare authoritatively that there is only one God.

The Gospels Teach There Is Only One God

Numerous passages from Scripture teaching the unity of God could be cited, but these few verses will suffice to prove the truth of this important doctrine. Moses, the great lawgiver of the Jews, declared, "Thou shalt have no other gods before me" (Exodus 20:3). Moses also declared the unity of God in the famous words of the "Shema," the daily affirmation for thousands of years of righteous Jews throughout the world: "Hear, O Israel: The Lord our God is one Lord" (Deuteronomy 6:4). The prophet Isaiah also declared the unity of God in his prophetic words: "I am the Lord: that is my name: and my glory will I not give to another, neither my praise to graven images" (Isaiah 42:8). "To whom will ye liken me, and make me equal, and compare me, that we may be like?" (Isaiah 46:5). The prophet Malachi wrote of one God when he said, "Have we not all one father? hath not one God created us?" (Malachi 2:10).

One of the most important attributes of Jesus as the Son of God is that He is both eternal and uncreated. In other words, there was never a time when God did not exist. Therefore, God has no beginning and no end. The Scriptures reveal the eternal nature of God in many passages, including the words of King David in the Psalms: "Before the mountains were brought forth, or ever thou hadst formed the earth and the world, even from everlasting to everlasting, thou art God" (Psalms 90:2). Jesus Christ confirmed His eternal nature in these words: "Verily, verily, I say unto you, Before Abraham was, I am" (John 8:58).

Furthermore, the Bible teaches us that God is omnipresent, which means that He is simultaneously everywhere throughout His creation, not only in awareness but in His actual divine presence. This omnipresence of God was alluded to by King Solomon at the building of the Temple, as recorded in the book of Kings: "But will God indeed dwell on the earth? Behold, the heaven and heaven of heavens cannot contain thee; how much less this house that I have builded?" (1 Kings 8:27).

The Scriptures also declare that God is unchangeable, that His nature will remain the same forever. The prophet Malachi wrote, "For I am the Lord, I change not" (Malachi 3:6). This inspired declaration by Malachi confirms that God's nature, as expressed in the Trinity in unity, did not change when the Son incarnated in the body of the Christ child, Jesus of Nazareth, two thousand years ago. In other words, the Father, the Son, and the Holy Spirit have always existed as the Trinity.

The Father, Jesus the Son, and the Holy Spirit Are Equally God

Now that we have examined the passages that affirm there is only one God, we need to explore the other passages of Scripture that also teach us clearly that God the Father, God the Son, and God the Holy Spirit, are all identified and named as God. Paul wrote the following letter referring to both the Father and Jesus as God: "To Timothy, my dearly beloved son: Grace, mercy, and peace, from God the Father and Christ Jesus our Lord" (2 Timothy 1:2). Paul again affirms that both are God in his letter to the Church at Philippi: "And that every tongue should confess that Jesus Christ is Lord, to the glory of God the Father" (Philippians 2:11). In the Gospel of John we find a clear declaration by the beloved disciple, John, that both Jesus and the Father are God. "No man hath seen God at any time; the only begotten Son, which is in the bosom of the Father, he hath declared him" (John 1:18).

Jesus Christ, the Son of God, Created the Universe

However, while John reveals that Jesus and the Father are both God, he also reveals that it was Jesus, the Son of God, as the Word (*logos*) of God, who created the entire universe and everything within it. A careful examination of the Scriptures reveals that the act of creation was committed to Jesus, the Son of God. "In the beginning was the Word, and the Word was with God, and the Word was God. The same was in the beginning with God. All things were made by him; and without him was not any thing made that was made" (John 1:1–3). This teaching is confirmed by Paul's letter to the Ephesian Church: "And to make all men see what is the fellowship of the mystery, which from the beginning of the world hath been hid in God, who created all things by Jesus Christ" (Ephesians 3:9). The Psalmist David alludes to the fact that the Son is the One who created all things by identifying the Creator as "the Word of the Lord": "By the word of the Lord were the heavens made; and all the host of them by the breath of his mouth"

(Psalms 33:6). Later in this chapter we will examine the scriptural evidence that "the Word of the Lord" is often used as an Old Testament title for the Son of God, the second person of the Trinity. David declares, "By the word of the Lord were the heavens made; and all the host of them by the breath of his mouth" (Psalms 33:6).

The Bible continually refers to the Holy Spirit as a distinct person of the Godhead who teaches, acts, witnesses about Christ, and dwells within the spirit of the believer as the Spirit of God. At the end of His earthly ministry, Jesus Christ promised His disciples that He would send them "a Comforter" to guide and direct them after He ascended to heaven. "And I will pray the Father, and he shall give you another Comforter, that he may abide with you for ever; Even the Spirit of truth; whom the world cannot receive, because it seeth him not, neither knoweth him: but ye know him; for he dwelleth with you, and shall be in you" (John 14:16–17). This passage reveals the three divine persons of the Trinity. However, this verse also clearly identifies the Holy Spirit as the person of God the Comforter, who will empower the believers. King David also wrote about the divine Holy Spirit as a separate person of the Trinity when he appealed to God (the Father) in the following words: "Cast me not away from thy presence; and take not thy holy spirit from me" (Psalms 51:11). Additionally, in the New Testament, Jesus identified the Holy Spirit as both God and as a distinct person of the Trinity. Jesus taught about the Holy Spirit as God in His conclusion to the Lord's Prayer, which was addressed to "Our Father." Jesus taught, "If ye then, being evil, know how to give good gifts unto your children: how much more shall your heavenly Father give the Holy Spirit to them that ask him?" (Luke 11:13). These Scriptures obviously teach the threefold nature of God as we describe it under the word "Trinity."

The Bible Teaches the Trinity

We have examined the scriptural teaching that there is only one God. In addition, we have examined the Scriptures that teach that the Father, the Son, and the Holy Spirit are three distinct persons of the Godhead. We need now to look at the Scriptures that reveal the three persons as one God. One of the most significant passages revealing this teaching about the Trinity is found at the beginning of the ministry of Jesus when John baptized our Lord. The Gospel of Matthew records, "And Jesus, when he was baptized, went up straightway out of the water: and, lo, the heavens were opened unto him, and he saw the Spirit of God descending like a dove, and lighting upon him: And lo a voice from heaven, saying, This is my beloved Son, in whom I am well pleased" (Matthew 3:16–17). In this well-loved passage we observe Jesus, the Son of God, being baptized by John and the Holy Spirit of God descending upon Him. Simultaneously, God the Father speaks from heaven saying, "This is my beloved Son."

This critical passage reveals the three distinct persons of the Trinity acting as individuals, yet in perfect harmony as the triune God. It is significant that at the end of His ministry on earth, Jesus Christ instructed His disciples by giving them His Great Commission: "Go ye therefore, and teach all nations, baptizing them in the name of the Father, and of the Son, and of the Holy Ghost" (Matthew 28:19). Since baptism is the most profound profession of faith, devotion, and worship, which is due only to God, the words of Jesus confirm that "the Father, the Son, and the Holy Ghost" are equally God, as taught in the biblical doctrine of the Trinity. This teaching of the Trinity also appears in the final benediction, in which the apostle Paul concludes his second inspired letter to the church at Corinth. Paul gave them his blessings in the names of the three persons of God, as revealed in the Trinity, "The grace of the Lord Jesus Christ, and the love of God, and the communion of the Holy Ghost, be with you all. Amen" (2 Corinthians 13:14).

The Early Church Taught the Divine Nature of Jesus

Universally, the early Church upheld the biblical doctrine of the Divine nature of Jesus Christ from the Day of Pentecost in A.D. 32 throughout the last two thousand years. An examination of the early Church writings will verify their unwavering support for this teaching found in the writings of both the Old and New Testament. The real value of these ancient Christian writings is that they are the best interpreters of the doctrine of the Trinity as it was preached by Jesus and the apostles. As some of these early Christians were taught by those who personally knew the apostles, they would have been in an excellent position to understand the true meaning of the New Testament teachings. Some critics of the doctrine of the Trinity have complained that the word "Trinity" cannot be found in the actual Hebrew or Greek words of the Scriptures. However, the truth of this doctrine is taught clearly from Genesis to Revelation. Many scholars believe that the word "Trinity" was used for the first time in reference to this biblical doctrine during a Church council held at Alexandria, Egypt in A.D. 317. However, the history of the early Church reveals that this doctrine of the Trinity was taught by Jesus Christ, His disciples, and the apostles. The Trinity of God was the universal belief of the Church from the very beginning of the Christian era. For example, the secular Greek writer Lucian, in his book *Philopatris*, written in A.D. 160, confirmed the well-known belief of the Christians in the Trinity. Lucian described the first generations of Christians confessing their faith in God in the following words: "The exalted God . . . Son of the Father, Spirit proceeding from the Father, One of Three, and Three of One."[1]

Some critics and theologians have claimed that the doctrine of the Trinity and the Divinity of Jesus Christ was unknown until the Council of Nicca in A.D. 325, where they claim it was invented by the unanimous collusion of the Church fathers in that council. However, this claim is totally contradicted by the many writings of the early Church from the time of Christ to A.D. 325. Some passages from several of these writers can establish this fact.

One of the earliest of the manuscripts written by church leaders is the *Shepherd of Hermas*. Hermas was a brother of Pius, the Bishop of Rome. Some scholars believe Hermas is the person mentioned in the apostle Paul's epistle to the Romans (16:14). Hermas wrote, "The Son of God is more ancient than any created thing, so that He was present in council with His Father at the creation."[2] Justin Martyr's writing declares that the doctrine of the pre-existence of Jesus as God was proclaimed with great clarity from the earliest ages of the Church. Justin and many of the early Church fathers wrote that it was Jesus Christ who appeared as God to Moses in the burning bush. He criticized the Jews for confusing the roles of God the Father with that of His Son in the passages of the Old Testament. Justin Martyr wrote,

> The Jews, who think that it was always God the Father who spoke to Moses, (whereas He who spoke to him was the Son of God, who is also called an Angel, and an apostle) are justly convicted both by the prophetical spirit, and by

Christ himself, for knowing neither the Father nor the Son. For they, who say that the Son is the Father, are convicted of neither knowing the Father, nor of understanding that the God of the universe has a Son: who, being the first-born Word of God, is also God.[3]

Justin Martyr also wrote the following statement in his *Dialogue With Trypho*. He establishes a general rule that wherever God appears or converses with any man in the Old Testament, as in Genesis 17:22, et cetera, we should understand that the passage is referring to Jesus as God the Son. "Now that Christ is Lord, and substantially God the Son of God, and in times past appeared potentially as a man and an angel, and in fiery glory as He appeared in the bush, and at the judgment of Sodom, has been proved by many arguments."[4]

In A.D. 351 the Council of Sirmium was held to deal with a number of heresies that were beginning to plague the Church. This council established a creed as a clear statement of the teaching of the Church regarding Christ's Divinity and the Trinity. In one of its comments on this subject we find the following words: "If any one say that the Father did not speak the words, 'Let us make man,' to His Son, but that he spoke them to Himself, let him be anathema."[5] The declaration "Let him be anathema" means "Let him be accursed or cut off from the Church." This strong statement reveals the Divinity and pre-existence of Jesus Christ as an essential doctrine of the early Church.

Notes

1. Lucian of Samosata, *Philopatris* (A.D. 160).
2. Shepherd of Hermas, *Similitude*, 3 vols. 1:118.
3. Edward Burton, ed., *Testimonies of the Ante-Nicene Fathers to the Divinity of Christ* (Oxford: University Press, 1829).
4. Edward Burton, ed., *Testimonies of the Ante-Nicene Fathers to the Divinity of Christ* (Oxford: University Press, 1829) 52–53.
5. The Council of Sirmium, *Ath. de Synodis* (A.D. 351) 1:743.

14

The Evidence of Transformed Lives

The most powerful evidence of Jesus' existence as the Son of God is the life-changing impact this truth has on the lives of men and women who have placed their faith and trust in Him.

Jesus' life and His Word have held the undying attention of many brilliant men over the ages. Tertullian, an early Church writer who lived in the second century, devoted his life to the study of Scripture every day and night. By the end of his life Tertullian had memorized most of the Bible by heart, including the punctuation! A profound love of Jesus motivated the early Christians who lived with the constant threat of persecution. Bishop Eusebius, the great historian of the early Church, wrote about one persecuted Christian whose eyes were burned out because he refused to deny Christ during one of the ten great waves of persecution against the early Church. This blind Christian saint could repeat large portions of the Bible from memory. A century later the great Christian theologian of the early Church, St. Augustine, wrote: "I have read in Plato and Cicero sayings that are very wise and very beautiful; but I never read in either of them: 'Come unto me all ye that labour and are heavy laden.'"

The French Christian writer Desiderius Erasmus wrote, "By a

Carpenter mankind was made, and only by that Carpenter can mankind be remade." Thomas Beza, a translator of the Scriptures in 1585, had such a profound love of the words of Jesus that, at the age of eighty, he could still repeat from memory all of the New Testament epistles in the Greek language. Two of the leading Reformers during the Protestant Reformation, Cranmer and Ridley, found their faith immeasurably strengthened by memorizing the entire New Testament during the time of their persecution.

Henry Drummond wrote about the remarkable influence of Jesus' life: "Christ built no church, wrote no book, left no money, and erected no monument! yet show me ten square miles in the whole world without Christianity, where the life of man and the purity of women are respected and I will give up Christianity." Another writer, Henry Benjamin Whipple, declared, "All we want in Christ, we shall find in Christ. If we want little, we shall find little. If we want much, we shall find much; but if, in utter helplessness, we cast our all on Christ, He will be to us the whole treasury of God."

The great men who founded the United States of America, including George Washington, were strongly influenced by their faith in Jesus Christ. President Washington once declared, "It is impossible to rightly govern the world without God and the Bible." The preacher Earle W. Crawford gave a sermon entitled "God Is With Us," (recorded in *Pulpit Preaching)* in which he shared his conviction about Jesus of Nazareth: "The Christian faith is firmly rooted in the incarnation, in the conviction that, 'God was in Christ, reconciling the world unto himself.' To believe in Christ is to believe that God has come to earth to dwell with men. . . . In Jesus, we meet the living. Jesus is more than a religious genius or a holy man or a spiritual pioneer. To believe in Christ is to believe that the living God has come."

Another great writer and brilliant scientist, Lord Francis Bacon, wrote a pivotal book, *The Advancement of Learning,* in which he called for a study to be made of Bible prophecy to systematically show how God had precisely fulfilled the predictions made over thousands of years. Filled with wonder at the creation of the world, Bacon wrote, "Thy creatures, O Lord, have been my books, but thy Holy Scriptures much more. I have sought thee in the courts, fields and gardens; but I have found thee, O God, in thy sanctuary, thy temples." Although Bacon acknowledged the awesome evidence about God the Creator revealed by science and nature, he discovered that the most profound knowledge of God is found in detailed study of His written Word, the Holy Scriptures.

The Impact of Jesus on the Lives of the apostles

What could possibly account for the sudden transformation from an attitude of helplessness, fear, and despair among the eleven disciples at the cross to an attitude of joy and bold confidence in declaring the good news of the risen Savior that these men demonstrated for the rest of their lives to the whole of the known world? The only rational answer is that they personally witnessed the resurrection of Jesus of Nazareth with their own eyes and personally experienced His supernatural empowerment through the Holy Spirit — a claim the writers of the New Testament repeatedly made: they were eyewitnesses or had spoken first hand to eyewitnesses. For example, Luke the physician tells us that his written account is based on eyewitness reports: "Even as they delivered them unto us, which from the beginning were eyewitnesses, and ministers of the word" (Luke 1:2). The apostle Peter confirmed that he personally witnessed the glory and majesty of Jesus in His resurrection body: "For we have not followed cunningly devised fables, when we made known unto you the power and coming of our Lord Jesus Christ, but were eyewitnesses of his majesty" (2 Peter 1:16).

The history of the persecution of the Church, which began within thirty years of Christ's death on the cross, during the reign of Emperor Nero, reveals that the followers of Jesus were known for going to their painful deaths with hymns and prayers on their lips. Is it probable — is it even possible — to imagine that hundreds of thousands of intelligent people would endure torture and martyrdom rather than deny their faith in the risen Jesus if they had the slightest doubt that He was truly God? Is it likely that they would have accepted martyrdom unless they truly believed that His resurrection, attested to by eyewitnesses, was the guarantee that they too would arise one day through Christ's victory over death and sin? The only logical explanation is that these people were absolutely convinced that Jesus was the Son of God because they were eyewitnesses themselves, or because they had heard trustworthy accounts of the death and resurrection of Jesus from eyewitnesses. The remarkable growth of the Christian faith, despite the most horrendous persecution, is proof enough that these people were supernaturally motivated to reach the world with the Gospel of Jesus Christ. It is estimated that a significant portion of the Roman Empire became followers of Jesus within one hundred years of His resurrection.

Quotations to Meditate Upon

The purpose of Christianity is not to avoid difficulty, but to produce a character adequate to meet it when it comes. It does not make life easy; rather it tries to make us great enough for life.

— James L. Christensen

Christianity is not a puzzle to be solved, but a way of life to be adopted. It is not a creed to be memorized, but a Person to follow.

— Anonymous quotation

Still as of old
Men by themselves are priced —
For thirty pieces Judas sold
Himself, not Christ.

— Hester H. Cholmondeley

He changed sunset into sunrise.

— Clement of Alexandria

Jesus Christ is in the noblest and most perfect sense the realized ideal of humanity.

— Johann Gottfried von Herder

All that I am I owe to Jesus Christ revealed to me in His divine Book.

— David Livingstone

Sin will keep you from this Book. This Book will keep you from sin.

— Dwight L. Moody

15

The Impact of Jesus' Life on World History

Other books were given for our information, the Bible was given for our transformation.

— The Defender

The impact that Jesus of Nazareth had on the history of the world can be gleaned from observations of the impact He had on the great men in history. While there are voluminous articles in the *Encyclopedia Britannica* about Alexander the Great, Julius Cæsar, Napoleon, Aristotle, and Plato, the amount of historical material and analysis about the teachings of Jesus far exceeds the attention given to any other individual in the history of man. In fact the *Encyclopedia Britannica* uses over twenty thousand words to tell us the story about His life, teaching, and His impact on the lives of billions of people on every continent in every century for the last two thousand years. Even the atheist writer H. G. Wells, who openly blasphemed the name of Jesus, realized that he could not ignore the influence of Christ on history. He reserved ten pages of his monumental volume *Outline of History* to discuss the life of the Nazarene.

The brilliant writer and former president, Thomas Jefferson, wrote about the life of Jesus: "His parentage was obscure; His condition poor; His education null; His natural endowments great; His life correct and innocent; He was meek, benevolent, patient, firm, disinterested, and of the sublimest eloquence." Professor Alexander Stewart wrote, "He who would worthily write the life of Christ must have a pen dipped in the imaginative sympathy of a poet, in the prophet's fire, in the artist's charm and grace and in the reverence and purity of the saint."[1]

Samuel Taylor Coleridge wrote, "For more than a thousand years the Bible collectively taken, has gone hand in hand with civilization, science, law — in short, with the moral and intellectual cultivation of the species, always supporting and often leading the way." Another genius, Herder, wrote, "Jesus Christ is in the noblest, and most perfect sense, the realized ideal of humanity."[2]

Writer Joseph Ernst Renan commented on the mystery that God used the new religion of Christianity to transmute the truths of ancient Judaism into a form that would reach the entire gentile world with the revelation of God's plan to redeem humanity from the curse of sin. Renan wrote, "It is through Christianity that Judaism has really conquered the world. Christianity is the masterpiece of Judaism, its glory and the fullness of its evolution."[3]

Another writer, Thomas Carlyle, expressed his personal response to the personality of Christ, "Jesus of Nazareth, our divinest symbol! Higher has the human thought not reached." Carlyle declared that Jesus was, "a symbol of quite perennial, infinite character, whose significance will ever demand to be anew inquired into, and anew made manifest."[4]

The author of *Doctor Zhivago*, Boris Pasternak, once wrote, "It is possible to be an atheist, it is possible not to know whether God exists, or why, and yet believe... that history as we know it now began with Christ and that Christ's Gospel is its foundation."[5] The seeming familiarity of Jesus oftens stands in the way of men honestly examining His life and teaching. Winifred Kirkland wrote, "Today the greatest single deterrent to knowledge of Jesus is his familiarity. Because we think we know him, we pass him by." The great writer Charles Lamb once wrote, "If Shakespeare should come into this room, we would all rise; but if Jesus Christ should come in, we would all kneel."

The Bible's Transformation of Society

The social situation in England in the early 1700s, before the Evangelical Revival led by John and Charles Wesley, was a moral abyss. In 1738 in his book *Discourse Addressed to Magistrates and Men in Authority*, Bishop George Berkeley wrote that the level of public morality and religion had collapsed in Britain "to a degree that has never been known in any Christian country. . . . Our prospect is very terrible and the symptoms grow worse from day to day." Berkeley spoke of a torrent of evil that flooded the land:

> which threatened a general inundation and destruction of these realms. . . . The youth born and brought up in wicked times without any bias to good from early principle, or instilled opinion, when they grow ripe, must be monsters indeed. And it is to be feared that the age of monsters is not far off.[6]

As you read the history of the England of two centuries ago, consider the spiritual and moral parallel with the spiritual breakdown of our own North American society as we begin the new millennium. Many writers, including Daniel Defoe, Alexander Pope, and Samuel Johnson confirm that England was on the point of moral collapse in the early 1700s, much as North America and Europe are today. In the previous century, the official state-sponsored Church of England had severely suppressed true Christians through strict laws (such as the Act of Conformity), forbidding Nonconformist ministers (independent pastors who were not endorsed by the Church of England) from teaching or preaching. Many of the greatest preachers in England were driven out of their churches for refusing to accept these laws. The French athiest philosopher Voltaire understood the fundamental role that the Holy Scriptures played in the growth and preservation of true Christianity. Voltaire cynically wrote, "If we would destroy the Christian religion, we must first of all destroy man's belief in the Bible."

The Great Plague of 1665 killed one in every five people in London. Everyone who could fled London, including most of the ministers and bishops of the official Church of England and the government. The apostate government of England passed the infamous Five Mile Act, which prohibited any of the expelled clergy from preaching within five miles of their former church, in an attempt to prevent people from hearing the Gospel message from a biblically based minister. Many of the independent nonconformist pastors ignored the laws and returned to help their dying congregations by preaching that the only hope for mankind was to trust in Jesus Christ. Over four thousand pastors were thrown into prison for disregarding this law. Finally, in 1714, the Schism Act prohibited anyone from preaching anywhere without a special license from his bishop. The result of the suppression of the preaching of the Gospel was the descent of England into a morass of immorality, perversion, and widespread moral collapse. Writer Thomas Carlyle wrote his verdict on eighteenth century English society: "stomach well alive, soul extinct." The writer Mark Pattison also gave his summation: "decay of religion, licentiousness of morals, public corruption, profaneness of language — a day of rebuke and blasphemy." As the moral code broke down, with the teaching of the Gospel repressed and the crime rate rising, the ruling classes naturally responded by fearfully demanding severe laws to restrain criminals. The parallel with today's demand for "law and order," "three strikes and you're out," and the doubling of the American prison population in only two decades is uncannily similar.

At a time when writer William E. Blackstone was proudly writing about the glory of England's "unmatched Constitution," both adults and children were subject to one hundred and sixty capital criminal laws that resulted in hanging. If anyone shoplifted more than one shilling, stole one sheep, harmed a tree, gathered fruit from someone's property, or snared a rabbit on someone's estate, they were hanged. The evangelist Charles Wesley reported in his *Journal* that he preached in one jail to fifty-two people awaiting execution on death row, including one ten-year-old child. Public drunkenness was so widespread that many young adults and children died as alcoholics. Millions of children and women were working in appalling labor conditions in dangerous factories and mines for unbelievably low wages. England was a moral and spiritual wasteland.

Yet, into this spiritual cesspool, God sent His last, best hope for England. John and Charles Wesley began to preach about Jesus of Nazareth. In 1769 John Wesley started the Sunday School movement, which ultimately flourished throughout England. The preaching of the Wesley brothers and their fellow ministers of the Gospel produced a spiritual revival. As a young missionary, John Wesley was sent out in 1735 on a mission to Georgia in the young American colonies. Wesley wrote to his friend as he began his long sailing journey, "Sir, if the Bible be not true, I am as fool and madman as you can conceive; but if it be of God I am sober-minded." On one occasion, when Wesley addressed three thousand people, he declared these words from the prophet Isaiah 61:1–2:

> The spirit of the Lord is upon me, because he hath appointed me to preach the Gospel to the poor; he hath sent me to heal the broken-hearted; to preach deliverance to the captive, and recovery of sight to the blind; to set at liberty them that are bruised, to proclaim the acceptable year of the Lord.[7]

The spiritual energy supernaturally released by this renewed preaching about Jesus by many dedicated ministers, including John Milton and John Bunyan, literally transformed the soul of that nation. John Wesley proclaimed the need to allow the Gospel to transform society and each individual soul as well: "We know no Gospel without salvation from sin. . . . Christianity is essentially a social religion; to turn it into a solitary religion is indeed to destroy it." He declared that "a doctrine to save sinning men, with no aim to transform them into crusaders against social sin, was equally unthinkable."[8]

In addition to the personal transformations, this evangelical revival transformed all aspects of English society. Many features of modern Western society that we take for granted today were the result of the great spiritual move of God produced by the Wesleyan Revival. As Christ transformed individual sinners, these reformed men and women took up the task of reforming their society. The imprisonment of debtors and children was made illegal. Schools were opened in every parish in the nation to every child who wanted to learn. Harsh penal laws and child labor in mines and factories were eliminated as a result of new laws passed by Christian parliamentarians based on the teaching of Jesus. The evangelical movement created the first hope for prosperity and self-respect that the forgotten masses of England had ever known. England was quickly restored to greatness. Universal free schools, charities, and free hospitals were formed by Christians who found their motivation in following Jesus. The great preacher and Christian writer Jonathan Edwards described the incredible influence of the transforming power of Jesus Christ on English society: "There is no leveler like Christianity, but it levels by lifting all who receive it to the lofty table-land of a true character and of undying hope both for this world and the next."

Bishop Davidson declared that Wesley was "one of the greatest Englishmen who ever lived" and stated that "Wesley practically changed the outlook and even the character of the English nation." In truth, it was the return to Jesus' Gospel teaching that transformed England. A fascinating story is recounted about an ambassador of a prince of an African nation who was granted an audience with Queen Victoria. During his interview with the deeply religious monarch, the ambassador asked her about the secret of the manifest greatness of England among the many nations throughout the world. Queen Victoria is reported to have pointed to the Bible on her desk and said, "Tell your prince that this book (the Bible) is the secret of England's greatness." It may come as a great suprise to many Americans that the well-known phrase most Americans recognize from their own Declaration of Independence was actually first articulated by the Christian Bible translator John Wycliffe in the preface to his and Hereford's translation of the English Bible: "The Bible is for the government of the people, by the people, and for the people."

An inscription at the eastern entrance to the Rockefeller Center in New York City acknowledges the profound impact Jesus has had on humanity's destiny and upon our quality of life. The inscriptions reads, "Man's ultimate destiny depends not on whether he can learn new lessons or make new discoveries and conquests, but on his acceptance of the lesson taught him close upon two thousand years ago."

However, when we compare the spiritual attitude of that reformed English society of two centuries ago to the contemporary attitudes of indifference and opposition to the Bible throughout the Western nations today, we recognize the vast moral changes that have occurred as a result of the continuing attack on the authority of the Word of God in this century. We are as much in need today for an evangelical revival as was England two hundred years ago.

Jesus' Impact on Women and Children

The Gospel of John records that three women, each named Mary, were present at the crucifixion of Jesus.

> Now there stood by the cross of Jesus His mother, and His mother's sister, Mary the wife of Cleophas, and Mary Magdalene. When Jesus therefore saw His mother, and the disciple [John] standing by, whom He loved, He saith unto His mother, Woman, behold thy son! Then saith He to the disciple [John], Behold thy mother! And from that hour that disciple took her unto his own home. (John 19:25–27)

This moving passage reveals the profound love of Jesus for His mother, Mary, and for His loyal friend John. In the primitive attitudes of the ancient Middle East, it was common for a Jewish man to comment, "Thank God that I was not born a woman" as part of his customary morning prayers. Some of the peoples in the ancient Middle East denied that women even possessed souls. The status of women in the centuries preceding the life of Jesus was very restricted in comparison to that of men. In contrast to this widespread ancient attitude that tended to minimize the role of women, Jesus surrounded Himself with women disciples who were often the first to recognize Him as their Messiah and respond to His message about the need for personal repentance. In this way, Jesus elevated forever the role and status of women by treating them as equal in spiritual and social value to men. Edith Hamilton wrote that "the Bible is the only literature in the world up to our century which looks at women as human beings, no better and no worse than men." The prominent position of women as followers of Jesus and His respectful treatment of women ultimately led to a transformation of the rights and roles for women in Western society.

By surrounding Himself with young children and declaring that "of such is the kingdom of God," the Lord changed forever the way adults would look at children. This was a revolutionary change from the prevailing ancient cultural attitude that held children to be of little value. Jesus forever elevated the precious value of every single person, regardless of their social position, capabilities, age, sex, or race, because every one of us is made in the image of God. The transforming principles taught by Jesus motivated Christian reformers during the past several centuries to finally put an end to the institution of slavery. If we examine the lives and attitudes of the great reformers of the past and present, we will often find that the wellspring of their motivation to improve society is routed in a personal love of Jesus Christ.

His Impact on Other Societies

The transforming power of the Gospel of Jesus Christ is best exemplified in the nations of central Africa that British and American missionaries explored during the last century. Missionaries Dr. David Livingstone and Henry M. Stanley wrote that over half of all of the hundreds of tribes they encountered during thousands of miles of exploration through eighteenth century central Africa practiced cannibalism and other unspeakable pagan practices prior to the introduction of the Gospel. Truly, these peoples had sat "in darkness and in the shadow of death" until the glorious light of Jesus entered their lives. From 1800 on, thousands of faithful European and North American Christians gave up their family ties, their promising careers, and worldly success to travel halfway around the world as missionaries to share the wonderful truth of Jesus Christ. As a result of their faithful labors, hundreds of thousands of African pastors and national workers are now completing the Great Commission of Jesus Christ throughout the vast continent of Africa, where more than five hundred million people now live. Today, mission organizations estimate that over one thousand new churches are built every week in Africa and Asia. Some studies indicate that up to half of Africa's population will be followers of Jesus Christ during the first years of the new millennium.

The marvellous power of the Gospel of Jesus to spiritually transform both individuals and whole societies is well documented in the story of the events on Pitcairn Island. The story of *Mutiny on the Bounty* has been retold many times in print and in several famous movies. The fugitive sailors from the mutiny on the British ship known as the *Bounty* took refuge on Pitcairn Island, hoping to escape the vengeance of the British navy. The following account from a quotation in the *Gospel Herald* (*7700 Illustrations*) tells a side of the story not commonly known:

One part that deserves retelling was the transformation wrought by one book. Nine mutineers with six native men and twelve native (Tahitian) women put ashore on Pitcairn Island in 1790. One sailor soon began distilling alcohol. And the little colony was plunged into debauchery and vice. Ten years later, only one white man survived, surrounded by native women and half-breed children. In an old chest from the Bounty, this sailor one day found a Bible. He began to read it and then to teach it to the others. The result was that his own life and ultimately the lives of all those in the colony were changed. Discovered in 1808 by the USS *Topas*, Pitcairn had become a prosperous community with no jail, no whisky, no crime, and no laziness.

Tragically, during the last forty years, the Bible has been relegated to the dusty bookshelves of our homes and the libraries of our nations. Our modern educational establishments, government, courts, and even some churches no longer considered the Bible relevant or authoritative. Someone once wisely wrote, "Men do not reject the Bible because it contradicts itself but because it contradicts them" (*The Defender*).

We have sown a wind of secularism, modernism, and shifting moral values. As a direct result, we are now reaping a whirlwind of immorality, sexually transmitted disease, corruption, and violent crime. The only hope that exists for our individual, national, spiritual, and institutional recovery is to return to the spiritual values that originally formed the foundation of North American national life — the teaching of Jesus Christ, as found in the Word of God.

One Solitary Life

Years ago an anonymous writer summed up the extraordinary influence and impact the solitary life of Jesus of Nazareth had produced on mankind. While many of us have read this beloved passage, it is worth repeating because it reveals the awesome influence of the life of Jesus as the Son of God.

He was born in an obscure village, the child of a peasant woman. Until He was thirty, He worked in a carpenter shop and then for three years He was an itinerant preacher. He wrote no books. He held no office. He never owned a home. He was never in a big city. He never travelled two hundred miles from the place He was born. He never did any of the things that usually accompany greatness. The authorities condemned His teachings. His friends deserted Him. One betrayed Him to His enemies for a paltry sum. One denied Him. He went through the mockery of a trial. He was nailed upon a cross between two thieves. While He was dying, His executioners gambled for the only piece of property He owned on earth: His coat. When He was dead He was taken down and laid in a borrowed grave.

Nineteen centuries have come and gone, yet today He is the crowning glory of the human race, the adored leader of hundreds of millions of the earth's inhabitants. All the armies that ever marched and all the navies that were ever built and all the parliaments that ever sat and all the rulers that ever reigned — put together — have not affected the life of man upon this earth so profoundly as that One Solitary Life.

Notes

1. Alexander Stewart, *All The Men Of The Bible* (Grand Rapids: Zondervan Publishing House, 1958).

2. Herder, *Herzog's Encyclopædia* 5:751.

3. Joseph Ernst Renan, *History of Israel* (1893).

4. Thomas Carlyle, *Sartor Resartus* 137, 140.

5. Boris Pasternak, *Doctor Zhivago* (New York: Random Books, 1958).

6. George Berkeley, *Discourse Addressed to Magistrates and Men in Authority* (1738).

7. John Wesley, *Journal* 31 Mar. 1739.

8. Henry Carter, *The Methodist* 174.

16

The Verdict Is Yours

Jesus Christ lived His life in poverty. He never travelled more than a few hundred miles from the tiny village of Bethlehem, where He was born. He never wrote a book, nor launched a political movement, yet His life and teachings have transformed the lives of hundreds of millions of men, women, and children over the last two thousand years.

A German theologian, Wilhelm M. L. De Wette, spoke of the importance of Jesus Christ in his preface to his *Commentary on the Book of Revelation*, published before his death in 1849:

> This only I know, that there is salvation in no other name than in the name of Jesus Christ, the Crucified, and that nothing loftier offers itself to humanity than the God-manhood realized in Him, and the kingdom of God which He founded — an idea and problem not yet rightly understood and incorporated into the life, even of those who, in other respects, justly rank as the most zealous and the warmest Christians I know. Were Christ in deed and in truth our Life, how could such a falling away from Him be possible? Those in whom He lived would witness so mightily for Him, through their whole life, whether spoken, written, or acted, that unbelief would be forced to silence.

The evidence presented in this book supports the argument that Jesus is the Messiah. If Jesus did exist and was the Son of God, we are left with a fundamental decision: Will we accept or reject Him?

Jesus: The Great Debate provides powerful scientific, archeological, and historical information that supports the claims of the Gospel writers that Jesus is the Son of God. However, there are many people, including some readers of this book, who will still claim they can't accept Him. The problem is not really a problem of "belief"; rather, it is a lack of willingness to accept information that challenges long-held positions. While such people can recognize the strong evidence supporting the historicity of Jesus of Nazareth, they cannot bring themselves to accept the inevitable conclusion that He is the true Messiah because they would have to abandon their previously held agnostic position to which they are emotionally and intellectually committed.

God never told us, "Believe in the Gospels and you shall be saved." The demons of hell know that the Gospel record is true, but this knowledge will not save them. It is significant that God commands us, "Believe on the Lord Jesus Christ, and thou shall be saved, and thy house" (Acts 16:31).

Who Do You Say That I Am?

When Jesus came into the coasts of Cæsarea Philippi, he asked his disciples, saying,

> Whom do men say that I the Son of man am? And they said, Some say that thou art John the Baptist: some, Elias; and others, Jeremias, or one of the prophets. He saith unto them, But whom say ye that I am? And Simon Peter answered and said, Thou art the Christ, the Son of the living God. (Matthew 16:13–16)

Then Jesus asked, "Whom say you that I am?" If Jesus is truly the Son of God as He claims, this question is the most fundamental and important question you and I will ever answer. If we reject the only salvation that God has ever offered us, then we will end our lives as unrepentant sinners, and we will have chosen to go to our deaths in permanent rebellion against God.

Throughout the pages of the Scriptures, we read the claim that

Jesus is the Messiah, the Son of God. The Bible declares that His death on the cross was the only acceptable sacrifice that could pay the full price of our sins. The apostle Paul warns all of us, "For the wages of sin is death; but the gift of God is eternal life through Jesus Christ our Lord" (Romans 6:23). As a result of our sins, each of us has walked away from God in disobedience. The problem is this: How can we ever be reconciled to a holy God when we have been rebelling against Him all our lives? The apostle Paul confirmed this when he declared, "For all have sinned, and come short of the glory of God" (Romans 3:23).

Many people have never seriously considered the claims of the Gospels about Jesus Christ. They have never even thought about the matter. Their denial of the authority of the Scriptures has shielded them against asking the following questions: What if the Gospel is true? What if Jesus really is the Son of God? What if there truly is a heaven and hell to be faced at the end of this life? In light of the evidence presented in this book, we need to carefully consider the implications. If the Bible is truly the Word of God, then every one of us will someday stand before Jesus Christ at the end of our life to answer His question: Who do you say that I am?

On that day, those who have accepted Christ's offer of salvation through His sacrifice on the cross will bow their knees willingly to Jesus, knowing that their sins are forgiven by God. Their destiny will be to live joyfully with Christ forever in heaven. However, those who have chosen to reject the Gospels and Christ's gift of salvation will be forced by their irrevocable decision to bear their own punishment in hell forever. Many in our modern society are offended by the fact that the Bible says that there is only one possible way to be saved. However, the apostle Paul spoke about the absolute necessity of faith in Jesus Christ: "Neither is there salvation in any other: for there is none other name under heaven given among men, whereby we must be saved" (Acts 4:12).

Many suggest that, as long as we are sincere, we will surely make it to heaven. This is a seductive lie from the pit of hell. The Word of God declares that sincerity is not enough. If you are sincere in your faith, but have chosen to place your faith in a false religion, then you are sincerely wrong and lost for eternity. Why would Jesus Christ have willingly gone to the cross for your sins if there were other equally valid ways to be reconciled to God?

One of the religious leaders of Israel named Nicodemus came to Jesus secretly one night to ask Him how he could be assured of salvation. The gospel of John records the answers Jesus gave to Nicodemus. Jesus told him, "Ye must be born again" (John 3:7). He explained to Nicodemus, "Whosoever believeth in him should not perish, but have eternal life. For God so loved the world, that he gave his only begotten Son, that whosoever believeth in him should not perish, but have everlasting life" (John 3:15–16). Every one of us is a sinner who, therefore, stands condemned by God. Jesus said, "He that believeth on him is not condemned: but he that believeth not is condemned already, because he hath not believed in the name of the only begotten Son of God" (John 3:18).

If you have never accepted Jesus Christ as your personal Savior, I pray that the evidence in *Jesus: The Great Debate* will persuade you that God has inspired the writers of the Gospels to present His offer of salvation to all who will accept Jesus as their Lord and Savior.

If you are a Christian, I challenge you to use the evidence in this book, *Jesus: The Great Debate,* when you witness to your friends about your faith in Christ. The proof that Jesus of Nazareth is the true Messiah may not convince anyone to place their faith in Him, but it may remove the false intellectual barriers created by decades of erroneous information instilled in the minds of those who would otherwise seriously consider His claims as the true Messiah. Only by taking a fresh look at the historical evidence about Jesus, can open minds and hearts begin to consider whether or not they want to accept Christ as their Savior.

You have seen the evidence. What is your verdict in the great debate about Jesus? The decision is yours.

Selected Bibliography

Allen, Charlotte. *The Human Christ*. New York: The Free Press, 1998.

Anderson, Sir Robert. *Human Destiny*. London: Pickering & Inglish, 1913.

Ball, Rev. C. J. *Light From The East*. London: Eyre and Spottiswoode, 1899.

Bartlett, John R. *The Bible: Faith and Evidence*. London: British Museum Press, 1990.

Bentwich, Norman. *Fulfilment in the Promised Land*. London: The Soncino Press, 1938.

Blomberg, Craig. *The Historical Reliability of the Gospels*. Leicester: Inter-Varsity Press, 1987.

Blunt, Rev. J. J. *Undesigned Coincidences in the Old and New Testament*. London: John Murray, 1876.

Borg, Marcus. *Meeting Jesus Again for the First Time*. San Francisco: HarperSanFrancisco, 1995.

Borg, Marcus and N. T. Wright. *The Meaning of Jesus*. San Francisco: HarperSanFrancisco, 1999.

Bready, J. Wesley. *England: Before and After Wesley.* London: Hodder and Stoughton Ltd., 1939.

Bulst, Werner. *The Shroud of Turin.* trans. Stephen McKenna, C.Ss.R. and James J. Galvin, C.Ss.R. Milwaukee: The Bruce Publishing Company, 1957.

Burrows, Millar. *The Dead Sea Scrolls of St. Marks Monastery.* New Haven: The American Schools of Oriental Research, 1950.

Burton, Rev. Edward. *Testimonies of the Ante-Nicene Fathers to the Divinity of Christ.* Oxford: University Press, 1829.

Case, Shirley Jackson. *The Historicity of Jesus.* Chicago: The University of Chicago Press, 1912.

Charlesworth, James H. *Jesus Within Judaism.* New York: Doubleday, 1988.

Charlesworth, James H., ed. *The Messiah.* Minneapolis: Fortress Press, 1992.

Chilton, Bruce and Craig A. Evans, ed. *Studying the Historical Jesus.* Leiden: Brill, 1998.

Cobern, Camden M. *The New Archeological Discoveries.* London: Funk & Wagnalls Co., 1929.

Cornfeld, Gaalyah. *Archæology of the Bible: Book by Book.* London: Adam and Charles Black, 1977.

Crossan, John Dominic. *The Historical Jesus.* San Francisco: HarperSanFrancisco, 1992.

Driver, S. R. and A. Neubauer, translators. *The Fifty-third Chapter of Isaiah According to The Jewish Interpreters,* 2 vol. New York: Ktav Publishing House, Inc., 1969.

Duncan, J. Garrow. *Digging Up Biblical History,* vol. I & II. London: Society For Promoting Christian Knowledge, 1931.

Edersheim, Rev. Alfred, *The Life and Times of Jesus the Messiah,* 1 vol. New York: Longmans, Green, and Co., 1899.

Eisenman, Robert. *The Dead Sea Scrolls and the First Christians.* Shaftesbury: Element Books Limited, 1996.

Eisler, Robert. *The Messiah Jesus and John the Baptist.* London: Methuen & Co. Ltd., 1931.

Evans, Craig A. *Jesus*. Grand Rapids: Baker Book House, 1992.

Evans, Craig A. *Life of Jesus Research*. Leiden: E.J. Brill, 1996.

Eusebius. *The History of the Church from Christ to Constantine*. New York: Dorset Press, 1965.

Finegan, Jack. *Archeological History of the Ancient Middle East*. New York: Dorsett Press, 1979.

Finegan, Jack. *Light From the Ancient Past*. Princeton: Princeton University Press, 1946.

Finegan, Jack. *The Archeology of the New Testament*. Princeton: Princeton University Press, 1992.

Flavius, Josephus. *Antiquities of the Jews*. Grand Rapids: Kregal Publications, 1960.

Flusser, David. *Judaism and the Origins of Christianity*. Jerusalem: The Magnes Press, 1988.

Frend, William H. C. *The Archæology of Early Christianity*. London: Geoffrey Chapman, 1996.

Funk, Robert W. *Honest to Jesus*. San Francisco: HarperSanFrancisco, 1996.

Funk, Robert W. and The Jesus Seminar. *The Acts of Jesus*. San Francisco: HarperSanFrancisco, 1998.

Garza-Valdes, Dr. Leoncio A. *The DNA of God?* London: Hodder & Stoughton, 1998.

Gaussen, L. *The Divine Inspiration of the Bible*. Grand Rapids: Kregel Publications, 1971.

Geikie, Cunningham. *The Holy Land and the Bible*. New York: James Pott & Co. Publishers, 1891.

Goguel, Maurice. *Jesus and the Origins of Christianity*, 1 vol. New York: Harper Brothers, 1960.

Goldstein, Rabbi Morris. *Jesus in the Jewish Tradition*. New York: The Macmillan Company, 1950.

Gollancz, Victor. *From Darkness to Light*. London: Victor Gollancz Limited, 1956.

Grant, Michael. *Jesus*. New York: Charles Scribner's Sons, 1977.

Greenstone, Julius H. *The Messiah Idea in Jewish History.* Philadelphia: The Jewish Publication Society of America, 1948.

Habermas, Gary R. *The Historical Jesus.* Joplin: College Press Publishing Co., 1996.

Heller, Dr. John H. *Report on the Shroud of Turin.* Boston: Houghton Mifflin Company, 1983.

Johnson, Luke Timothy. *The Real Jesus.* San Francisco: HarperSanFrancisco, 1997.

Keith, Alexander. *Evidence of the Truth of the Christian Religion.* London: T. Nelson and Sons, 1846.

Keith, Alexander. *Christian Evidences: Fulfilled Bible Prophecy.* Minneapolis: Klock & Klock Christian Publishers, Inc., 1984.

Kenyon, Sir Frederic. *The Bible and Archæology.* London: George G. Harrap & Co. Ltd., 1940.

Kersten, Holger and Elmar R. Gruber. *The Jesus Conspiracy.* Shaftesbury: Element Books Limited, 1992.

Klausner, Joseph. *Jesus of Nazareth.* New York: The MacMillan Company, 1926.

Klausner, Joseph. *The Messianic Idea in Israel.* New York: The Mcmillan Company, 1955.

Lewis, C. S. *Selected Books.* London: HarperCollins Publishers, 1999.

Little, Paul. *Know Why You Believe.* Downers Grove: InterVarsity Press, 1988.

Mancini, Ignazio. *Archæological Discoveries.* Jerusalem: Franciscan Printing Press, 1984.

Martin, Raymond. *The Elusive Messiah.* Boulder: Westview Press, 1999.

McBirnie, William Steuart. *The Search for the Tomb of Jesus.* Montrose: Acclaimed Books, 1978.

McCrone, Walter. *Judgment Day for the Shroud of Turin.* Amherst: Prometheus Books, 1999.

McDowell, Josh. *More Than a Carpenter*. Wheaton: Tyndale House Publishers, Inc., 1973.

McDowell, Josh. *Evidence That Demands a Verdict*. Arrowhead Springs: Campus Crusade For Christ, 1972.

Meier, John P. *A Marginal Jew*, 2 vol. New York: Doubleday, 1994.

Montefiore, C. G. *Rabbinic Literature and Gospel Teachings*. New York: Ktav Publishing House, Inc., 1970.

Morris, Henry M. *Many Infallible Proofs*. El Cajun: Master Books, 1974.

Morris, Henry M. *The Bible and Modern Science*. Chicago: Moody Press, 1968.

Morris, Henry M. *The Biblical Basis for Modern Science*. Grand Rapids: Baker Book House, 1984.

Morris, Herbert W. *Testimony of the Ages*. St. Louis: William Garretson & Co., 1884.

Palestine Exploration Fund. Quarterly Statement. London: Richard Bentley & Son, 1876.

Palestine Exploration Fund. Quarterly Statement. London: Richard Bentley & Son, 1877.

Palestine Exploration Fund. Quarterly Statement. London: Richard Bentley & Son, 1879.

Palestine Exploration Fund. Quarterly Statement. London: A.P. Watt & Son, 1895.

Patai, Raphæl. *The Messiah Texts*. Detroit: Wayne State University Press, 1979.

Pax, Wolfgang E. *In the Footsteps of Jesus*. Bnei Brak: Steimatzky, 1997.

Petrie, Flinders. *Seventy Years in Archeology*. New York: Henry Holt and Co., 1932.

Porter, J. R. *Jesus Christ*. London: Duncan Baird Publishers, 1999.

Post, Rev. George E. *Flora of Syria, Palestine, and Sinai*. Beirut: Syrian Protestant College, 1883.

Price, Randall. *The Stones Cry Out*. Eugene: Harvest House Publishers, 1997.

Proctor, William. *The Resurrection Report.* Nashville: Broadman & Holman Publishers, 1998.

Riehm, Dr. Edward. *Messianic Prophecy.* Edinburgh: T. & T. Clark, 1900.

Riggans, Walter. *Yeshua Ben David.* Crowborough: Marc, 1995.

Robinson, John A. T. *Redating the New Testament.* Philadelphia: The Westminster Press, 1976.

Rops, Daniel. *Jesus and His Times.* New York: E. P. Dutton & Co., Inc., 1954.

Rule, William Harris. *Biblical Monuments.* Croydon: Werteimer, Lea and Co., 1873.

Saller, Fr. Sylvester J. *Excavations at Bethany.* Jerusalem: Franciscan Printing Press, 1982.

Sayce, A. H. *Records of the Past,* 5 vol. London: Samuel Bagster & Sons, Ltd., 1889.

Scholem, Gershom, *The Messianic Idea in Judaism.* New York: Schocken Books, 1971.

Schonfield, Hugh J. *The Mystery of the Messiah.* London: Open Gate Press, 1998.

Schonfield, Hugh J. *The Passover Plot.* New York: Bernard Geis Associates, 1965.

Sheppard, Lancelot C. *Prophecy Fulfilled — The Old Testament Realized in the New.* New York: David McKay Co. Inc., 1958.

Smith, William. *A Dictionary of the Bible.* Boston: D. Lothrop & Co., 1878.

Spong, John Shelby. *Resurrection: Myth or Reality?* San Francisco: HarperSanFrancisco, 1971.

Stevenson, Kenneth E. and Gary R. Habermas. *The Shroud and the Controversy.* Nashville: Thomas Nelson Publishers, 1990.

Stevenson, Kenneth E. and Gary R. Habermas. *Verdict On The Shroud.* Wayne: Banbury Books, Inc., 1981.

Stoner, Peter W. *Science Speaks.* Chicago: Moody Books, 1963.

Strobel, Lee. *The Case for Christ.* Grand Rapids: Zondervan Publishing House, 1998.

Thiede, Carsten Peter and Matthew D'Ancona. *Eyewitness to Jesus.* New York: Doubleday, 1996.

Theissen, Gerd and Annette Merz. *The Historical Jesus.* Minneapolis: Fortress Press, 1996.

Thompson, J. A. *The Bible and Archeology.* Grand Rapids: Eerdmans Publishing Co., 1972.

Thompson, William M. *The Land and the Book.* Hartford: The S. S. Scranton Co., 1910.

Unger, Merrill, F. *Archeology and the Old Testament.* Grand Rapids: Zondervan Publishing Co., 1954.

Vermes, Geza. *Discovery in the Judean Desert.* New York: Desclee Co., 1956.

Vermes, Geza. *The Dead Sea Scrolls in English.* London: Penguin Books, 1988.

Vincent, Rev. J. H. *Curiosities of the Bible.* Chicago: R. C. Treat., 1885.

Vos, Howard. *Can I Trust The Bible?* Chicago: Moody Press, 1963.

Wells, G. A. *The Historical Evidence for Jesus.* Buffalo: Prometheus Books, 1988.

Wilson, Bill. *A Ready Defense — The Best of Josh McDowell.* San Bernardino: Here's Life Publishers, Inc., 1990.

Wilson, C. W. *Golgotha and the Holy Sepulchre.* London: Harrison and Sons, 1906.

Wislon, Ian. *Holy Faces, Secret Places.* New York: Doubleday, 1991.

Wilson, Ian. *Jesus: The Evidence.* San Francisco: Harper and Row Publishers, 1984.

Wilson, Ian. *The Blood and the Shroud.* London: Weidenfeld & Nicolson, 1998.

Wilson, Ian. *The Mysterious Shroud.* Garden City: Doubleday & Company, Inc., 1986.

Wilson, Ian. *The Shroud of Turin.* Garden City: Doubleday & Company, Inc., 1978.

Witherington, Ben. *The Jesus Quest.* Downers Grove: InterVarsity Press, 1997.

Wright, N. T. *Jesus and the Victory of God.* Minneapolis: Fortress Press, 1996.

Yahuda, A. S. *The Accuracy of the Bible.* London: William Heinemann Ltd., 1934.

Young, Brad H. *Jesus the Jewish Theologian.* Peabody: Hendrickson Publishers, 1997.

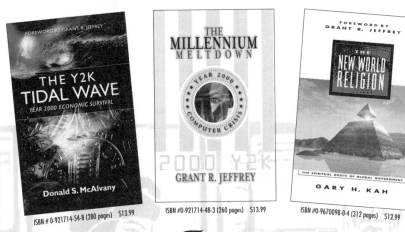

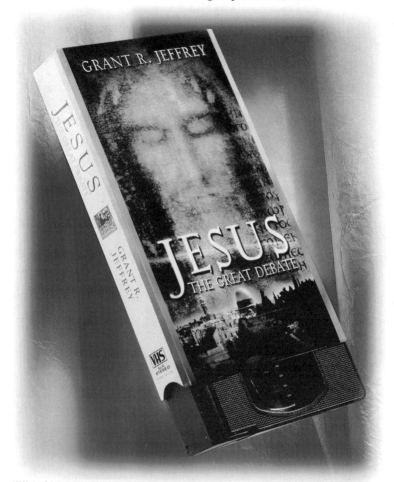

Ministry Resources

Available in Christian bookstores everywhere

Quantity	Code	Description		Price	Total
		Softback Books			
	BK-3	Messiah – War in the Middle East & The Road to Armageddon		$12.99	
	BK-4	Apocalypse – The Coming Judgment of the Nations		$12.99	
	BK-5	Prince of Darkness – Antichrist and the New World Order		$13.99	
	BK-6	Final Warning – Economic Collapse and Coming World Government		$13.99	
	BK-7	Heaven – The Mystery of Angels		$12.99	
	BK-8	The Signature of God – Astonishing Biblical Discoveries		$13.99	
	BK-9	Yeshua – The Name of Jesus Revealed in the Old Testament		$11.99	
	BK-10	Armageddon – Appointment With Destiny		$12.99	
	BK-11	His Name is Jesus – The Mysterious Yeshua Codes		$12.99	
	BK-12	The Handwriting of God – Sacred Mysteries of the Bible		$13.99	
	BK-13	The Millennium Meltdown – Year 2000 Computer Crisis		$13.99	
	BK-14	The New World Religion (Gary H. Kah)		$12.99	
	BK-15	The Y2K Tidal Wave (Donald S. McAlvany)		$13.99	
	BK-16	Jesus, The Great Debate		$13.99	
		ANY THREE BOOKS OR MORE	**EACH**	**$11.00**	
		Hardcover Books			
	HC-H	Heaven – The Mystery of Angels		$15.99	
	W-50	Mysterious Bible Codes		$19.99	
	W-51	Flee The Darkness (Grant R. Jeffrey and Angela Hunt)	*Fiction*	$17.99	
	W-52	By Dawn's Early Light (Grant R. Jeffrey and Angela Hunt)	*Fiction*	$18.99	
		Executive Edition *(pocket-sized witnessing pack)*			
	EE-1	The Signature of God (78 pages, 3 booklets per pack)		$9.99	
		Videos			
	V-5	The Rebirth of Israel and The Messiah		$19.99	
	V-6	The Antichrist and The Mark of The Beast		$19.99	
	V-7	The Rapture and Heaven's Glory		$19.99	
	V-8	The Coming Millennial Kingdom		$19.99	
	V-9	The Search for The Messiah		$19.99	
	V-13	Archeological Discoveries: Exploring Beneath the Temple Mount		$19.99	
	V-14	Prince of Darkness and The Final Inquisition		$19.99	
	V-15	Secret Agenda of The New World Order and The Tribulation		$19.99	
	V-16	Rush to Armageddon		$19.99	
		ANY TWO VIDEOS OR MORE	**EACH**	**$17.00**	
	V-19	The Millennium Meltdown		$19.99	
	V-20	Jesus, The Great Debate		$19.99	
		Total this page (to be carried forward)			

continued overleaf

Quantity	Code	Description	Price	Total
			Total from previous page	
		Double-length Videos		
	V-17	The Signature of God – Astonishing Biblical Discoveries	$29.99	
	V-18	Mysterious Bible Codes	$29.99	
	VP-1	Final Warning, Big Brother Government	$29.99	
		Audio Cassettes		
	AB-14	The Signature of God (2 tapes)	$15.99	
	AB-15	Mysterious Bible Codes (2 tapes)	$15.99	
	AB-16	The Millennium Meltdown (2 tapes)	$15.99	
	AB-17	Jesus, The Great Debate (2 tapes)	$15.99	
		Computer Programs		
	BC	Unlocking the Bible Codes (on CD-ROM; for IBM-compatible computers only) (*shipping and handling included*)	$69.99	
	PIB	**Product Brochure**	No charge	
		One low shipping and handling fee for the above (per order)	$4.95	$4.95
		Zondervan Prophecy Marked Reference Study Bible Grant R. Jeffrey, General Editor		
	KJV	Hardcover	$34.99	
	KJV	Bonded Leather: Black	$59.99	
	KJV	Bonded Leather: Burgundy	$59.99	
	KJV	Top Grain Leather: Black	$69.99	
	NIV	Hardcover	$34.99	
	NIV	Bonded Leather: Black	$59.99	
	NIV	Bonded Leather: Burgundy	$59.99	
		Shipping and handling fee for Bibles (per order)	$5.95	$5.95
		Oklahoma residents add 7.5% sales tax		

All prices are in U.S. dollars   Additional shipping charges will apply to orders outside North America.

Grand Total [ ]

PLEASE PRINT

Name _____

Address _____

City _____ State _____ Zip _____

Phone _____ Fax _____

Credit card number _____

Expiry date _____

U.S. orders: mail along with your check or money order to:
Frontier Research Publications
P.O. Box 470470, Tulsa, OK 74147-0470
U.S. credit card orders: call 1-800-883-1812

Canadian orders: call or write for pricing to:
Frontier Research Publications
P.O. Box 129, Station "U", Toronto, Ontario M8Z 5M4
Canadian VISA card orders: call 1-800-853-1423

Prices effective July 1, 1999